Favorite Recipes
of 1986

Favorite Recipes
of 1986

Heritage House INC.

Credits

Home Economics Editorial Advisory Board: Charlotte Boyette, Marilyn Butler, Sandra Crouch, Paula Hartsfield, Katherine Jensen, Frances King, Carolyn Kratz, Sue Smith

Essayist: Joan Dew
Creative Director: Phil Sankey

Heritage House, Inc.

Publisher: Thomas Milam
Editor-in-Chief: Mary Jane Blount
Editors: Georgia Brazil, Mary Cummings, LaNita Stout
Editorial Assistant: Jane Hinshaw
Project Manager: Paula Cometto
Production Manager: John Moulton
Production Coordinator: Teresa Fitzgerald
Typography: William E. Maul, Sharon K. Whitehurst

Photography

Cover, Hershey Foods Corporation; Page 1, Idaho Potatoes; Page 2, Coco Ribe; Page 19, Argo and Kingsford's cornstarch; Page 20, Hershey Foods Corporation; Page 53, National Live Stock and Meat Board; Page 54, Argo and Kingsford's cornstarch; Page 71, The Rice Council; Page 72, Spanish Green Olive Commission; Page 105, United Fresh Fruit and Vegetable Association; Page 106, The Dow Chemical Company, makers of SARAN WRAP™ brand plastic film; Page 123, Florida Tomato Exchange; Page 124, Ocean Spray Cranberries, Inc.; Page 157, Cape Granny Smith Apples; Page 158, Argo and Kingsford's cornstarch; Page 175, Argo and Kingsford's cornstarch; Page 176, Jell-O brand gelatin, Jell-O brand pudding and pie filling, Birds Eye Cool Whip non-dairy whipped topping.

Library of Congress Catalog Number is as follows: 86-25708
ISBN: 0-87197-216-6

Manufactured in the United States of America
First Printing 1986

Recipes for Cover on pages 176, 198, 212, 213, 214 and 215.
Recipe for Page 1 on page 49.
Recipes for Page 2 on pages 109, 156 and 181.

Contents

Winter	8
Menus	12
January	14
February	30
March	42
Spring	58
Menus	62
April	64
May	80
June	94
Summer	112
Menus	116
July	118
August	134
September	146
Fall	160
Menus	164
October	166
November	184
December	200
Calorie Chart	218
Index	220

Introduction

*F*avorite Recipes of 1986 is the second in a series of annual cookbooks from Heritage House, a division of The Southwestern Company. In keeping with our 119-year old tradition, we continue to publish quality books which will be a positive influence on American family life.

This collection of recipes includes an assortment of both traditional favorites and new influences reflecting the trends of 1986. Some recipes are updated versions of familiar dishes while others are certain to become modern classics. All are easy to use and to read.

Favorite Recipes of 1986 is arranged according to nature's calendar with twelve monthly divisions grouped into four seasons. Each season features both foods which are at their peak of flavor and availability and recipes which are appropriate for the time of year. Each begins with a delightful essay recalling the nostalgia of the changing seasons as well as suggesting celebrations featuring nature's abundance. Each includes a section highlighting the season's best food choices with information to help you choose and store top quality fruits, vegetables, and meats. And each season includes menu suggestions for every occasion and for cooks with different skill levels.

To increase their usefulness, the recipes have been analyzed and coded with symbols to show at a glance which are perfect for your family's needs, schedule, and budget. The symbols are easy to recognize and use.

Quick and Easy

For the "on the go" days in your active life, these recipes take only minutes from thought to table.

Nutritional

These recipes include nutritious foods offering the most in vitamins and minerals while minimizing sodium, cholesterol, and calories.

Economical

According to the seasonal food listings, these recipes offer exceptional taste and variety and are easy on your budget.

Microwave

These recipes include microwave instructions for all or part of the preparation, saving time and energy.

Make Ahead

Made hours, days, or weeks ahead, these recipes let you relax and enjoy special dinners as well as daily meals.

Outdoor Cooking

These recipes take the cooking outdoors for easy preparation and good times with family and friends.

Alert

To ensure your success, these recipes alert you that special attention or care might be necessary.

Joan Dew captures the ways in which the changing seasons shape our lives in four charming essays. They evoke memories of childhood favorites and celebrate holidays past and present. A nationally known writer with articles appearing in over fifty magazines including _Good Housekeeping_, _Redbook_, and _Ladies Home Journal_, Ms. Dew has been writing about food for twenty years. She has been a newspaper, magazine, and television food and restaurant critic for the past seven years and recently collaborated with reknown restaurateur, Mario Ferrari, on the book, _On Wine and Food_. She is also author of the autobiographies of Tammy Wynette and Minnie Pearl and of _Singers & Sweethearts: The Women in Country Music_.

Mary Jane Blount, Editor-in-Chief for Heritage House, has edited over 150 cookbooks during the past twenty years, including books for National and State Grange Organizations, 4-H Clubs, and the Home Economics Teachers of America. The Home Economics Advisory Board, consisting of leaders in the field of Home Economics, works with Ms. Blount and her staff to keep them abreast of the current needs and preferences of homemakers nationwide. This group of professionals collaborate on books involving thousands of recipes annually for Heritage House, The Southwestern Company, and Great American Opportunities.

Dozens of experts from all across the country have combined their talents to bring you this volume of recipes and food ideas. It is their hope that you will prepare and serve many delicious family and party dishes for those you love—whatever the season.

Winter

*A*t no time during our seasonal cycle is food so important as it is in Winter. Only a few generations ago, the amount of food stored away for Winter could actually mean life or death for settlers. Now, Winter foods are as close as the nearest supermarket, and, thanks to modern transportation and technology, we have almost all types of foods available year-round. Yet, even with frozen Spring asparagus in abundance in January, most of us would prefer fresh seasonal vegetables—ripe acorn squash stuffed with sausage, apple, and onion; a flavorful casserole of potatoes, turnips, and carrots; tasty parsnip, artichoke, and eggplant gratin.

Winter brings out the need to mother and be mothered. We crave the foods of our childhood—*comfort* foods. As freezing rains and bone-chilling winds send us indoors for protection, we want dishes that stick to the ribs: hearty stews; savory pot roasts with rich natural gravy and mounds of fluffy mashed potatoes; beef and chicken potpies in golden crusts; bowls of steaming soup and spicy chili. This Winter craving for childhood *comfort* foods is so deeply ingrained it can have its effect even in the tropics. I experienced this while living in the West Indies. In mid-Winter the temperature there hovers in the high 70's, and balmy breezes carry the exotic fragrance of ripening fruit. Nevertheless, come January and February, when others were feasting on succulent papaya and sweet pineapple for breakfast, I found myself in the kitchen frying country ham, making red-eye gravy, baking cheese grits, and stirring up a batch of buttermilk biscuits. My body was in the tropics, but my taste buds were back in the Georgia of my childhood where Winter at my grandmother's house focused on *sturdy* foods. To this day I have never smelled anything as heady and intoxicating as the aromas that wafted from her cozy kitchen—yeast dough set in the cupboard to rise; sweet potato pie just out of the oven; chicken frying in the iron skillet; simmering Brunswick stew.

The Winter season begins with the grand tradition of celebrating the end of the old year, the beginning of the new. New Year's Eve is the perfect time for parties featuring the best in snack foods—fancy canapés and tasty hors d'oeuvres; miniature sandwiches of roast beef and turkey on homemade buttered rolls.

Valentine's, the most romantic of holidays, comes just in time to brighten the darkest Winter. The occasion calls for *romantic* foods— chicken breasts in Champagne sauce; Rock Cornish game hens with apple-grape stuffing; elegant raspberry soufflé (so easy to make with frozen raspberries) or a wickedly rich dessert of chocolate, one of the ultimate *comfort* foods.

We need party foods during the Winter season to brighten our spirits, but the tastes we long for the most are the basic, solidly satisfying dishes of the day-to-day table: hearty Winter soups or meat loaf, as varied as the imagination.

If you are lucky enough to live in an area where Winter snows turn the outdoors into a white wonderland, you know that a day on the ski slopes or sledding down steep hills makes for ravenous appetites. What better way to satisfy snow-hunger than a bowl of hearty seafood chowder teamed with crusty homemade bread or a delicious cassoulet, the classic French peasant stew made from dried white beans and meat, traditionally duck or lamb. I prefer mine made with pork and garlicy sausage, such as kielbasa, and served with big chunks of corn bread oozing sweet butter. It's the perfect one-pot meal for snowflake and icicle weather.

By the middle of Winter, we're looking for new ideas for salads. The abundance of fresh salad vegetables we took for granted all Summer is but a distant memory. Finding substitutes is a challenge best met by creative combinations of the fresh vegetables available with frozen or canned ingredients that add pizazz to salads, such as tiny green peas or artichoke hearts. Fresh mushrooms marinated in a walnut-oil dressing with lemon juice and lots of chopped parsley is so refreshing it has become a year-round favorite at our house. Other Winter winners include broccoli and red bean salad; slaw of red and white cabbage with apples and chopped nuts; kidney and garbanzo beans with chopped red onion; and curly endive in a garlic-oil and vinegar dressing.

The most inviting Winter kitchens have a sunny window for growing fresh herbs which give a delightful lift to winter vegetables, stews, and soups. These indoor miniature herb gardens take very little care and only a small amount of space. One windowsill will do if it gets direct sun for several hours a day. If no sunny sill is available, herbs picked in the Summer—oregano, marjoram, rosemary, and sage—may be hung upside down to dry for use all Winter. Tied with bright ribbons, they also make charming kitchen decor. Greener herbs, such as basil, parsley, tarragon, and dill are better preserved by puréeing the leaves with a little oil in a blender, then freezing in small containers or in ice cube trays. When you're ready to season, pop an herb ice cube into the pot!

On the worst freezing Winter days, when schools are closed and the cookie monsters at your house are bored and restless, bring out the marshmallows and hot dogs and have a fireplace wiener roast; let them make fudge or decorate a cake; have a "tea party." A mug of hot chocolate with pecan shortbread cookies will do wonders for icy-day dispositions. And moms of cookie monsters might want to put a note on the refrigerator door with these encouraging words from the poet Shelley:

O, Wind
If Winter comes, can Spring be far behind?

Winter Foods

Winter foods feature hearty vegetables, jewel-tone citrus fruit, and fresh shellfish to spark menus when days are cold and sunshine is scarce. Choosing the best foods available is more important now when there are fewer choices and a greater need for nourishment than in any other season.

Grapefruit: Choose heavy, firm, smooth, thin-skinned Florida or Texas grapefruit which are free from puffiness and pointed stem ends. Store in refrigerator.

Lemons and Limes: Choose plump, heavy, smooth-skinned lemons and limes with rich color which are free from soft spots and mold. Store in refrigerator. Serve at room temperature.

Oranges: Choose firm, heavy, smooth-skinned Navel and Temple oranges regardless of color which are free from puffiness and soft spots. Store in refrigerator.

Winter Pears: Choose firm (not hard), well-colored, and well-shaped Bosc or Comice pears which are free from bruises and soft spots. Ripen at room temperature. Store in refrigerator.

Brussels Sprouts: Choose firm, compact, bright-green Brussels sprouts with tight heads and no yellowing or puffiness. Store in airtight bag in refrigerator.

Mushrooms: Choose clean creamy-white or light tan mushrooms which are free from spongy or discolored spots. Store in refrigerator. Wipe with damp cloth but do not wash to clean.

Endive: Choose firm, tight, crisp endive stalks which are pale-yellow or white with tightly clinging leaves. Store, tightly wrapped in plastic, in refrigerator.

Parsnips: Choose firm, smooth, smallish parsnips which are clean and free from soft spots. Store, wrapped in plastic, in refrigerator.

Spinach: Choose fresh, crisp, dark-green spinach which is free from wilting and bruising. Store in plastic bag in refrigerator.

Shellfish: Choose clams and oysters with tightly closed shells or those which close when tapped. Choose crab and crayfish which move their legs and feel heavy for their size. Scallops should be creamy-colored. Shrimp should be firm and moist. All shellfish should smell fresh and ammonia-free. Store in very cold refrigerator, and use as soon as possible.

Menus

BREAKFASTS

Super Bowl Brunch

A Festive Brunch for Eight

Crab Meat Strata	22
Cheese Popovers	38
Tomato Juice with Lime Slices	

Handwarmer Breakfast

A Hearty Breakfast for Six

Food Processor Cheese Soufflé	205
Grilled Canadian Bacon	
Peanut Butter-Bran Muffins	26
Cocoa Mocha Mix	29

Make-Ahead Breakfast

An Easy Breakfast for Two to Six

Night-Before Yeast Waffles	27
Crock•Pot Apple Butter	15
Broiled Link Sausages	
Sliced Oranges	

LUNCHES

Thermos Lunch

A Toteable Lunch for Three

Smoky Beef Chowder	15
Burrito Sandwiches	17
Pear Wedges	
Apple-Orange Squares	41

Everyone's Irish Potato Luncheon

A St. Patrick's Day Luncheon for Six

O'Topper Potatoes	49
Lucky Fruited Green Salad	45
Irish Cream Brownies	57
Irish Coffee	

DINNERS

14	Caviar Appetizer Pie	*New Year's Eve*
17	Beef Tenderloin with Mushroom Stuffing	*Dinner*
48	Broccoli Puff	
23	Deviled Black-Eyed Peas	
40	Strawberry Angel Dessert with Raspberry Sauce	*A Company Dinner for Eight*
29	Mock Champagne	

New Year's Eve Dinner — *A Company Dinner for Eight*

32	Taco Pot Roast	*Fiesta*
38	Pepper-Rice Casserole	*Dinner*
28	Southwestern Fruit Delight	
56	Pear-Cheese Cake	*An Oven Dinner for Four*

Fiesta Dinner — *An Oven Dinner for Four*

33	Baked Chili	*Fix and Forget*
32	Sunshine Vegetable Salad	*Dinner*
	Hot Tortillas	
57	Hurry-Up Peach Pie	*An Easy Dinner for Six*

Fix and Forget Dinner — *An Easy Dinner for Six*

SUPPERS

44	Vegetable Chowder	*Winter Soup*
16	Super Slaw	*Supper*
26	Baked Onion Loaf	
27	Cranberry-Pear Crisp	*A Fireside Supper for Six*

Winter Soup Supper — *A Fireside Supper for Six*

34	Cornish Game Hens with Wild Rice	*Sweetheart*
37	Belgian Endive with Dijon Sauce	*Supper*
40	Strawberry Yogurt and Rice Parfaits	
41	Cold Quack	*A Valentine's Day Supper for Two*

Sweetheart Supper — *A Valentine's Day Supper for Two*

January

Caviar Appetizer Pie

Sonia K. Lowitz, Maryland

6	**hard-boiled eggs, shredded**
	Pepper to taste
1½	**tablespoons mayonnaise**
1	**avocado, mashed ***
2	**tablespoons minced red onion**
1	**large jar black caviar**
	Cocktail rye bread
	* Seasonal

Combine eggs, pepper and mayonnaise in bowl; mix well. Do not add salt. Chill in refrigerator for several hours. ** Layer avocado, onion and egg mixture in pie plate. Spread caviar over layers. Serve with cocktail rye bread. Yield: 8 servings.

** *Make ahead to this point.*
Note: May use a combination of red and black caviar. Place red caviar in center surrounded by black caviar.

Mushroom Party Snacks

Pat Henry, North Carolina

16	**ounces fresh mushrooms ***
¾	**cup mashed potatoes ***
¼	**cup cottage cheese**
2	**tablespoons dry onion soup mix**
2	**teaspoons milk**
	* Seasonal

Wash mushrooms; pat dry. Remove and chop stems. Combine mushroom stems, mashed potatoes, cottage cheese, soup mix and milk in bowl; mix well. Spoon into mushroom caps. Chill in refrigerator if desired. ** Place on baking sheet. Bake at 375 degrees for 15 minutes. Arrange on serving plate. Yield: 3 dozen.

** *Make ahead to this point.*

Crock•Pot Apple Butter

May Smith, Ohio

Combine applesauce, cider, sugar and spices in Crock•Pot; mix well. Cook on Low for 12 hours or until of desired consistency. Mixture will thicken when cool. **Spoon into hot sterilized jars, leaving ½-inch headspace. Seal with 2-piece lids.** Process in boiling water bath for 10 minutes. Yield: 12 cups. ✔4 🍎 🐦 🍲 ✳

8	*cups applesauce* *
4	*cups apple cider* *
2	*cups sugar*
¼	*teaspoon each allspice, cloves*
1	*teaspoon cinnamon*
	* Seasonal

Barley-Cheese Soup

Jennifer Ellis, California

Combine broth, broccoli, carrots, onion, barley, garlic, salt, pepper and 2 cups water in 4-quart glass bowl. Cover with waxed paper. Microwave on High for 18 to 20 minutes or until barley is tender, stirring once. Combine flour and ½ cup milk; mix well. Stir into vegetable mixture. Stir in remaining 1 cup milk. Microwave, covered, on High for 5 minutes or until thickened, stirring once. Stir in cheese. Let stand, covered, for 3 to 5 minutes before serving. Yield: 6 servings. ✔4 🍎 🐦 ≋

1	*10-ounce can condensed chicken broth*
2	*cups chopped broccoli* *
1	*cup sliced carrots* *
½	*cup chopped onion*
½	*cup quick-cooking pearl barley*
1	*small clove of garlic, minced*
1	*teaspoon salt*
⅛	*teaspoon pepper*
⅓	*cup flour*
1½	*cups milk*
1½	*cups chopped Swiss cheese*
	* Seasonal

Smoky Beef Chowder

Chuck Frey, Texas

Sauté celery and onion in margarine in saucepan or microwave on High until tender. Stir in flour, salt and basil. Stir in milk. Cook until thickened, stirring constantly, or microwave, stirring twice. Chop beef finely. Add beef and cheese to cooked mixture. Cook until cheese melts, stirring constantly, or microwave, stirring twice. Stir in parsley. Serve immediately or keep hot in thermos. Yield: 3 servings. ✔4 🍎 🐦 ≋ 🍲

½	*cup finely chopped celery*
1	*onion, finely chopped*
2	*tablespoons margarine*
3	*tablespoons flour*
	Salt to taste
¼	*teaspoon basil*
3	*cups milk*
3	*ounces thinly sliced smoked beef*
¾	*cup shredded American cheese*
1	*tablespoon chopped parsley*

Citrus Fruit Salad

Marie Booth, Texas

½ cup grapefruit sections *
1 cup orange sections *
3 bananas, sliced
1 cup miniature marshmallows
2 cups fresh pineapple chunks *
¼ cup shredded coconut
6 cherries, chopped
1 cup whipping cream
* Seasonal

Combine, grapefruit, oranges, bananas, marshmallows, pineapple, coconut and cherries in bowl. Fold in stiffly whipped cream gently. Spoon into serving bowl. Serve immediately. Yield: 6 servings.

Super Slaw

Connie Krueger, Texas

1 medium head cabbage *
1 can water chestnuts
¼ cup shredded red cabbage *
2 carrots, grated *
½ cup chopped celery
½ cup chopped green pepper
1 apple, chopped *
½ cup white raisins
½ cup chopped pecans
2 cups pineapple tidbits *
1 8-ounce jar poppy seed
   dressing
   * Seasonal

Shred cabbage. Drain and chop water chestnuts. Combine shredded cabbage, carrots, celery, green pepper, apple, water chestnuts, raisins, pecans and pineapple in bowl; mix well. Chill for several hours. ** Add poppy seed dressing; toss lightly. Chill for 1 hour longer.
Yield: 6 servings.

** *Make ahead to this point.*

Chicken and Rice Salad

Helen Heath, Indiana

1 6-ounce package rice
2 cups chopped cooked chicken *
1 cup seedless green grapes *
1 cup sliced celery
¾ cup chopped nuts
2 tablespoons minced onion
¼ cup (or more) mayonnaise
¼ cup lemon juice
1 orange, sliced *
2 lemons, sliced *
1 cluster grapes
   * Seasonal

Cook rice using package directions. Chill in refrigerator. Combine rice, chicken, 1 cup grapes, celery, nuts and onion in bowl; mix lightly. Add enough mayonnaise to moisten. Add lemon juice; mix well. Chill for several hours. ** Arrange orange and lemon slices around top edge of lettuce-lined serving bowl. Spoon chicken mixture into center. Chill if desired. ** Garnish with grape cluster.
Yield: 6 servings.

** *Make ahead to this point.*

Broccoli and Beef Salad

Cut broccoli into flowerets; slice stems ¼ inch thick. Stir-fry broccoli stems in hot oil in wok for 1 minute. Add flowerets. Stir-fry for 2 minutes. Cook, covered, for 2 to 3 minutes or until tender-crisp. Place broccoli in serving bowl. Stir-fry red pepper for 2 minutes. Add to broccoli. Stir-fry mushrooms for 3 to 4 minutes. Add to broccoli mixture. Cut roast beef into slivers. Add roast beef and water chestnuts to vegetables; mix well. Mix vinegar, soy sauce and hot peppers in bowl. Pour over beef. Chill for several hours.
Yield: 6 servings.

2 *pounds fresh broccoli* *
¼ *cup oil*
1 *sweet red pepper, cut into strips*
2 *cups sliced mushrooms* *
1 *pound rare roast beef*
8 *ounces sliced water chestnuts*
¼ *cup vinegar*
¼ *cup reduced-sodium soy sauce*
1 *to 2 tablespoons dried hot peppers*
* Seasonal

Burrito Sandwiches

JoRie Jeffries, New Mexico

Soften tortillas in microwave, in oven or on stove top using package directions. Layer turkey, cheese, ham and lettuce on tortillas. Brush avocado slices with lemon juice. Arrange over lettuce. Drizzle salad dressing over avocado. Roll tortillas to enclose filling. Wrap in plastic wrap. Chill until serving time.
Yield: 3 sandwiches.

3 *flour tortillas*
4 *ounces thinly sliced turkey breast* *
4 *ounces thinly sliced Swiss cheese*
4 *ounces thinly sliced baked ham*
1 *cup shredded lettuce*
1 *avocado, thinly sliced* *
1 *teaspoon lemon juice*
¼ *cup Thousand Island salad dressing*
* Seasonal

Beef Tenderloin with Mushroom Stuffing

Marilyn Kasmiersky, Texas

Sauté chopped onion, celery and sliced mushrooms in margarine in skillet for 10 minutes or microwave in glass bowl on High until tender. Cool. Combine bread crumbs, seasonings and sautéed vegetables in bowl; mix lightly. **Slice tenderloin ¾ through lengthwise to form pocket.** Spoon in stuffing lightly; secure with toothpicks. Arrange bacon diagonally over top. Refrigerate, tightly covered, for several hours if desired. ** Place on rack in roasting pan. Roast at 350 degrees for 1 hour for medium-rare. Place on serving platter. Cut into slices.
Yield: 8 servings.

** *Make ahead to this point.*

1 *medium onion*
½ *cup chopped celery*
4 *ounces mushrooms* *
¼ *cup margarine*
2 *cups soft bread crumbs*
   Salt to taste
⅛ *teaspoon pepper*
½ *teaspoon basil*
⅛ *teaspoon parsley flakes*
1 *3-pound beef tenderloin*
4 *slices bacon*
* Seasonal

Crock•Pot Pizza Casserole
Iola Elliott, Ohio

1	**pound ground beef**
1	**onion, chopped**
2	**16-ounce cans pizza sauce**
2½	**cups grated mozzarella cheese**
1	**7-ounce package macaroni, cooked**
8	**ounces sliced pepperoni**
4	**ounces mushrooms ***
	* Seasonal

Brown ground beef and onion in skillet or microwave, stirring until crumbly; drain. Combine with pizza sauce, cheese, macaroni, pepperoni and mushrooms in Crock•Pot; mix well. Cook on Low for 3 hours or until of desired consistency. Yield: 6 servings.

Baked Ribs and Sauerkraut
Carol Majors, Michigan

4	**cups sauerkraut**
2	**medium apples, chopped ***
1	**cup chopped celery**
1	**medium onion, chopped**
2	**teaspoons brown sugar**
3	**pounds spareribs**
	Salt and pepper to taste
½	**cup raisins**
	* Seasonal

Combine sauerkraut, apples, celery, onion and brown sugar in bowl; mix well. Place half the ribs in baking pan. Spread sauerkraut mixture over ribs. Place remaining ribs on top. Season with salt and pepper. Refrigerate for several hours if desired. ** Bake at 350 degrees for 1½ hours. Drain. Place on serving platter. Sprinkle with raisins. Yield: 5 servings.

** *Make ahead to this point.*

Easy Cassoulet
Edna Wagner, California

1	**10-ounce package frozen whole green beans**
1	**16-ounce package kielbasa**
1	**medium onion, chopped**
2	**tablespoons oil**
1	**16-ounce can white beans**
1	**cup milk**
3	**tablespoons mustard**
⅛	**teaspoon crushed red pepper**

Cook green beans in saucepan or microwave using package directions. Brown kielbasa with onion in oil in skillet. Add green beans, white beans, milk, mustard and red pepper. Cook until heated through, stirring occasionally. Arrange kielbasa and vegetables on warm serving platter. Yield: 4 servings.

Note: May substitute smoked sausage for kielbasa.

Chicken Breasts Stuffed with Crab Meat

Marlene Hawks, Maryland

Flatten chicken breasts with meat mallet. Combine crab meat, eggs, mayonnaise, mustard, dry mustard, parsley flakes, celery seed and seasonings in bowl; mix well. Spoon onto chicken breasts. Roll to enclose filling; secure with toothpicks. Dip in beaten egg whites; coat with cornflakes. Place in greased 9x13-inch baking dish. Bake at 350 degrees for 1 hour or microwave on High until chicken is tender, turning dish twice. Yield: 8 servings.

- 8 *chicken breast filets* *
- 1 *pound crab meat* *
- 2 *eggs, beaten*
- 1½ *tablespoons mayonnaise*
- 1 *teaspoon prepared mustard*
- 1 *teaspoon dry mustard*
- 1 *tablespoon parsley flakes*
- 1 *teaspoon celery seed*
- *Salt to taste*
- 1 *teaspoon Old Bay seasoning*
- 2 *egg whites, beaten*
- 1½ *cups crushed cornflakes*
- * Seasonal

Upside-Down Pizza

Ryan Burrow, New Mexico

Soak cracked wheat in boiling water to cover in bowl for 5 minutes; drain. Prepare bread mix using package directions. Stir in cracked wheat. Let dough rest according to package directions. Combine tomatoes, green pepper, tomato paste and seasonings in saucepan. Simmer, covered, for 10 minutes. Add chicken, olives and mushrooms. Sprinkle cheeses in 8 greased 10 to 12-ounce baking dishes. Spoon chicken mixture over cheese. Divide dough into 8 portions. Roll each ¾ inch larger than baking dish. Place on dishes, turning down edges to seal. Bake at 375 degrees for 15 minutes or until light brown. Invert onto serving plates. Yield: 8 servings.

- 2 *tablespoons cracked wheat*
- 1 *16-ounce package whole wheat bread mix*
- 1 *14-ounce can tomatoes*
- 1 *green pepper, chopped*
- 1 *6-ounce can tomato paste*
- 2 *teaspoons crushed fennel seed*
- 1 *teaspoon each oregano, basil*
- ½ *teaspoon pepper*
- 3 *cups chopped cooked chicken* *
- 8 *ounces sliced black olives*
- 1 *12-ounce can sliced mushrooms, drained*
- ½ *cup Parmesan cheese*
- 2 *cups shredded mozzarella cheese*
- * Seasonal

Haddock-Shrimp Bake

Hilda Wolbaugh, Ohio

Place fillets in rectangular glass baking dish with thick portion toward outer edge of dish. Spoon soup over fillets. Microwave on High for 4 to 6 minutes, turning once. Combine remaining ingredients in bowl; mix well. Sprinkle over fillets. Microwave on High for 2 to 4 minutes or until fish flakes easily. Yield: 4 servings.

- 1½ *pounds fresh haddock fillets* *
- 1 *can cream of shrimp soup*
- ½ *cup melted butter*
- 1 *teaspoon onion powder*
- ½ *teaspoon Worcestershire sauce*
- ¼ *teaspoon garlic salt*
- 1¼ *cups Ritz cracker crumbs*
- * Seasonal

Recipes on pages 38 and 39.

Crab Meat Strata

Mary A. Yenney, Maryland

6	tablespoons margarine, softened
6	slices bread
1	pound crab meat *
½	cup chopped celery
½	cup finely chopped onion
½	cup finely chopped parsley
¾	cup mayonnaise
12	ounces Swiss cheese, shredded
5	eggs, beaten
3	cups milk
1	4-ounce jar chopped pimento
¼	teaspoon dry mustard
	Salt and pepper to taste
	* Seasonal

Spread margarine on both sides of bread. Arrange in 9x13-inch baking dish. Combine crab meat, celery, onion, parsley and mayonnaise in bowl; mix well. Spoon over bread. Sprinkle with shredded cheese. Combine eggs, milk, pimento and seasonings in bowl; mix well. Pour over cheese. Chill, covered, in refrigerator overnight. ** Bake at 350 degrees for 1 hour. Yield: 8 servings.

** *Make ahead to this point.*

Cheesy Tuna and Rice Dish

Betty Dexter, Ohio

¼	cup butter
3	tablespoons flour
¼	teaspoon salt
	Dash of pepper
1	large can evaporated milk
1½	cups shredded Cheddar cheese
2	tablespoons Parmesan cheese
1⅓	cups minute rice
1	tablespoon chopped parsley
	Paprika and cayenne pepper to taste
½	teaspoon each oregano, salt
1	16-ounce can tomatoes, drained
1	small onion, chopped
1	7-ounce can tuna

Melt butter in saucepan or microwave. Blend in flour, salt and pepper. Stir in evaporated milk. Cook until thickened, stirring constantly, or microwave, stirring twice. Add cheeses. Stir until cheeses melt. Combine rice, parsley and remaining seasonings in greased rectangular baking dish. Add 1⅓ cups water. Layer ⅔ of the tomatoes and all the onion, tuna and cheese sauce over rice. Top with remaining tomatoes. Refrigerate if desired. ** Bake at 375 degrees for 15 to 20 minutes or microwave on High until rice is tender. Yield: 6 servings.

** *Make ahead to this point.*

Easy Hopping John

Jim Noble, Texas

1	can cream of onion soup
¼	teaspoon garlic salt
½	teaspoon Tabasco sauce
1	10-ounce package frozen black-eyed peas
1½	cups cubed ham
1½	cups minute rice

Combine soup, 1 soup can water, garlic salt and Tabasco sauce in large saucepan. Add black-eyed peas and ham. Simmer, covered, for 40 minutes. Add 1½ cups water and minute rice. Simmer, covered, for 5 minutes. Let stand for 5 minutes. Yield: 5 to 6 servings.

Deviled Black-Eyed Peas
Mary Ann Chase, California

Cook black-eyed peas on stove top or in microwave using package directions; drain well. Combine oil, vinegar, onions, parsley, crushed garlic, basil, oregano, dry mustard, pepper and red pepper in bowl; mix well. Add warm peas; mix well. Chill, tightly covered, for 12 hours. ** Slice green pepper into rings. Arrange green pepper rings in serving bowl. Spoon black-eyed peas into bowl.
Yield: 6 servings.

** *Make ahead to this point.*

1	*10-ounce package frozen black-eyed peas*
2/3	*cup oil*
5	*tablespoons red wine vinegar*
2	*onions, chopped*
1	*cup chopped parsley*
2	*cloves of garlic, crushed*
2	*teaspoons basil*
1	*teaspoon oregano*
1/2	*teaspoon dry mustard*
1/2	*teaspoon pepper*
	Dash of red pepper flakes
1	*green pepper*

Veggie Chili
Linda Alpern, Maryland

Sauté garlic, onion, celery and cabbage in butter in large saucepan. Add carrots, zucchini, broccoli, mushrooms and cauliflower. Simmer for 10 minutes. Add corn, tomatoes, salt and pepper and Worcestershire sauce. Simmer for 5 minutes. Stir in tomato purée, kidney beans and chili powder. Simmer for 30 to 45 minutes or until of desired consistency. Spoon into serving bowls. Sprinkle with Swiss and provolone cheeses. Yield: 10 to 14 servings.

6	*cloves of garlic, minced*
1	*onion, finely chopped*
1/2	*stalk celery, chopped*
1/2	*head green cabbage, chopped* *
1/4	*head red cabbage, chopped* *
1/2	*cup butter*
4	*carrots, sliced* *
4	*zucchini, sliced*
1	*stalk broccoli, chopped* *
1	*pound mushrooms, chopped* *
1/2	*head cauliflower, chopped*
2 1/2	*cups corn*
2	*tomatoes, chopped*
	Salt and pepper to taste
2	*tablespoons Worcestershire sauce*
4	*cups tomato purée*
4	*cups cooked kidney beans*
	Chili powder to taste
	Grated Swiss cheese
	Grated provolone cheese
	* Seasonal

Mushroom Fritters

Marie Davidson, California

1 cup chopped fresh mushrooms *
2 tablespoons minced green onion
1 tablespoon minced pimento
1 cup buttermilk baking mix
1 egg yolk, beaten
¼ cup sour cream
¼ teaspoon salt
¼ teaspoon celery seed
1 egg white, stiffly beaten
Oil for deep frying
* Seasonal

Combine mushrooms, green onion, pimento and baking mix in bowl; mix lightly. Add mixture of egg yolk, sour cream and seasonings; mix well. Fold in stiffly beaten egg white gently. Drop by tablespoonfuls into 375-degree oil. Deep-fry for 2 minutes or until golden brown on both sides, turning once. Drain on paper towels.
Yield: 24 fritters.

Mustard Green Patties

Clara Shepherd, Michigan

2 pounds fresh mustard greens *
3 eggs, beaten
¼ cup Parmesan cheese
¼ cup flour
2 tablespoons minced onion
Salt and pepper to taste
½ cup fine dry bread crumbs
2 tablespoons oil
* Seasonal

Cook mustard greens in 1 cup boiling water in covered saucepan until tender. Drain well; chop finely. Combine with eggs, cheese, flour, onion and seasonings in bowl; mix well. Shape into patties. Coat with crumbs. Chill in refrigerator if desired. ** Brown on both sides in oil in skillet. Drain on paper towels.
Yield: 12 patties.

** *Make ahead to this point.*

Parsnip Soufflé

Mrs. William Brown, Ohio

¼ cup melted butter
¼ cup flour
⅓ cup evaporated milk
⅓ cup parsnip cooking liquid
2 cups mashed cooked parsnips *
3 eggs, beaten
* Seasonal

Blend butter and flour in saucepan or glass bowl. Stir in evaporated milk and cooking liquid gradually. Cook until thickened, stirring constantly, or microwave on Medium-High, stirring twice. Remove from heat. Add mashed parsnips and beaten eggs; mix well. Pour into greased 1-quart casserole. Bake at 350 degrees for 40 minutes.
Yield: 6 to 8 servings.

Glorious Potatoes
Margaret Olmsted, Michigan

Slice potatoes ¼ inch thick. Cook in water to cover in saucepan for 15 minutes or microwave until tender. Drain and mash. Add milk, butter, cream cheese, sour cream and salt and pepper; mix well. Spoon into serving dish. Garnish with chives. Yield: 4 servings. ✔

Preparation suggestion: May shape into patties and brown for 5 minutes on each side in a small amount of oil in skillet.

3   **large potatoes, peeled** *
¼   **cup milk**
2   **tablespoons butter**
3   **ounces cream cheese with chives, softened**
¼   **cup sour cream**
    Salt and pepper to taste
1   **teaspoon snipped chives**
    * Seasonal

Two-Alarm Grits
Sheryl Simpson, Texas

Cook grits in 8 cups boiling salted water in large saucepan until thickened, stirring constantly. Remove from heat. Add butter and cheese. Stir until cheese melts. Add Sherry, Worcestershire and Tabasco sauces, eggs and chilies; mix well. Spoon into buttered baking dish. Chill for several hours if desired. ** Bake at 350 degrees for 1 hour. Yield: 8 servings. ✔ 🥄 🍳

** *Make ahead to this point.*

2   **cups grits**
    Salt to taste
1½ **sticks butter**
1   **roll garlic cheese**
2   **tablespoons Sherry**
1   **teaspoon Worcestershire sauce**
1   **teaspoon Tabasco sauce**
2   **eggs, beaten**
1   **7-ounce can chopped green chilies**

Sour Cream Noodles
Dana Meyer, California

Cook noodles according to package directions; drain. Rinse with cold water; drain well. Combine cottage cheese, sour cream, onion and seasonings in large bowl; mix well. Add noodles; mix gently. Pour into greased 9x13-inch baking dish. Sprinkle cheese over top. Chill, covered, in refrigerator for several hours if desired. ** Bake, uncovered, at 350 degrees for 40 minutes or until bubbly. Yield: 8 servings. ✔ 🍎 🍳

** *Make ahead to this point.*

1   **8-ounce package noodles**
2   **cups cottage cheese**
2   **cups sour cream**
½   **cup chopped onion**
    Dash of Tabasco sauce
2   **teaspoons Worcestershire sauce**
1   **teaspoon salt**
⅛   **teaspoon garlic powder**
½   **cup shredded sharp Cheddar cheese**

Brown Rice Pilau

Dorothy Wisniewski, Michigan

2	beef bouillon cubes
1	teaspoon parsley flakes
½	teaspoon celery salt
⅜	teaspoon pepper
⅔	cup brown rice
½	cup chopped celery
8	ounces mushrooms, sliced *
1	small onion, chopped
1	tablespoon butter
1	tablespoon soy sauce
1	can sliced water chestnuts
	* Seasonal

Combine bouillon cubes, seasonings and 1½ cups water in saucepan. Bring to a boil. Stir in rice; reduce heat. Simmer, covered, until rice is tender. ** Sauté celery, mushrooms and onion in butter in skillet or microwave until tender. Add soy sauce and drained water chestnuts; mix well. Add rice. Heat to serving temperature, stirring frequently. Spoon into serving dish. Yield: 4 servings.

** *Make ahead to this point.*

Baked Onion Loaf

Kaye Windsor, California

2	cups buttermilk baking mix
1	small can French-fried onions
1½	cups shredded Monterey Jack cheese
4	eggs, beaten
1	can cream of onion soup

Combine baking mix and ½ cup water in bowl; mix well. Pat into greased 7x11-inch baking dish. Sprinkle half the onions and cheese over dough. Blend eggs and soup. Pour over onions and cheese. Top with remaining onions and cheese. Bake at 375 degrees for 25 minutes. Cut into squares. Serve hot. Yield: 6 servings.

Peanut Butter-Bran Muffins

Kim Sutherlin, Indiana

2½	cups bran flakes
1¼	cups milk
1	cup flour
½	cup packed brown sugar
1	tablespoon baking powder
½	teaspoon salt
1	egg, beaten
⅓	cup oil
⅓	cup peanut butter
½	cup finely chopped pecans

Combine cereal and milk in small bowl. Let stand for 3 minutes; mix well. Combine flour, brown sugar, baking powder and salt in bowl. Add egg, oil, peanut butter, cereal mixture and pecans; mix well. Spoon into greased muffin cups. Bake at 400 degrees for 20 minutes. Yield: 12 to 14 muffins.

Quick Batter Mix Rolls

Pat Dorman, New Mexico

Combine roll mix, shortening and 1 cup lukewarm water in bowl; mix well. Batter will be soft. Spoon into greased muffin cups. Let rise for 15 to 20 minutes or until doubled in bulk. Bake at 400 degrees for 15 minutes or until golden brown. Yield: 1 dozen.

3 **cups Batter Roll Mix**
4 **teaspoons melted shortening**

Batter Roll Mix

Combine yeast, milk powder, flour, baking powder, sugar and salt in bowl; mix well. Store in airtight container. Yield: 10 cups.

3 **packages or 3 tablespoons dry yeast**
1 **cup nonfat dry milk powder**
10 **cups flour**
2 **tablespoons baking powder**
½ **cup sugar**
2 **tablespoons salt**

Night-Before Yeast Waffles

Shirley Young, California

Dissolve yeast in ½ cup warm milk in bowl. Add eggs, flour, sugar, oil, salt and milk; mix well. Refrigerate, covered, overnight. ** Bake in hot waffle iron according to manufacturer's instructions. Serve with apple butter or syrup. Batter may be stored in refrigerator for 2 weeks. Yield: 10 waffles.

** *Make ahead to this point.*

1 **package or 1 tablespoon dry yeast**
½ **cup warm milk**
2 **eggs**
3 **cups flour**
1 **tablespoon sugar**
½ **cup oil**
1 **teaspoon salt**
2 **cups milk**

Cranberry-Pear Crisp

Michelle Britten, Texas

Combine pears, cranberries, sugar, flour and cinnamon in casserole; mix well. Bake, covered, at 350 degrees for 45 minutes or microwave on High until cranberries burst. Combine butter and brown sugar in saucepan. Cook until sugar melts, stirring constantly. Stir in oats. Sprinkle over cranberry mixture. Bake, uncovered, for 15 minutes longer. Serve warm or cold. Yield: 6 servings.

4 **firm pears, peeled, sliced ***
2 **cups cranberries**
1 **cup sugar**
¼ **cup flour**
½ **teaspoon cinnamon**
¼ **cup melted butter**
½ **cup packed brown sugar**
1 **cup quick-cooking oats**
   * Seasonal

Southwestern Fruit Delight

Kenna Kiser, Texas

½   cup tangerine sections *
½   cup chopped fresh pineapple *
1   apple, thinly sliced *
1   pear, thinly sliced *
1   banana, sliced
3   tablespoons pineapple juice *
1   teaspoon Fruit-Fresh
½   cup confectioners' sugar
1   teaspoon poppy seed
     * Seasonal

Combine tangerine sections, pineapple, apple, pear and banana in bowl; mix gently. Blend remaining ingredients in small bowl. Fold into fruit mixture gently. Chill, covered, overnight. Yield: 4 servings.

Ruby Red Grapefruit Cake

Kay Lynn Van Winkle, Texas

1   2-layer package white cake mix
1   envelope unflavored gelatin
¾   cup oil
¾   cup ruby red grapefruit juice *
4   eggs
1   cup ruby red grapefruit
     sections *
     * Seasonal

Combine cake mix, dry gelatin, oil and grapefruit juice in mixer bowl; mix well. Add eggs 1 at a time, beating well after each addition. Add grapefruit sections. Beat for 30 seconds longer. Tint with red food coloring if desired. Pour into greased and floured tube pan. Bake at 300 degrees for 1 hour. Cool in pan on wire rack for 10 minutes. Invert onto cake plate. Cool completely. Frost as desired or garnish with light sifting of confectioners' sugar.
Yield: 12 to 16 servings.

Maple Syrup Cake

Martha Warner, Michigan

2   eggs
1   cup packed brown sugar
1   cup maple syrup
1   teaspoon baking powder
1   teaspoon soda
1   cup sour cream
1   teaspoon vanilla extract
2   cups flour

Combine eggs and brown sugar in mixer bowl; mix well. Stir in maple syrup, baking powder, soda and sour cream. Add vanilla and flour; mix well. Pour into greased 9x13-inch cake pan. Bake at 325 degrees for 40 minutes or until cake tests done. Cool on wire rack. Cut into squares.
Yield: 24 servings.

Quick Saucepan Brownies

Jean Yost, Ohio

Melt chocolate chips and margarine in saucepan over low heat, stirring frequently. Remove from heat. Add baking mix, condensed milk and egg; mix well. Stir in walnuts. Pour into greased and floured 9x13-inch baking pan. Bake at 350 degrees for 20 minutes or until brownies pull from side of pan. Cool for 15 minutes. Cut into squares. Cool completely before serving.
Yield: 3 to 4 dozen.

1 *cup semisweet chocolate chips*
¼ *cup margarine*
2 *cups buttermilk baking mix*
1 *can sweetened condensed milk*
1 *egg, beaten*
1 *cup chopped walnuts*

Sugarless Apple Pie

Greta Cornell, California

Blend apple juice concentrate and cornstarch in saucepan. Cook over low heat until thickened, stirring constantly. Add butter, cinnamon and salt; mix well. Cook apples in a small amount of water in saucepan until tender-crisp. Add lemon juice and cooked mixture; mix gently. Spoon into pastry-lined 9-inch pie plate. Top with remaining pastry; seal edge and cut vents. Brush with milk. Bake at 350 degrees for 30 to 40 minutes or until golden brown.
Yield: 6 servings.

12 *ounces frozen apple juice concentrate, thawed*
3 *tablespoons cornstarch*
1 *tablespoon butter*
½ *teaspoon cinnamon*
   Pinch of salt
5 *large Golden Delicious apples, peeled, thinly sliced **
3 *tablespoons fresh lemon juice*
1 *recipe 2-crust pie pastry*
   * Seasonal

Mock Champagne

Combine grape juice and ginger ale in pitcher. Serve immediately in tall slender glasses over crushed ice.
Yield: 8 cups.

4 *cups white grape juice, chilled **
4 *cups ginger ale, chilled*
   * Seasonal

Cocoa Mocha Mix

Karen Rasengren

Combine all ingredients in bowl; mix well. Store in covered jar. Add 3 tablespoons cocoa mix to 1 cup boiling water in mug; mix well.
Yield: Enough mix for 10 cups cocoa.

1 *cup nondairy coffee creamer powder*
¼ *cup instant coffee granules*
½ *cup instant cocoa mix*
⅓ *cup sugar*
¼ *teaspoon cinnamon*
⅛ *teaspoon nutmeg*

February

Curried Cheese Bites

Nancy Mayes, Texas

1	**cup finely shredded sharp Cheddar cheese**
½	**cup chopped ripe olives**
½	**cup minced onion**
½	**teaspoon pepper**
1	**teaspoon curry powder**
¾	**cup mayonnaise**
6	**English muffins, split**

Combine cheese, olives and onion in bowl. Add seasonings and mayonnaise; mix well. Store in airtight container in refrigerator. ** Spread on split muffin halves. Cut each into 6 wedges. Place ½ inch apart on baking sheet. Bake at 350 degrees until topping is bubbly. Arrange on serving plate. Serve hot. Yield: 6 dozen.

** Make ahead to this point.

Fruity Popcorn Crunch

Jesse Skinner, Michigan

6	**cups popped popcorn**
1	**cup dry-roasted peanuts**
⅓	**cup shredded coconut**
¼	**cup honey**
2	**tablespoons melted butter**
¾	**cup chopped dried apricots**
¾	**cup raisins**

Combine popcorn, peanuts and coconut in 9x13-inch baking pan. Drizzle with mixture of honey and butter; mix gently. Bake at 300 degrees for 20 minutes, stirring every 5 minutes. Cool. Stir gently to separate. Add apricots and raisins; mix gently. Store in airtight container.
Yield: 8 cups.

Ten-Minute Crab Bisque

Doris Owen, Maryland

Cook frozen vegetables in saucepan or microwave according to package directions. Combine soups, half and half, Sherry and Worcestershire sauce in large saucepan; mix well. Bring to a simmer, stirring frequently. Add Japanese vegetables, crab meat, tomato and butter. Heat to serving temperature, stirring frequently. Ladle into soup bowls. Garnish with croutons and chopped parsley.
Yield: 6 servings. 🍏 ≋

1 *10-ounce package frozen Japanese-style vegetables*
1 *can Cheddar cheese soup*
1 *can New England clam chowder*
2 *soup cans half and half*
3 *tablespoons dry Sherry*
1 *teaspoon Worcestershire sauce*
8 *ounces crab meat, flaked ***
1 *tomato, peeled, chopped*
1 *tablespoon butter*
   Garlic-flavored croutons
   Chopped parsley
   * Seasonal

Sausage and Vegetable Chowder

Catharine Bates, California

Brown sausage in skillet over medium heat; drain and slice. Rinse and drain kidney beans. Drain and chop tomatoes. Combine sausage, beans, tomatoes, onion, potato, green pepper and carrot in large saucepan. Add bay leaf, garlic, seasonings and 2 cups water; mix well. Simmer, covered, for 30 minutes, stirring occasionally. Add zucchini. Simmer, covered, for 5 minutes. **Discard bay leaf.** Ladle into soup bowls. Yield: 10 servings. 🍏 ✳

1 *pound sweet Italian sausage*
1 *16-ounce can kidney beans*
1 *20-ounce can tomatoes*
1 *onion, chopped*
1 *potato, peeled, chopped*
½ *cup chopped green pepper*
1 *carrot, thinly sliced*
1 *bay leaf*
1 *clove of garlic, crushed*
¼ *teaspoon each thyme, basil and oregano*
   Salt and pepper to taste
1 *cup sliced zucchini*

Winter Fruit Salad Cups

Dana Meyer, California

Cut apples and bananas into bite-sized pieces. Peel and section tangerines. Combine fruits, coconut and walnuts in bowl. Blend sour cream with half the whipped topping in small bowl. Fold into fruit mixture gently. Chill in refrigerator if desired. ** Spoon into lettuce cups on salad plates. Top with dollop of remaining whipped topping.
Yield: 8 servings.

** Make ahead to this point.

2 *tart apples ***
2 *bananas*
2 *tangerines ***
2 *cups fresh pineapple chunks ***
½ *cup shredded coconut*
¼ *cup chopped walnuts*
¼ *cup sour cream*
1 *8-ounce carton whipped topping*
   Crisp lettuce cups
   * Seasonal

Sunshine Vegetable Salad

Kathie Lane, Nebraska

2	**bunches broccoli ***
½	**cup raisins**
½	**cup sunflower seed**
½	**cup chopped green onions**
½	**cup alfalfa sprouts**
½	**cup mayonnaise**
2	**tablespoons vinegar**
2	**tablespoons sugar**
¼	**cup milk**
8	**slices bacon**
	* Seasonal

Combine broccoli, raisins, sunflower seed, green onions and alfalfa sprouts in serving bowl; toss lightly. Blend mayonnaise, vinegar, sugar and milk in small bowl. Pour over vegetables. Chill, covered, for 2 hours to overnight. ** Cook bacon in skillet or microwave until crisp. Drain and crumble. Add to salad just before serving. Toss lightly.
Yield: 6 servings.

** *Make ahead to this point.*

Ship Ahoy Scallop Salad

1	**cup sour cream**
½	**cup mayonnaise**
1	**teaspoon dry mustard**
2	**teaspoons lemon juice**
2	**teaspoons drained capers**
2	**tablespoons chopped parsley**
½	**teaspoon basil**
4	**carrots, sliced ***
3	**cups small Brussels sprouts ***
¼	**cup oil**
½	**teaspoon salt**
¼	**teaspoon pepper**
4	**teaspoons lemon juice**
2	**onions, sliced**
3	**cups sliced cooked scallops ***
	Red onion rings
	Romaine lettuce
	* Seasonal

Blend sour cream and mayonnaise in small bowl. Add dry mustard, 2 teaspoons lemon juice, capers, parsley and basil; mix well. Chill, covered, until serving time. Cook carrots and Brussels sprouts separately in saucepan or microwave; drain and chill. ** Combine oil, salt, pepper and 4 teaspoons lemon juice in small bottle with shaker top. Separate onion slices into rings. Layer onion rings, carrots, scallops and sliced Brussels sprouts in glass salad bowl, sprinkling each layer with oil mixture. Garnish with red onion rings. Toss salad at the table just before serving. Serve on romaine-lined salad plates with sour cream dressing.
Yield: 4 servings.

** *Make ahead to this point.*

Taco Pot Roast

Robin Mock, Texas

1	**3-pound rump roast**
1	**can cream of mushroom soup**
1	**envelope taco seasoning mix**
½	**teaspoon minced garlic**
⅔	**cup red wine**

Place roast in baking dish or Crock•Pot. Spread soup over top. Sprinkle with seasoning mix and garlic. Add wine. Seal baking dish tightly with foil. Bake at 325 degrees for 3 hours or until tender.
Yield: 4 servings.

Preparation suggestion: Roast may also be baked in Crock•Pot on Low for 8 hours or on High for 3 hours.

Baked Chili

Susan Brown, Oklahoma

Brown beef, onions and green peppers in Dutch oven, stirring constantly. Stir in tomatoes, salt, paprika, cayenne pepper, cloves, bay leaves, chili powder, cumin, chopped red peppers and oregano. Bake, covered, at 300 degrees for 2 hours or until beef is tender. **Remove bay leaves.**
Yield: 6 servings.

2	*pounds beef, chopped*
2	*pounds onions, chopped*
2	*green peppers, chopped*
7	*cups chopped tomatoes*
2	*cans Ro-Tel tomatoes*
	Salt to taste
¼	*teaspoon paprika*
¼	*teaspoon cayenne pepper*
3	*whole cloves*
2	*bay leaves*
2	*tablespoons chili powder*
1	*teaspoon cumin*
4	*red peppers, chopped*
1	*teaspoon oregano*

Stroganoff Sandwiches

Joe Weems, Texas

Brown ground beef with onion and green pepper in skillet, stirring frequently; drain. Add salt, garlic powder, mustard and sour cream. Cook until heated through, stirring constantly. Do not boil. Slice tops from loaves; scoop out to form shallow shells. Spoon ground beef mixture into shells. Arrange green pepper, tomato and cheese over ground beef. Replace tops. Chill, wrapped in plastic wrap, if desired. **
Microwave wrapped sandwiches on Medium for 3 minutes or until heated through or place unwrapped sandwiches on baking sheet. Remove tops; place cut side up on baking sheet. Bake at 350 degrees for 10 minutes or until heated through. Broil until cheese bubbles if desired. Replace tops; place on serving plate.
Yield: 6 sandwiches.

*** Make ahead to this point.*

1	*pound ground beef*
1	*onion, chopped*
½	*green pepper, chopped*
1	*teaspoon salt*
¼	*teaspoon garlic powder*
1	*tablespoon mustard*
1	*cup sour cream*
6	*individual loaves French bread*
6	*to 12 green pepper rings*
6	*to 12 tomato slices*
6	*slices sharp cheese, cut into triangles*

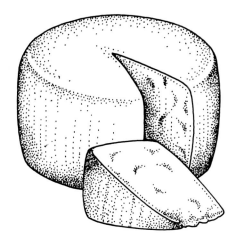

French Meat Loaf

Ginger Brinsfield, Maryland

1	**large round loaf French bread**
2	**pounds ground beef**
1	**onion, chopped**
½	**cup chopped celery**
	Salt and pepper to taste
1	**8-ounce can tomato sauce**
2	**eggs, beaten**
4	**ounces Cheddar cheese, sliced**

Cut 1 thick slice from side of bread. Scoop out center to form shell. Crumble bread; set bread crumbs and shell aside. Brown ground beef with onion and celery in skillet, stirring frequently; drain. Add salt, pepper and tomato sauce; mix well. Cool slightly. Stir in bread crumbs and eggs. Spoon into bread shell. Place loaf on baking sheet. Replace bread slice, securing with toothpicks. Arrange cheese slices on top. Place on baking sheet. Bake at 350 degrees for 30 minutes. Place on serving plate. Cut into slices.
Yield: 6 to 8 servings.

Stuffed Acorn Squash

Bobby Lou King, California

2	**acorn squash ***
½	**pound sausage**
2	**tablespoons chopped onion**
¼	**cup chopped celery**
2	**tablespoons chopped green pepper**
1½	**cups bread crumbs**
2	**tablespoons melted butter**
	* Seasonal

Cut squash into halves; discard seed. Place cut side down in shallow baking dish. Bake at 350 degrees for 45 minutes or until tender. Scoop out and mash pulp; reserve shells. Brown sausage with onion, celery and green pepper in skillet, stirring constantly; drain. Add to squash; mix well. Add ¾ cup bread crumbs or enough to make of desired consistency. Spoon into shells. Chill, tightly covered, for several hours if desired. ** Place on baking sheet. Toss remaining crumbs with butter. Sprinkle over stuffing. Bake at 350 degrees for 10 minutes or until crumbs are golden.
Yield: 4 servings.

** Make ahead to this point.

Cornish Game Hens with Wild Rice

Wendy Utley, Texas

1	**package long grain and wild rice mix**
1	**can cream of mushroom soup**
1	**can French onion soup**
½	**cup chopped celery**
½	**cup chopped onion**
2	**Cornish game hens**
2	**tablespoons melted margarine**

Prepare rice mix using package directions. Add soups, celery and onion; mix well. Stuff game hens with rice mixture. Spoon remaining rice into 9x11-inch baking dish. Arrange game hens on top. Brush with margarine; cover with foil. Refrigerate for several hours, if desired. ** Bake at 350 degrees for 1¼ hours or until tender.
Yield: 2 servings.

** Make ahead to this point.

Crock•Pot Turkey Gumbo

Luella Johnson, California

Cook turkey in skillet, stirring until crumbly. Combine with celery, onion, green pepper, okra, tomatoes, corn, seasonings and bacon in Crock•Pot. Mix oil and flour in saucepan. Cook over medium heat until medium brown, stirring constantly. Stir in broth gradually. Cook until thickened, stirring constantly. Pour into Crock•Pot; mix well. Cook on High for 3 to 4 hours. Add shrimp. Cook for 10 minutes longer. **Discard bay leaves.** Ladle over hot rice in soup bowls. Yield: 14 servings.

1	*pound ground fresh turkey*
3	*stalks celery, sliced*
1	*onion, chopped*
1	*green pepper, chopped*
1	*10-ounce package frozen sliced okra*
1	*16-ounce can stewed tomatoes*
½	*cup whole kernel corn*
2	*cloves of garlic, crushed*
1	*teaspoon Tabasco sauce*
1	*teaspoon basil*
½	*teaspoon thyme*
2	*bay leaves*
1	*teaspoon salt*
3	*slices crisp-fried bacon, crumbled*
⅓	*cup oil*
½	*cup flour*
4	*cups chicken broth*
6	*ounces cooked shrimp **
8	*cups cooked rice*

* Seasonal

Coquilles St. Jacques

Vicki Landrus, California

Combine green onions, mushrooms and butter in 2-quart glass casserole. Microwave on High for 2 to 3 minutes or until tender, stirring twice. Add scallops, wine, pimento and seasonings; mix well. Microwave on Medium for 7 minutes, stirring 3 times. Blend flour and cream. Stir into casserole. Microwave for 5 minutes or until sauce is thickened and scallops are tender. Let stand for 5 minutes. **Discard bay leaf.** Serve over rice. Yield: 4 servings.

2	*green onions, sliced*
1	*cup sliced mushrooms **
3	*tablespoons butter*
1	*pound fresh scallops **
½	*cup white wine*
1	*tablespoon chopped pimento*
½	*teaspoon salt*
	Pepper to taste
1	*bay leaf*
3	*tablespoons flour*
¼	*cup light cream*
2	*cups hot cooked rice*

* Seasonal

Mushroom Tetrazzini

Karen Perry, Ohio

8	*ounces mushrooms, sliced* *
1	*onion, chopped*
6	*tablespoons butter*
3	*tablespoons flour*
1	*teaspoon salt*
	Pepper to taste
2	*cups milk*
¼	*cup Sherry*
1	*cup shredded provolone cheese*
½	*cup chopped parsley*
8	*ounces spaghetti, cooked*
½	*cup shredded provolone cheese*
	* Seasonal

Sauté mushrooms and onion in butter in skillet. Sprinkle with flour, salt and pepper; mix well. Stir in milk and Sherry gradually. Cook until thickened, stirring constantly. Add 1 cup cheese and parsley. Cook until cheese melts, stirring constantly. Pour over hot cooked spaghetti in 2-quart baking dish. Sprinkle with remaining ½ cup cheese. Bake at 350 degrees or microwave until cheese melts.
Yield: 4 main-dish or 6 side-dish servings.

Maple-Flavored Baked Beans

Florence Linebaugh, Michigan

8	*cups drained cooked navy beans*
1	*cup catsup*
1½	*to 2 cups maple syrup*
½	*pound bacon, chopped*
2	*teaspoons salt*
¼	*teaspoon pepper*

Combine beans, catsup, maple syrup, bacon, salt and pepper in 3-quart casserole. Stir in 1 cup water. Bake at 300 degrees for 4 hours or until thickened.
Yield: 20 servings.

Nutty Brussels Sprouts

Exean Freeny, California

2	*pounds Brussels sprouts* *
½	*cup sliced almonds*
2	*tablespoons butter*
⅛	*teaspoon thyme*
1	*can cream of chicken soup*
	* Seasonal

Cook Brussels sprouts in a small amount of water in saucepan or microwave on High just until tender; drain well. ** Sauté almonds in butter in skillet until golden brown. Add thyme and soup. Heat until well blended, stirring constantly. Add Brussels sprouts. Heat to serving temperature. Pour into serving dish. Yield: 6 servings.

** *Make ahead to this point.*

Belgian Endive with Dijon Sauce

Ruthe Messenger, California

Combine endive, salt, onion and 3 tablespoons water in saucepan. Simmer for 10 minutes. Drain, reserving liquid. Add enough water to reserved liquid to measure ¼ cup. Arrange endive and onion in small baking dish. Combine sour cream, flour, sugar and mustard in bowl; mix well. Stir in reserved liquid. Spoon sour cream mixture over endive. Chill in refrigerator. ** Combine bread crumbs, chives and butter in bowl; mix well. Sprinkle over casserole. Bake at 325 degrees for 30 minutes.
Yield: 2 servings.

** *Make ahead to this point.*
Note: May substitute 1 bunch celery for endive. Trim, cut into fourths and simmer until tender.

2	**Belgian endive ***
⅛	**teaspoon salt**
½	**onion, sliced**
½	**cup sour cream**
1	**tablespoon flour**
1	**teaspoon sugar**
1½	**tablespoons Dijon mustard**
2	**tablespoons fine dry bread crumbs**
1	**tablespoon chopped chives**
1½	**teaspoons butter, melted**
	* Seasonal

Speedy Potato Puffs

Alice Capen, California

Bring 1 cup water to a boil in saucepan or microwave. Add 3 tablespoons margarine and seasoned salt. Remove from heat. Stir in sour cream, milk and potato flakes. Let stand for 2 minutes. Whip with fork until fluffy. Cool slightly. Add eggs; mix well. Shape into 3-inch balls. Roll in melted margarine; coat with mixture of crumbs and poultry seasoning. Arrange on buttered baking sheet. Bake at 400 degrees for 15 minutes or until golden brown.
Yield: 12 to 15 puffs.

3	**tablespoons margarine**
½	**teaspoon seasoned salt**
½	**cup sour cream**
¼	**cup milk**
2¾	**cups potato flakes**
2	**eggs, beaten**
3	**tablespoons melted margarine**
½	**cup fine dry bread crumbs**
½	**teaspoon poultry seasoning**

Barley-Mushroom Casserole

Ken Burkman, Ohio

Sauté barley, mushrooms and onion in margarine in skillet over low heat for 15 minutes or until golden brown. Pour into casserole. Stir in broth. Bake at 350 degrees for 1 hour or until liquid is absorbed.
Yield: 6 servings.

1	**cup barley**
2	**cups sliced mushrooms ***
½	**cup chopped onion**
1	**stick margarine**
2	**cans beef broth**
	* Seasonal

Pepper-Rice Casserole

Maxine Barlow, California

1½	cups cooked rice
¼	cup chopped onion
¼	cup chopped celery
2	tablespoons chopped jalapeño pepper
½	cup milk
1	egg plus 1 egg yolk
2	tablespoons oil
1	tablespoon chopped parsley
	Salt and pepper to taste
¼	cup grated Cheddar cheese

Combine rice, vegetables, milk, eggs, oil, parsley and seasonings in bowl; mix well. Pour into greased 8-inch square baking dish. Sprinkle with cheese. Refrigerate if desired. **
Bake at 250 degrees for 2 hours.
Yield: 4 servings.

** *Make ahead to this point.*

Mini Chip Cranberry-Nut Bread

Photograph for this recipe on page 20.

2	cups flour
1	cup sugar
1½	teaspoons baking powder
1	teaspoon salt
½	teaspoon soda
¾	cup orange juice
1	teaspoon grated orange rind
2	tablespoons shortening
1	egg
1	cup chopped fresh cranberries
¾	cup chopped nuts
1	cup semisweet miniature chocolate chips
1	cup confectioners' sugar
1	teaspoon butter
1	tablespoon milk
½	teaspoon vanilla extract

Combine flour, sugar, baking powder, salt and soda in large bowl. Add orange juice, orange rind, shortening and egg; mix well. Stir in cranberries, nuts and chocolate chips. Pour into greased loaf pan. Bake at 350 degrees for 60 to 65 minutes or until bread tests done. Cool for 10 minutes. Remove to wire rack to cool completely. Combine confectioners' sugar, butter, milk and vanilla in bowl; mix well. Drizzle over bread.
Yield: 12 servings.

Cheese Popovers

Wanda Stacke, Wisconsin

1	cup flour
½	teaspoon salt
2	eggs, slightly beaten
1	cup milk
1	cup grated cheese

Sift flour and salt into bowl. Combine eggs and milk in small bowl; mix well. Add to dry ingredients. Beat until smooth. Fill hot buttered muffin cups ⅓ full. Sprinkle with cheese. Add enough remaining batter to fill each cup ⅔ full. Bake at 425 degrees for 20 minutes. Reduce temperature to 350 degrees. Bake for 15 to 20 minutes longer or until golden brown. Yield: 8 servings.

Applesauce Muffins

Marilyn Routh, North Carolina

Cream butter and sugar in bowl until light and fluffy. Add eggs, applesauce and vanilla; mix well. Add mixture of flour, soda and spices; stir just until moistened. Stir in nuts and raisins. Spoon into paper-lined muffin cups. Bake at 350 degrees for 10 minutes or until brown. Store unused batter in covered container in refrigerator for up to 1 week. Yield: 4 dozen.

2	*sticks butter, softened*
2	*cups sugar*
2	*eggs*
2	*cups applesauce *
1	*teaspoon vanilla extract*
4	*cups flour*
2	*teaspoons each soda, cinnamon*
1	*teaspoon each cloves, allspice*
1	*cup chopped nuts*
½	*cup raisins*

* Seasonal

Mushroom Bread

Janice Jobson, Maryland

Separate rolls into triangles. Fit into 9-inch pie plate; do not seal edges. Spread mushrooms evenly in prepared pie plate. Drizzle margarine over mushrooms. Sprinkle with marjoram and cheese. Bake at 375 degrees for 20 minutes or until golden brown. Let stand for 5 to 10 minutes. Break into wedges. Yield: 8 wedges.

1	*package refrigerator crescent rolls*
2	*cups sliced mushrooms *
¼	*cup melted margarine*
¼	*teaspoon marjoram*
¼	*to ½ cup Parmesan cheese*

* Seasonal

Mini Chip Swirl Buns

Photograph for this recipe on page 20.

Dissolve yeast in ¼ cup warm water. Combine with buttermilk, egg, 1¼ cups flour, ¼ cup softened butter, sugar, baking powder and salt in large mixer bowl. Blend at low speed. Beat at medium speed for 2 minutes. Stir in enough remaining flour to make dough easy to handle. Knead on floured surface for 5 minutes. Roll into 9x16-inch rectangle. Combine brown sugar, 3 tablespoons melted butter and nuts in bowl; mix well. Spread over dough. Sprinkle with chocolate chips. Roll as for jelly roll from long side; pinch edge to seal. Cut into ½-inch slices. Arrange cut side up in circle on greased baking sheet. Let rise, covered, for 1 hour or until doubled in bulk. Bake at 350 degrees for 20 minutes. Cover outer edge with foil. Bake for 5 to 10 minutes longer. Glaze if desired. Serve warm. Yield: 11 servings.

1	*package or 1 tablespoon dry yeast*
⅔	*cup buttermilk*
1	*egg*
1¼	*cups flour*
¼	*cup butter, softened*
¼	*cup sugar*
1	*teaspoon baking powder*
1	*teaspoon salt*
1¾	*to 2 cups flour*
½	*cup packed brown sugar*
3	*tablespoons melted butter*
¾	*cup chopped nuts*
¾	*cup semisweet miniature chocolate chips*

Pear Tart

D'Lyn Loessin, Texas

¾	*cup flour*
3	*tablespoons sugar*
¼	*teaspoon allspice*
6	*tablespoons butter*
1	*envelope unflavored gelatin*
½	*cup orange juice* *
3	*ripe pears, puréed* *
3	*tablespoons brown sugar*
¼	*teaspoon salt*
⅛	*teaspoon allspice*
¼	*cup orange marmalade*
3	*ripe pears, thinly sliced* *
¼	*cup orange marmalade*
	* *Seasonal*

Mix flour, sugar and ¼ teaspoon allspice in bowl. Cut in butter until crumbly. Knead until mixture forms ball. Press over bottom and side of 9-inch tart pan; prick with fork. Bake at 400 degrees for 10 minutes or until golden. Cool on wire rack. Soften gelatin in orange juice in saucepan. Cook over low heat until gelatin dissolves, stirring constantly. Remove from heat. Add pear purée, brown sugar, salt, ⅛ teaspoon allspice and ¼ cup marmalade to gelatin mixture; blend well. Chill for 45 minutes, stirring occasionally. Pour into prepared tart pan. Chill, covered, until set. ** Arrange sliced pears over top. Brush with melted marmalade. Chill until serving time. Yield: 12 servings.

** *Make ahead to this point.*

Strawberry Angel Dessert

Marilyn Senn, Maryland

16	*ounces frozen strawberries, thawed*
8	*ounces cream cheese, softened*
½	*cup confectioners' sugar*
2	*cups whipping cream*
½	*cup confectioners' sugar*
1	*angel food cake, cubed*
10	*ounces frozen raspberries, thawed*
½	*cup sugar*
2	*teaspoons cornstarch*
½	*cup currant jelly*

Drain strawberries, reserving ½ cup juice. Combine strawberry juice, cream cheese and ½ cup confectioners' sugar in mixer bowl. Beat for 3 minutes. Beat whipping cream and ½ cup confectioners' sugar until stiff peaks form. Fold half the whipped cream gently into cream cheese mixture. Fold in strawberries and cake. Spoon into glass serving bowl. Chill for 2 hours. ** Drain raspberries, reserving juice. Add enough water to reserved juice to measure 1 cup. Press raspberries through sieve. Combine raspberry purée, reserved juice, sugar, cornstarch and jelly in saucepan. Cook until thickened, stirring constantly. Cool. Decorate dessert with remaining whipped cream and fresh strawberries. Spoon into dessert dishes. Serve with cooled raspberry sauce. Yield: 8 servings.

** *Make ahead to this point.*

Strawberry Yogurt and Rice Parfaits

Lynn Covington, Texas

½	*cup strawberry yogurt*
¾	*cup cooked rice, chilled*
5	*ounces frozen strawberries, thawed*
	Whipped topping

Combine yogurt and rice in bowl; mix well. Chill, covered, in refrigerator. ** Layer rice and strawberries alternately in parfait glasses. Garnish with whipped topping. Yield: 2 servings.

** *Make ahead to this point.*

Apple Pie

Photograph for this recipe on page 54.

Line pie plate with pastry, leaving 1-inch overhang. Combine sugar, cornstarch, cinnamon, apples and lemon juice in bowl; toss to coat. Spoon into prepared pie plate. Dot with margarine. Top with remaining pastry, fluting edge and cutting steam vents. Bake at 425 degrees for 50 minutes or until golden brown.
Yield: 6 to 8 servings. 🐦 🥘

1	recipe 2-crust pie pastry
¾	cup sugar
1	tablespoon Argo cornstarch
1	teaspoon cinnamon
6	cups sliced peeled apples *
1	tablespoon lemon juice
1	tablespoon Mazola margarine
	* Seasonal

Apple-Orange Squares

Erin Balzano, New Mexico

Combine margarine and brown sugar in saucepan or glass bowl. Heat or microwave until well blended, stirring occasionally. Combine with applesauce, egg, orange rind and 1 teaspoon vanilla in bowl. Add mixture of flour, baking powder, soda and salt; mix well. Stir in pecans. Pour into greased and floured 7x12-inch baking dish. Bake at 350 degrees for 25 minutes. Combine remaining ingredients in bowl; mix well. Spread over warm layer. Cool. Cut into squares. Yield: 1½ dozen. ✔4 🐦 ≋ 🥘

6	tablespoons margarine
1	cup packed brown sugar
½	cup applesauce *
1	egg, beaten
1	teaspoon shredded orange rind
1	teaspoon vanilla extract
1¼	cups flour
1	teaspoon baking powder
¼	teaspoon each soda, salt
½	cup chopped pecans
1½	cups confectioners' sugar
2	tablespoons orange juice *
½	teaspoon vanilla extract
	* Seasonal

Cold Quack

Prexy Pegram, Texas

Combine all ingredients in pitcher; mix well. Chill in refrigerator. ** Serve over crushed ice.
Yield: 2 servings. ✔4 🐦 🥘

*** Make ahead to this point.*

1	10-ounce can Fresca
1	10-ounce can sugar-free black cherry cola
1	tablespoon apple cider *
1	tablespoon cider vinegar
	* Seasonal

March

Curried Appetizer Tidbits

Emily Hall, Maryland

1	**8-ounce package brown and serve sausage links**
1	**13-ounce can syrup-pack pineapple tidbits**
¼	**teaspoon curry powder**
¼	**teaspoon seasoned salt**

Cut sausages in half crosswise. Place in microwave browning dish preheated according to manufacturer's instructions. Microwave on High for 1 minute. Turn sausages over. Add drained pineapple. Sprinkle with seasonings. Microwave for 1½ minutes. Keep warm in chafing dish.
Yield: 8 to 10 servings.

Golden Broccoli Dip

Jane Brown, Hawaii

1	**bunch broccoli, chopped ***
1	**can golden mushroom soup**
1	**cup chopped mushrooms ***
⅛	**teaspoon garlic powder**
	Salt to taste
8	**ounces Velveeta cheese**
	Assorted crackers
	Bite-sized fresh vegetables
	* Seasonal

Cook broccoli in a small amount of water in saucepan until tender-crisp. Combine soup, well-drained broccoli, mushrooms and seasonings in blender container. Process until well mixed. Pour into glass bowl. Chill, covered, for several hours if desired. ** Add cheese. Microwave on High until cheese melts, stirring occasionally. Pour into chafing dish. Serve hot with crackers and vegetables.
Yield: 4 cups.

** Make ahead to this point.

Smoked Oyster Roll
Rosann Seibel, Maryland

Drain and chop oysters. Combine cream cheese, mayonnaise, Worcestershire sauce and garlic powder in mixer bowl. Beat until smooth. Spread into ½-inch thick rectangle on plastic wrap. Cover with finely chopped oysters; roll as for jelly roll. Chill, wrapped in plastic wrap, for 45 minutes. Press pecans over roll. Wrap in plastic wrap. Store in refrigerator. ** Place unwrapped roll on serving plate. Cut into slices. Serve with crackers. Yield: 32 slices.

** *Make ahead to this point.*

2	*cans smoked oysters*
16	*ounces cream cheese, softened*
2	*tablespoons mayonnaise*
2	*teaspoons Worcestershire sauce*
⅛	*teaspoon garlic powder*
1	*cup chopped pecans*
	Assorted crackers

Mexican Won Tons

Cut cheese into ½-inch cubes. Place 1 cheese cube and ½ teaspoonful drained chilies on each won ton skin. Fold into triangle; moisten edges and seal tightly. Deep-fry in 375-degree oil until golden brown; drain on paper towels. Arrange on serving plate. Serve hot with chilled guacamole or salsa. Yield: 8 servings.

1	*pound Monterey Jack cheese*
1	*4-ounce can chopped green chilies*
1	*package won ton skins*
	Oil for deep frying
1	*recipe favorite guacamole*
	Red or green chili salsa

Taco Beef Soup
Joann Kikel, Oregon

Cook ground beef and onion in saucepan or large glass bowl in microwave until brown, stirring frequently; drain. Add tomatoes, beans, tomato sauce, seasoning mix and 1½ cups water. Bring to a simmer, covered, over medium heat or in microwave on High. Simmer for several minutes. Ladle into serving bowls. Garnish with avocado, shredded cheese, chips and sour cream as desired.
Yield: 6 servings.

½	*pound ground beef*
¼	*cup chopped onion*
1	*16-ounce can tomatoes*
1	*8-ounce can kidney beans*
1	*8-ounce can tomato sauce*
2	*tablespoons taco seasoning mix*
1	*avocado, chopped* *
	Cheddar cheese, shredded
	Corn or tortilla chips
	Sour cream
	* *Seasonal*

Vegetable Chowder

Photograph for this recipe on page 19.

1	*cup chopped celery*
1	*cup chopped onion*
1	*clove of garlic, minced*
¼	*cup Mazola margarine*
4	*cups beef bouillon*
3	*cups chopped potatoes **
1	*17-ounce can whole kernel corn*
1	*16-ounce can tomatoes*
2	*cups sliced carrots **
½	*teaspoon celery seed*
½	*teaspoon thyme*
½	*teaspoon salt*
2	*tablespoons cornstarch*
	* Seasonal

Sauté celery, onion and garlic in margarine in stockpot. Add bouillon, potatoes, corn, tomatoes, carrots and seasonings. Simmer, covered, for 30 minutes or until vegetables are tender. Stir in mixture of cornstarch and ¼ cup cold water. Bring to a boil over medium heat, stirring constantly. Cook for 1 minute longer. Ladle into soup bowls.

Yield: 6 servings.

Mama Cook's Brunswick Stew

Pearl Cook, Georgia

1	*pound beef chuck*
1	*pound pork shoulder **
1	*cup chopped onion*
1	*tablespoon oil*
3	*pounds chicken pieces **
1	*28-ounce can tomatoes*
1	*tablespoon sugar*
2	*teaspoons salt*
1	*teaspoon basil*
½	*teaspoon thyme*
½	*teaspoon freshly ground pepper*
1	*bay leaf, crushed*
3	*cups chopped peeled potatoes **
2	*cups corn*
2	*cups lima beans*
	* Seasonal

Cut beef and pork into ½-inch cubes. Brown with onion in oil in skillet; drain. Add chicken, undrained chopped tomatoes, sugar and seasonings. Simmer, covered, for 45 minutes or until chicken is tender. Add enough water during cooking to cover meats. Remove chicken; set aside to cool. Add potatoes. Bring to a boil. Reduce heat. Simmer, uncovered, for 30 minutes or until beef and pork are almost tender. Bone chicken; cut into ½-inch cubes. Add chicken, corn and lima beans to stew. Cook for 15 minutes longer or until beef and pork are tender. Adjust seasonings. Chill overnight to blend flavors. ** Reheat before serving.

Yield: 12 servings.

** Make ahead to this point.

Frozen Apricot Salad

Phyllis McBee, Kansas

1	*16-ounce can apricots*
½	*cup sugar*
½	*cup chopped pecans*
2	*8-ounce cartons peach yogurt*
1	*8-ounce carton plain yogurt*
	Cinnamon to taste

Drain and chop apricots. Combine with sugar, pecans and peach yogurt in bowl; mix well. Spoon into paper-lined muffin cups. Freeze until firm. Store in plastic bag in freezer. ** Remove paper; arrange frozen salads on chilled serving tray. Garnish with dollop of plain yogurt and sprinkle of cinnamon. Yield: 12 servings.

** Make ahead to this point.

Greek Salad

Amy Taylor, Texas

Soak dried beans in water in saucepan overnight. Add salt and pepper to taste. Cook for 1 hour or until tender. Drain well. Cook potatoes in boiling water until tender. Cool and chop. Cook peas and green beans on stove top or in microwave using package directions; drain. Combine navy beans, potatoes, peas, green beans, beets, pickles, drained capers and enough salad dressing to moisten; mix well. Chill overnight. ** Spoon salad onto romaine-lined serving plate. Garnish with mixture of mayonnaise and beet juice. Decorate with ripe olives.
Yield: 12 servings. 🍎 ≋ 🥘

** *Make ahead to this point.*

½ **cup dried white navy beans**
   Salt and pepper to taste
4 **unpeeled potatoes ***
1 **10-ounce package frozen green peas**
1 **10-ounce package frozen green beans**
1 **16-ounce can diced beets, drained**
6 **medium dill pickles, chopped**
1 **jar capers, drained**
½ **cup (or more) salad dressing**
   Romaine lettuce
¼ **cup mayonnaise**
1 **teaspoon beet juice**
1 **can ripe olives, drained**
   * Seasonal

Lucky Fruited Green Salad

Combine first 5 ingredients in covered jar; shake well. Chill dressing in refrigerator. Place greens in salad bowl. Slice peeled oranges thinly crosswise; cut slices in half. Arrange over greens. Sprinkle celery, green onions and almonds over top. Chill until serving time. ** Add dressing just before serving; toss lightly.
Yield: 6 servings. 🔺 🍎 🌏 🥘

** *Make ahead to this point.*

¼ **cup oil**
2 **tablespoons sugar**
2 **tablespoons malt vinegar**
¼ **teaspoon salt**
⅛ **teaspoon almond extract**
3 **cups torn lettuce**
3 **cups fresh spinach ***
3 **oranges, peeled**
1 **cup thinly sliced celery**
2 **tablespoons sliced green onions**
⅓ **cup toasted slivered almonds**
   * Seasonal

Spinach-Rotini Salad

Pamela Majoras, Ohio

Rinse spinach well; drain well. Tear into pieces. Combine spinach, mushrooms and pasta in salad bowl. Chill, covered, if desired. ** Combine vinegar, oil, salt and pepper in covered jar; shake vigorously. Pour desired amount of dressing over salad; toss gently. Serve immediately.
Yield: 4 to 6 servings. 🔺 🍎 🌏 🥘

** *Make ahead to this point.*

3 **bunches fresh spinach ***
1 **cup sliced mushrooms ***
2 **cups cooked rotini**
1 **cup red wine vinegar**
½ **cup oil**
½ **teaspoon each salt and pepper**
   * Seasonal

Molded Pasta Salad

Jacqueline Owings, Maryland

12	*ounces sliced ham*
4	*ounces sharp Cheddar cheese*
4	*cups cooked macaroni*
½	*cup chopped celery*
¼	*cup sliced green onions*
⅓	*cup chopped green pepper*
2	*tablespoons chopped pimento*
¼	*cup pickle relish*
½	*cup mayonnaise*
1	*tablespoon Dijon mustard*
	Salt to taste
6	*cups shredded lettuce*

Cut ham and cheese into thin strips. Combine with macaroni, celery, green onions, green pepper, pimento and drained relish in bowl. Add mixture of mayonnaise, mustard and salt; mix gently. Press into oiled mold. Refrigerate until serving time. ** Invert onto lettuce-lined plate.
Yield: 6 to 8 servings.

** *Make ahead to this point.*

Irish Pot Roast

Photograph for this recipe on page 53.

1	*3 to 5-pound boneless beef eye-of-chuck roast*
¼	*cup flour*
1	*teaspoon salt*
¼	*teaspoon pepper*
3	*tablespoons oil*
1	*teaspoon instant beef bouillon*
1	*teaspoon leaf thyme*
6	*medium potatoes*
1	*pound leeks*
½	*cup tea*
2	*tablespoons snipped parsley*

Coat roast with mixture of flour, salt and pepper. Reserve any remaining flour mixture. Brown roast in oil in heavy saucepan; drain. Add ¾ cup water, instant bouillon and thyme. Cook, tightly covered, over low heat for 1½ to 2½ hours or until almost tender. Peel potatoes; cut into halves. Add to pot roast. Cook, covered, for 40 minutes. Cut leeks into 2-inch pieces. Add to pot roast. Cook, covered, for 20 minutes or until roast and vegetables are tender. Arrange roast and vegetables on heated serving platter. Stir mixture of reserved flour and tea into pan juices. Cook until thickened, stirring constantly. Cook over low heat for 3 to 5 minutes. Garnish potatoes with parsley. Serve roast and vegetables with gravy.
Yield: 8 to 10 servings.

Reuben Casserole

Carolyn Simpson, California

1	*12-ounce can corned beef, drained*
¼	*cup (or more) Thousand Island dressing*
1	*16-ounce can sauerkraut*
8	*ounces Swiss cheese, shredded*
6	*slices rye bread*
¼	*cup melted margarine*

Layer flaked corned beef, salad dressing, sauerkraut and cheese in 8x12-inch baking dish. Toss crumbled bread with margarine. Sprinkle over layers. Chill in refrigerator if desired. ** Bake at 350 degrees for 30 minutes or microwave on High until heated through.
Yield: 6 servings.

** *Make ahead to this point.*

Argentinean Ground Beef

Clara Jensen, California

Sauté ground beef, onions, green pepper and garlic in skillet until vegetables are tender; drain. Drain beans, reserving liquid. Add beans, hominy and seasonings; mix well. Add enough reserved bean liquid to make of desired consistency. Simmer for 10 minutes. Pour into serving dish.
Yield: 4 servings.

1	*pound ground beef*
1½	*cups chopped onions*
1	*cup chopped green pepper*
3	*cloves of garlic, crushed*
1	*8-ounce can kidney beans*
1	*8-ounce can golden hominy*
1	*teaspoon salt*
1	*teaspoon basil*
½	*teaspoon pepper*
¼	*teaspoon sugar*
¼	*teaspoon oregano*
⅛	*teaspoon crushed red pepper flakes*

Ham and Broccoli Soufflé

Jean LaCross, Michigan

Drain broccoli; press out excess moisture. Sauté onion in margarine in skillet or microwave until tender. Add flour, salt and pepper; mix well. Stir in milk gradually. Cook until thickened, stirring constantly, or microwave, stirring twice. Stir a small amount of hot mixture into egg yolks; stir egg yolks into hot mixture. Cook over low heat for 2 minutes, stirring constantly, or microwave on Medium until thickened, stirring twice. Stir in broccoli, ham and cheese. Beat egg whites with cream of tartar until soft peaks form. Fold in broccoli mixture gently. Spoon into lightly greased 1½-quart soufflé dish. Bake in preheated 350-degree oven for 30 minutes or until knife inserted near center comes out clean. Serve immediately.
Yield: 4 servings.

2	*cups chopped cooked broccoli **
2	*tablespoons chopped onion*
3	*tablespoons margarine*
3	*tablespoons flour*
½	*teaspoon salt*
⅛	*teaspoon pepper*
1	*cup milk*
4	*egg yolks, beaten*
1	*cup finely chopped ham*
3	*tablespoons Parmesan cheese*
4	*egg whites*
1	*teaspoon cream of tartar*

* Seasonal

Buttermilk Chicken

Hazel Laterro, Ohio

Dip chicken in ¼ cup buttermilk. Coat with mixture of flour, salt and pepper. Melt margarine in 9x13-inch baking pan. Arrange chicken skin side down in prepared pan. Bake at 375 degrees for 30 minutes. Turn chicken over. Bake for 15 minutes longer. Blend 1¼ cups buttermilk and soup in bowl. Pour over chicken. Bake for 15 minutes longer or until tender. Yield: 4 servings.

1	*2½-pound chicken, cut up **
¼	*cup buttermilk*
¾	*cup flour*
1½	*teaspoons salt*
½	*teaspoon pepper*
¼	*cup margarine*
1¼	*cups buttermilk*
1	*can cream of chicken soup*

* Seasonal

Broiled Chicken and Fruit

1	cup melted butter
2	teaspoons cornstarch
2	teaspoons grated lemon rind
½	cup lemon juice
⅔	cup pineapple juice
¼	cup minced onion
2	teaspoons soy sauce
¼	teaspoon thyme
3	chickens, cut up *
¼	cup melted butter
	Salt and pepper to taste
12	pineapple slices *
12	peach halves
¾	to 1 cup apple butter *
	* Seasonal

Blend 1 cup butter, cornstarch, lemon rind and juices in saucepan. Add onion, soy sauce and thyme. Cook until thickened, stirring constantly. ** Arrange chicken pieces skin side down on rack in broiler pan. Brush with melted butter; sprinkle with salt and pepper. Broil 7 inches from heat source for 30 minutes or until light brown, basting occasionally with ¼ cup butter. Turn chicken over. Broil for 20 minutes longer. Arrange pineapple slices and peach halves filled with apple butter on rack. Brush with prepared sauce. Broil chicken and fruit for 5 minutes. Remove to serving platter. Serve with remaining sauce.

Yield: 12 servings.

** Make ahead to this point.

Chicken Breasts Italiano

Anita Zieman, Colorado

3	tablespoons butter
6	chicken breast filets *
1	package Italian-flavored Shake and Bake
12	ounces mushrooms *
3	tablespoons butter
¼	cup light cream
½	cup dry white wine
6	thin slices prosciutto
6	thin slices Swiss cheese
	* Seasonal

Melt 3 tablespoons butter in baking dish. Coat filets with Shake and Bake according to package directions; arrange in prepared dish. Bake at 400 degrees for 20 minutes. Slice mushrooms thinly. Sauté mushrooms in 3 tablespoons butter in skillet. Stir in cream and wine. Layer mushrooms, prosciutto and cheese over chicken. Bake for 5 minutes or until cheese melts.

Yield: 6 servings.

Broccoli Puff

Mary Allen, Georgia

2	pounds fresh broccoli *
1	can cream of mushroom soup
½	cup shredded Cheddar cheese
¼	cup milk
¼	cup mayonnaise
1	egg, beaten
1¼	cups dry bread crumbs
1	tablespoon melted butter
	* Seasonal

Trim broccoli. Cook broccoli in a small amount of water in saucepan for 5 minutes, or microwave on High until tender-crisp; drain. Arrange broccoli spears in greased 9x13-inch baking dish. Pour mixture of soup, cheese, milk, mayonnaise and egg over broccoli. Chill in refrigerator for several hours if desired. ** Sprinkle mixture of bread crumbs and butter over broccoli. Bake at 350 degrees for 45 minutes or until topping is golden.

Yield: 8 servings.

** Make ahead to this point.

O'Topper Potatoes

Photograph for this recipe on page 1.

Maxi Baked Potatoes

6   *baking potatoes*
   Sausage Topping
   Ratatouille Topping
   Tuna Topping

Bake potatoes at 400 degrees for 45 minutes to 1 hour or microwave on High until soft. Cut cross in top of each potato. Squeeze gently to open. Place on serving plate. Spoon topping of choice into each potato.
Yield: 6 servings.

Note: Oven-baked potatoes may be wrapped in foil for softer skins or rubbed with oil for crisper skins.

Sausage Topping

1   *pound sweet Italian sausage*
1   *red pepper, sliced*
1   *green pepper, sliced*
1   *onion, chopped*
1   *tablespoon curry powder*
2   *tablespoons Dijon mustard*
1½ *cups dry white wine*
8   *ounces mushrooms, sliced ***
1   *cup sour cream*
   * Seasonal

Sauté sausage in medium skillet until lightly browned. Add peppers and onion. Cook for 5 minutes. Stir in curry and mustard. Cook for 5 minutes longer. Add wine. Cook until slightly thickened. Stir in mushrooms and sour cream. Heat to serving temperature.
Yield: Enough for 6 potatoes.

Ratatouille Topping

1   *small eggplant, cubed*
1   *red onion, chopped*
3   *cloves of garlic, minced*
1   *green pepper, coarsely chopped*
1   *red pepper, coarsely chopped*
2   *tomatoes, coarsely chopped*
1   *cup cooked cut green beans*
1   *zucchini, slivered*
1   *cup sliced mushrooms ***
   * Seasonal

Sauté eggplant in a small amount of oil in large skillet over medium heat until tender. Add onion and garlic. Sauté for 1 minute. Add peppers. Cook for 1 minute longer. Add tomatoes and ½ cup water. Simmer for 3 minutes. Add green beans, zucchini strips and mushrooms. Cook until heated through. Yield: Enough for 6 potatoes.

Tuna Topping

2   *tablespoons melted butter*
3   *tablespoons flour*
2½ *cups milk*
½   *teaspoon dry mustard*
¼   *teaspoon hot pepper sauce*
2   *7-ounce cans tuna, drained*
¼   *cup chopped pitted black olives*
¼   *cup chopped pimento*

Combine butter and flour in saucepan; mix well. Cook over medium heat for 3 minutes, stirring constantly. Remove from heat. Stir in milk gradually. Cook until thickened, stirring constantly. Add mustard and hot pepper sauce. Fold in tuna, olives and pimento.
Yield: Enough for 6 potatoes.

Shrimp Casserole
Priscilla Teeter, Maryland

2 pounds large unpeeled fresh
  shrimp *
1 tablespoon lemon juice
3 tablespoons oil
¼ cup minced onion
¼ cup chopped green pepper
2 tablespoons butter
2 cups cooked rice
1 can tomato soup
1 cup heavy cream
½ cup Sherry
¼ cup slivered almonds
  Salt and pepper to taste
⅛ teaspoon mace
¼ cup sliced almonds
  Paprika to taste
  * Seasonal

Cook shrimp in water to cover in saucepan until pink; drain and peel. Place in bowl; sprinkle with lemon juice and oil. Chill in refrigerator. ** Sauté onion and green pepper in butter in skillet for 5 minutes. Add shrimp, rice, soup, cream, Sherry, slivered almonds, salt, pepper and mace; mix well. Spoon into greased 2-quart casserole. Top with sliced almonds and paprika. Chill in refrigerator if desired. ** Bake at 350 degrees for 50 minutes or until bubbly.
Yield: 6 servings.

** *Make ahead to this point.*

Skillet Cabbage
Cindi Wall, Texas

¼ cup bacon drippings
  or margarine
4 cups shredded cabbage *
2 cups chopped celery
2 onions, sliced
2 tomatoes, chopped
1 green pepper, chopped
2 tablespoons sugar
  Salt and pepper to taste
  * Seasonal

Preheat electric skillet to 375 degrees. Add bacon drippings. Heat for 1 minute. Add cabbage, celery, onions, tomatoes, green pepper, sugar and salt and pepper. Stir-fry for 5 minutes or until vegetables are tender-crisp.
Yield: 6 servings.

Mushroom and Potato Skillet
LaVerne McKeever, Maryland

1 pound potatoes *
8 ounces mushrooms, sliced *
1 small onion, minced
3 tablespoons butter
  Salt and freshly ground pepper
  to taste
½ cup sour cream
1 tablespoon minced dill
  * Seasonal

Cook unpeeled potatoes in boiling water until tender. Cool.** Sauté mushrooms and onion in butter in large skillet until tender. Peel and slice potatoes. Add to skillet. Sprinkle with seasonings. Cook over medium heat for 5 minutes or until heated through, turning occasionally with spatula. Add sour cream; mix gently. Spoon into serving dish. Sprinkle with dill.
Yield: 4 servings.

** *Make ahead to this point.*

Scalloped Potatoes

Leonore Fergus, Ohio

Microwave butter in 4-cup glass measure on High for 30 seconds. Blend in flour, salt and pepper. Stir in milk. Microwave for 8 to 10 minutes or until thickened, stirring once. Layer potatoes, onion and sauce alternately in greased 2-quart casserole. Sprinkle with cheese and paprika. Microwave, covered, on High for 17 to 19 minutes or until potatoes are tender. Let stand for 5 minutes before serving. Yield: 4 to 6 servings.

3 *tablespoons butter*
2 *tablespoons flour*
  Salt and pepper to taste
2 *cups milk*
3½ *to 4 cups thinly sliced potatoes* *
2 *tablespoons minced onion*
½ *cup shredded sharp cheese*
  Paprika to taste
  * Seasonal

Creamed Spinach

Lila Warrell, Indiana

Rinse spinach well; tear or chop if desired. Cook in a small amount of water in saucepan, or microwave on High in glass bowl for 10 minutes or until tender; drain. Stir in sour cream. Spoon into serving dish. Sprinkle with nutmeg. Yield: 6 to 8 servings.

2 *pounds fresh spinach* *
⅓ *cup sour cream*
½ *teaspoon nutmeg*
  * Seasonal

Creamed Vegetable Medley

JoAnn J. Kresky, Michigan

Combine soup, parsley, onion and salt in bowl; mix well. Add vegetables; mix well. Pour into 1½-quart casserole. Bake at 400 degrees for 35 minutes, or microwave on High for 10 to 12 minutes. Stir gently. Sprinkle with cheese. Bake or microwave until cheese melts. Yield: 6 servings.

1 *can cream of chicken soup*
¼ *cup chopped parsley*
1 *tablespoon instant minced onion*
  Salt to taste
2 *cups sliced carrots* *
2 *cups cauliflowerets* *
1 *10-ounce package frozen green peas, thawed*
1 *cup shredded sharp Cheddar cheese*
  * Seasonal

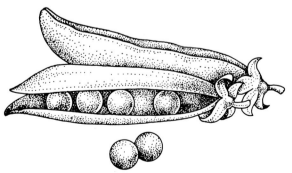

Twice as Nice Rice
Rene Givens, Michigan

½ cup wild rice
2 stalks celery, chopped
1 large onion, chopped
3 tablespoons butter
3 cups chicken broth
3 tablespoons chopped fresh
   parsley
½ teaspoon Kitchen Bouquet
   Salt and pepper to taste
¼ teaspoon sage
½ teaspoon basil
1 cup long grain rice
2 tablespoons slivered almonds

Sauté wild rice, celery and onion in butter in skillet until onion is tender. Add broth, parsley and seasonings. Bring to a boil; reduce heat. Simmer, covered, for 40 minutes. Add long grain rice. Bring to a boil. Simmer, covered, for 15 to 20 minutes. Add almonds. Spoon into serving dish. Yield: 4 servings.

Loquat Bread
Emma Michalk, California

3 eggs
½ cup oil
½ teaspoon vanilla extract
2 cups flour
2 teaspoons baking powder
1½ cups sugar
½ teaspoon salt
¼ teaspoon each cinnamon,
   allspice
2 cups chopped loquats *
½ cup chopped walnuts
½ cup flaked coconut
   * Seasonal

Line loaf pan with greased and floured waxed paper. Beat eggs, oil and vanilla in bowl. Add mixture of flour, baking powder, sugar, salt and spices; mix well. Add loquats, walnuts and coconut; mix well. Pour into prepared pan. Bake at 350 degrees for 45 minutes or until loaf tests done. Remove to wire rack. Cool completely before slicing. Yield: 1 loaf.

Pineapple Upside-Down Muffins
Ernest Tschoape, Texas

¼ cup packed brown sugar
2 tablespoons melted margarine
12 pecan halves
1½ cups bran flakes
1 8-ounce can crushed pineapple
¼ cup milk
1 egg
¼ cup oil
½ cup coarsely chopped pecans
1¼ cups flour
3½ teaspoons baking powder
1 teaspoon salt
⅓ cup sugar

Combine brown sugar and margarine in bowl; mix well. Spoon 1 scant teaspoonful into each greased muffin cup. Place 1 pecan half in each. Combine bran flakes, pineapple and milk in mixer bowl. Let stand for 2 minutes. Add egg and oil. Stir in chopped pecans. Add mixture of flour, baking powder, salt and sugar. Stir just until moistened. Spoon into prepared muffin cups. Bake at 400 degrees for 25 minutes or until brown. Invert onto serving plate. Yield: 1 dozen muffins.

Recipe on page 46.

Cheesy Potato-Rye Ring

Andrea Moore, Indiana

Combine rye and all-purpose flour. Mix ¾ cup flour mixture, onion salt, caraway seed and yeast in mixer bowl. Heat potato water, milk, molasses and margarine to 120 degrees in saucepan. Add to yeast mixture. Beat at medium speed for 2 minutes. Add potatoes and ½ cup flour mixture. Beat at high speed for 2 minutes. Stir in enough remaining flour mixture to make soft dough. Knead on floured surface for 8 to 10 minutes. Place in greased bowl, turning to grease surface. Let rise, covered, for 1 hour or until doubled in bulk. Shape into 20 balls. Place in greased bundt pan. Let rise, covered, for 1 hour. Sprinkle with cheese. Bake at 375 degrees for 30 minutes. Cool in pan for 10 minutes. Remove to wire rack to cool completely.
Yield: 1 loaf.

Preparation suggestion: Check microwave manufacturer's instructions for letting dough rise in microwave.

1	cup rye flour
3½	cups all-purpose flour
1½	teaspoons onion salt
2	teaspoons caraway seed
1	package or 1 tablespoon dry yeast
¼	cup potato cooking liquid
½	cup milk
¼	cup molasses
1	tablespoon margarine
1½	cups mashed cooked potatoes
1	cup grated Monterey Jack cheese

Multi-Grain Rolls

Becky Faust, Indiana

Dissolve yeast in ¼ cup lukewarm water and 1 tablespoon honey. Combine stock, oil, ½ cup honey, milk powder and salt in large bowl; mix well. Add oats, wheat germ, bran and whole wheat flour; mix well. Stir in yeast. Stir in as much unbleached flour as possible. Knead on floured surface for 15 to 20 minutes or until smooth and elastic, adding additional unbleached flour if necessary. Place in greased bowl, turning to grease surface. Let rise until doubled in bulk. Shape into rolls; place in greased baking pans. Let rise for 30 minutes or until doubled in bulk. Bake at 350 degrees for 20 minutes or until brown.
Yield: 3 dozen rolls.

2	packages or 2 tablespoons dry yeast
1	tablespoon honey
2	cups warm vegetable stock
½	cup oil
½	cup honey
2	cups instant dry milk powder
2½	teaspoons salt
1	cup oats
1	cup wheat germ
1	cup bran
2	cups whole wheat flour
3	cups unbleached flour

Onion-Poppy Seed Rolls

Delores Kluckman, Minnesota

Sauté onions in butter in skillet. Add sugar and poppy seed. Cook until sugar melts. Separate rolls. Spoon onion mixture onto each roll. Roll up from wide end. Place on baking sheet. Bake using package directions.
Yield: 8 rolls.

2	onions, sliced
¼	cup butter
¼	cup sugar
2	tablespoons poppy seed
1	package refrigerator crescent rolls

Recipe on page 41.

Hot Raspberry Soufflé

Joan Dew, Tennessee

2	**tablespoons sugar**
1	**10-ounce package frozen raspberries in syrup, thawed**
4	**egg whites, at room temperature**
½	**cup sugar**
1	**cup chilled whipping cream**
2	**tablespoons Grand Marnier**

Butter 6 individual soufflé dishes; sprinkle with 2 tablespoons sugar. Purée raspberries in food processor or blender. Beat egg whites until soft peaks form. Add ½ cup sugar 1 tablespoon at a time, beating constantly until stiff peaks form. Fold egg whites gently into raspberries. Spoon into prepared dishes. Bake in preheated 375-degree oven for 12 to 15 minutes or until puffed and light golden. Whip cream with Grand Marnier until soft peaks form. Serve soufflés hot with whipped cream. Yield: 6 servings.

Pear-Cheese Cake

Maggie Burgess, Maryland

1	**package quick nut bread mix**
1	**cup chopped canned pears**
1	**cup shredded Cheddar cheese**
½	**cup pear juice**
1	**egg**
1	**package oatmeal or spice cake mix**
3	**eggs**
⅓	**cup oil**

Combine nut bread mix, pears, cheese, pear juice and 1 egg in bowl; mix gently until blended. Combine cake mix, 3 eggs, oil and 1 cup water in mixer bowl. Beat at high speed for 2 minutes. Combine with pear mixture; mix gently. Pour into 3 greased and floured cake pans. Bake at 350 degrees for 35 minutes. Cool. Frost with Cream Cheese Frosting. Yield: 16 servings.

Cream Cheese Frosting

3	**ounces cream cheese, softened**
6	**tablespoons butter, softened**
1	**tablespoon milk**
1½	**teaspoons vanilla extract**
3	**cups sifted confectioners' sugar**
½	**can vanilla frosting**

Blend cream cheese and butter in bowl. Add milk, vanilla, confectioners' sugar and frosting. Beat until light and fluffy.

Pecan Shortbread Cookies

Patty Perry, California

½	**cup confectioners' sugar**
1	**cup butter, softened**
1	**teaspoon vanilla extract**
2	**cups cake flour**
¼	**teaspoon each salt, baking powder**
½	**cup minced pecans**

Sift confectioners' sugar. Cream butter until light and fluffy. Add confectioners' sugar gradually, beating until light and creamy. Blend in vanilla. Combine dry ingredients and pecans. Stir into creamed mixture. Chill in refrigerator. ** Roll dough to ¼-inch thickness. Cut into 1½-inch squares. Prick with fork. Place on cookie sheet lined with foil. Bake in preheated 350-degree oven for 20 minutes or just until light golden. Yield: 2 dozen.

** *Make ahead to this point.*

Irish Cream Brownies

Shirley Warnack, California

Melt chocolate with ½ cup butter in double boiler or microwave; mix well. Cool. Beat sugar with eggs in bowl. Add whiskey and cooled chocolate mixture; mix well. Stir in flour, salt and chocolate chips. Pour into buttered and foil-lined 8x8-inch baking pan. Bake at 325 degrees for 20 to 25 minutes or until brownies pull from side of pan. Cool for 2 hours or longer. Pierce with toothpick. Drizzle 3 tablespoons liqueur over brownies. Combine confectioners' sugar, 3 tablespoons butter and ¼ cup liqueur in bowl; mix well. Spread over brownies. Cut into rectangles.
Yield: 12 brownies.

Preparation suggestion: May flavor brownies and frosting with vanilla or peppermint extract to taste.

3 ounces baking chocolate
½ cup butter
1 cup sugar
2 eggs, beaten
1 tablespoon Irish whiskey
⅔ cup flour
¼ teaspoon salt
⅔ cup semisweet chocolate chips
3 tablespoons Irish cream liqueur
1 cup confectioners' sugar
3 tablespoons butter, softened
¼ cup Irish cream liqueur

Hurry-Up Peach Pie

Grady Spikes, Texas

Combine whipped topping, sour cream, sugar and cinnamon in bowl; mix well. Spoon ¾ of the pie filling into pie shell. Spoon whipped topping mixture over pie filling. Spoon remaining pie filling on top. Chill for 3 to 4 hours.
Yield: 6 to 8 servings.

8 ounces whipped topping
1 cup sour cream
¼ cup sugar
Dash of cinnamon
1 can peach pie filling
1 graham cracker pie shell

Piña Colada Flip

Eleanor Staber, Illinois

Chill pineapple juice, cream of coconut and club soda. Combine pineapple juice and cream of coconut in pitcher. Add ice cream; mix gently. Add club soda gradually. Serve in tall glasses. Garnish each with pineapple spear.
Yield: 6 servings.

3 cups pineapple juice *
8 ounces cream of coconut
1 12-ounce bottle of club soda
1 pint vanilla ice cream
6 fresh pineapple spears *
* Seasonal

Spring

*J*ust when the last cord of wood is nearly gone, the mufflers and mittens have all been lost, and heavy cold-weather foods are becoming tiresome, something miraculous happens. Chilly winds lose their biting edge, gray skies turn blue, and the first daffodils begin to peek through the soil. Spring has arrived, tugging at our sleeve, urging us out of doors to share in the magical splendor of nature's rebirth. The earth awakens, sending forth green shoots from dormant ground and leaves from bare branches. Our spirits lighten, and so does our taste in food.

Spring ushers in such a bountiful array of new foods that going to the market is more fun than going out to dinner. For me, asparagus epitomizes Spring. When it appears in the produce department, I greet it with the enthusiasm of seeing an old friend. I enjoy it hot or cold, steamed or stir-fried. I love it as soup, mousse, or soufflé. I even like it for breakfast in a fluffy omelet, sauced with cheese.

Warm Spring sun brings all the tender young vegetables to their best—tiny garden peas; young broccoli and spinach; cucumbers, tender green beans, and small red potatoes; garden lettuces and Vidalia onions (delicious sliced thin and layered on rye bread with homemade mayonnaise, salt, and freshly ground pepper!).

The best thing about Spring vegetables is that they are so naturally good they don't need to be fancied up with complicated recipes. Picked or purchased fresh, cooked just until tender and seasoned subtly, these delightful gifts of nature are as delicious as any sophisticated gourmet dish ever created.

But Spring's bounty doesn't end with vegetables. From April waters rushing from mountain streams come trout, which are at their absolute best when pan-fried in a skillet on the bank of the stream. Bluefish make their annual run up the Atlantic in Spring; silver salmon begin their swim upstream to spawn; Louisiana redfish come out of the bayous into the Gulf; and inland bass are biting in the lakes. Even meats are lighter in Spring: baby lamb, wonderful flavored with garlic, rosemary, and lemon; young capons; Rock Cornish game hens; succulent piglets; milk-fed veal.

One of my favorite rites of Spring is an April picnic, the first opportunity to eat out of doors after so many months in the kitchen. Old favorites, like pecan-chicken salad, and new discoveries, like dandelion and duck salad, find their way into the picnic basket, along with Spring crudités and flavorful dips such as green peppercorn-mustard dip or tapenade. The fun of a picnic is that the food be *interesting* as well as delicious and portable.

Easter is Spring's family celebration. While the children fill up on jelly beans and chocolate bunnies, we try to think of clever new ways to use the dozens of colorful hard-boiled eggs they retrieved earlier from the Easter Bunny's hiding places. Some go on the table for decoration; some are peeled and stuffed with variations from chopped bacon to minced radishes; others become garnishes for salads and cold lunches; and some go into old-fashioned egg salad.

When I was growing up, Easter dinner was always baked Virginia ham accompanied by homemade yeast rolls, those irresistible little pockets of buttery goodness. As an adult I've tried many menus for Easter Sunday, from a buffet brunch to a sit-down vegetarian dinner. But with all of these menus, Easter was soon forgotten. Except for little patches of pastel egg shells found for days afterwards in such unlikely places as the sugar jar, there were no leftover reminders of these special meals. Not so with ham! In fact, my grandfather's definition of eternity was two people and a ham. But none of us ever saw him push his plate away in the days following Easter when he was served scalloped ham and potatoes, my grandmother's ham muffins, or her delicious ham loaf with mustard dressing.

Mother's Day was created to pamper moms, and in my household it begins with breakfast in bed. Over the years I've been served some of the best burnt toast, soggy cereal, and cold coffee ever made. That most potent of flavorings—*love*—made them all taste wonderful to me. My favorite is a Mother's Day brunch menu that is both simple and elegant. Most of the work can be done the night before. Fresh berries in thick cream are served first, followed by scrumptious cheesy sausage casserole and maple-walnut muffins. It may not taste any better than burnt toast well-buttered with love, but it will look a lot prettier!

Afternoon tea, a ritual all but forgotten in this country for several generations, is now enjoying a comeback. It is especially appealing in the Springtime, preferably served on the porch, terrace, patio or under a big backyard shade tree. The tea should be steeped the English way, with loose tea leaves, and served from a teapot. With it, offer a platter of dainty tea sandwiches made from very fresh, thinly sliced bread. Favorite combinations include thinly sliced cucumber or chopped watercress with sweet butter; whipped cream cheese studded with bits of smoked salmon; chicken liver pâté with one thin slice of Vidalia onion; finely chopped hard-boiled egg with chopped black olives.

Weddings are romantic and sentimental occasions any time of year, but there is something special about ceremonies held in the Spring, when the earth is resplendent with new beginnings. Foods for prenuptial events should take advantage of the season's fresh fruits, vegetables, and flowers. Decorate a bridal shower cake with daffodils; serve a spectacular triple crown roast of lamb with asparagus custards for a rehearsal dinner.

Spring, above all, is the season that celebrates itself. Spring is Nature's coming-out party. And we're all invited!

Spring Foods

*S*pring gives us the freshest nature has to offer in tiny new vegetables, plump fruits and berries, and tender young veal, lamb, and pork. Whether picked in the garden or at the market, the delightful natural flavors of these foods are among the special pleasures of this season.

Mangoes: Choose fresh, firm mangoes which are free from wilting, gray patches, or black spots. Ripen at room temperature until very soft. Store in refrigerator.

Nectarines: Choose plump, firm, bright nectarines which are slightly soft along the seam and are free from patches and bruises. Ripen at room temperature. Store in refrigerator.

Pineapple: Choose plump, heavy pineapples with fresh green leaves, flat eyes, and fragrant aroma which yield to gentle pressure and are free from discoloration. Pineapples do not ripen after harvesting. Store in refrigerator. Use as soon as possible.

Plums: Choose slightly soft, plump plums with rich coloring which are free from bruises or sun browning. Ripen at room temperature. Store in refrigerator. Use as soon as possible.

Strawberries: Choose bright, firm strawberries which are free from soft spots or mold and have attached green caps. Store in refrigerator. Use as soon as possible. Rinse and remove hulls just before serving.

Asparagus: Choose straight, plump spears with bright green color, uniform thickness, compact tops, and moist bases. Wrap bases in damp towel. Store in plastic bag in refrigerator.

Broccoli: Choose crisp, moist broccoli with firm, compact, dark-green buds and firm, tender stalks. Store, wrapped in plastic wrap, in refrigerator.

Peas: Choose bright green, tender, crisp, velvety pea pods which are well-filled but not swollen and have fresh looking stem ends. Store, unshelled, in refrigerator.

New Potatoes: Choose small, firm, smooth new potatoes which are well-shaped and free from blemishes, green sunburn spots, and sprouts. Store in cool, dry place, not in refrigerator.

Spring lamb, pork and veal: Lamb should be firm, lean, and light pink; pork should be pinkish-gray with white fat; veal should be smooth, moist, and pink with little fat.

Menus

BREAKFASTS

Berry Lover's Breakfast

A Spring Breakfast for Six

Omelet Roll   102
Frosty Blackberry and Raspberry Cups
Hot Biscuits
Strawberry and Blueberry Freezer Jams   65, 81

Easter Brunch

A Holiday Brunch for Eight

Easter Brunch Lasagna   74
Frozen Fruit Cups   108
Butterscotch Breakfast Rolls   107

Breakfast-in-Bed

A Mother's Day Tray Breakfast for Four

Berry-Yogurt Grapefruit   80
Easy Egg and Cheese Casserole   87
May Poles   81
Coffee or Milk

LUNCHES

Light and Lovely Luncheon

A Low-Calorie Luncheon for Four

Honeydew Melon Wedges with Lime Slices
Oriental Crab Salad   97
Strawberry-Lemon Spritzer   79
Mocha Mousse   93

Pocket Lunch

A Packable Lunch for Three

Fruit Salad Pitas   98
Raisins and Nuts
Carrot and Celery Sticks
Chocolate Peppermint Crunchies   77

DINNERS

88	Spinach Soufflé	***Spring Vegetable***
96	Spring Vegetables Vinaigrette	***Feast***
	Dinner Rolls	
92	Lemon Cream and Berries	

A Garden Dinner for Four

67	Sunset Soup	***Fast and Fancy***
101	Linguine with Smoked Salmon Sauce	***Dinner***
	Green Salad with Italian Dressing	
92	Strawberry Tango	

An Easy Company Dinner for Six

99	Marinated Brisket	***A Family***
76	Crispy Cheese Potatoes	***Affair***
75	Green Beans Tartare	
107	Herb-Buttered Bread	
78	Butterscotch Carrot Cake	

A Father's Day Dinner for Eight

SUPPERS

83	Oriental Meat Loaf	***Last Minute***
74	Asparagus with Three-Cheese Sauce	***Supper***
	Steamed New Potatoes	
109	Easy Rhubarb Dessert	

A Microwave Supper for Four

98	Tortilla Roll-Ups	***Patio***
68	Pasta Salad with Herb Dressing	***Supper***
82	Pineapple-Berry Boats	
	Vegetable Juice Cocktail	

A Cool Buffet Supper for Six

April

Cornmeal-Cheddar Snaps

Osie Feusier, Ohio

½	cup all-purpose flour
½	cup whole wheat flour
½	teaspoon salt
¼	teaspoon red pepper
⅓	cup yellow cornmeal
1	stick margarine
1¼	cups grated sharp Cheddar cheese
1	teaspoon prepared mustard with horseradish

Sift flours, salt and red pepper into bowl. Stir in cornmeal. Cut in margarine until crumbly. Add cheese; mix well. Sprinkle mixture of mustard and 2 tablespoons water over dough; mix well with hands. Chill for 1 hour or longer. ** Roll ⅓ at a time very thin on floured surface. Cut as desired. Place on lightly greased baking sheet. Bake at 350 degrees for 12 minutes. Remove to wire rack to cool. Store in airtight container. Yield: 3 dozen.

** *Make ahead to this point.*

Bengali Cheese Spread

Grace Hanley, Maryland

6	ounces cream cheese, softened
4	ounces sharp Cheddar cheese, grated
¼	cup dry Sherry
½	teaspoon curry powder
¼	teaspoon salt
1	8-ounce jar chutney
2	green onions, minced *
	Sesame crackers
	* Seasonal

Combine cheeses, Sherry and seasonings in mixer bowl; beat until well blended. Press into oiled mold. Chill until firm. ** Unmold onto serving plate. Process chutney in blender until of desired consistency. Spoon over mold. Sprinkle green onions over top. Chill until serving time. Serve with crackers. Yield: 3 dozen appetizers.

** *Make ahead to this point.*

Tangy Tomato Dip
Norma Grace Bauer, Illinois

Combine tomato juice, onion, green pepper, seasonings and half the cottage cheese in blender container. Process until smooth. Add remaining cottage cheese. Process for 30 seconds or until of desired consistency. Pour into bowl. Add Parmesan cheese; mix well. Chill, covered, for several hours to several days. ** Pour into serving dish. Serve with vegetables and crackers.
Yield: 4½ cups.

** *Make ahead to this point.*

1½	cups tomato juice
1	medium onion, chopped
1	tablespoon chopped green pepper
1	teaspoon Beau Monde seasoning
1	tablespoon horseradish
¼	teaspoon garlic salt
2	teaspoons oregano
⅛	teaspoon pepper
1	24-ounce carton low-fat cottage cheese
¼	cup Parmesan cheese Bite-sized fresh vegetables * Assorted crackers * Seasonal

Tapenade
Joan Dew, Tennessee

Combine olives, anchovy fillets, garlic, capers, tuna, lemon juice and basil in blender container. Process until smooth. Add olive oil and mayonnaise very gradually, processing constantly. Chill, covered, in refrigerator for up to 1 week.
Yield: 1½ cups.

½	cup imported pitted ripe olives
2	or 3 anchovy fillets
1	clove of garlic
2	tablespoons drained oil-pack tuna
1	tablespoon lemon juice
1	cup (or more) fresh basil leaves
¼	cup imported virgin olive oil
¼	cup mayonnaise

Strawberry-Honey Freezer Jam

Combine strawberries, sugar and honey in bowl; mix well. Let stand for 10 minutes. Combine pectin and ¾ cup water in saucepan. Bring to a boil. Boil for 1 minute, stirring constantly. Stir into strawberries. Stir for 3 minutes. **Ladle into hot sterilized jars, leaving ½-inch headspace; seal with 2-piece lids.** Let stand at room temperature for 24 hours. Store in freezer.
Yield: 4¾ cups.

Note: May vary by adding 1 of the following to crushed strawberries: ½ cup chopped toasted almonds, pecans, pumpkin seed, sunflower seed or pine nuts; ¼ cup dry white Vermouth or Sherry; 2 tablespoons orange liqueur; 1 tablespoon minced crystallized ginger; 1 tablespoon grated lime or lemon rind; or 2 teaspoons almond extract.

2	cups crushed strawberries *
3	cups sugar
1	cup honey
1	box powdered fruit pectin * Seasonal

Mint Jelly
Marilyn Irrer, Michigan

2½	cups apple juice
1	tablespoon white vinegar
½	cup packed mint leaves
4	cups sugar
½	bottle pectin

Combine apple juice, vinegar and mint in saucepan. Simmer for 10 minutes. Strain, reserving liquid. Combine liquid, sugar and several drops of green food coloring. Cook for 2 minutes. Stir in pectin; remove from heat. **Pour into hot sterilized 4-ounce jelly jars, leaving ½-inch headspace; seal.** Process in boiling water bath for 5 minutes. Yield: 7 jars.

Beef and Meatball Soup
Melissa Peters, Michigan

1	pound stew beef
6	beef bouillon cubes
5	whole allspice
5	whole peppercorns
2	cups chopped cauliflower *
2	cups chopped carrots *
8	ounces fresh spinach *
2	leeks, chopped
8	ounces vermicelli
1	pound ground chuck
½	teaspoon allspice
	* Seasonal

Combine stew beef, bouillon cubes, whole allspice, peppercorns and 8 cups water in saucepan. Simmer for 2½ to 3 hours or until tender. Add cauliflower, carrots, spinach and leeks. Cook until vegetables are tender. Add vermicelli. Combine ground chuck, allspice and salt in bowl; mix well. Shape into marble-sized meatballs. Drop into simmering soup. Remove from heat. Let stand until vermicelli is tender and meatballs are cooked through. Ladle into soup bowls. Yield: 8 servings.

Chilled Carrot Soup

1	cup chopped onion
1½	teaspoons curry powder
2	tablespoons oil
3½	cups chicken broth
4	cups sliced carrots *
1	cup sliced celery
½	teaspoon cumin
½	teaspoon Tabasco sauce
1	bay leaf
1	cup low-fat milk
1	cup low-fat cottage cheese
	Celery sticks
	* Seasonal

Sauté onion with curry powder in oil in large saucepan for 3 to 5 minutes. Add broth, carrots, celery and seasonings. Simmer for 25 minutes or until vegetables are tender. **Discard bay leaf.** Process ¼ at a time in blender until smooth. Process cottage cheese and milk until smooth. Combine carrot mixture and cottage cheese mixture in pitcher. Chill until serving time. ** Pour into chilled mugs. Garnish each with celery. Yield: 7 cups.

** *Make ahead to this point.*

Sunset Soup

Merrill J. Egorin, Maryland

Combine soup and orange juice in blender container. Process for 10 seconds. Chill until serving time. Serve in chilled bowls garnished with orange slice and mint sprig. Yield: 6 servings. 🍴 🍎 🥄 🍲

2 cans tomato soup
2 soup cans orange juice *
1 orange, peeled, thinly sliced *
   Fresh mint sprigs
   * Seasonal

Menu suggestion: This soup is an especially good beginning for a seafood meal or warm weather buffet.

Crunchy Pea Salad

Peggy Baratta, Michigan

Cook peas in a small amount of water in saucepan or microwave just until tender; drain. Let stand until completely cool. Combine peas, onion and celery in bowl. Blend salad dressing, sour cream, sugar and seasonings in small bowl. Add to vegetables; mix gently. Chill until serving time. ** Stir in peanuts just before serving. Yield: 6 servings. 🍎 🥄 🍲

1 pound shelled fresh peas *
1 medium onion, chopped
2 stalks celery, chopped
½ cup salad dressing
½ cup sour cream
2 teaspoons sugar
2 teaspoons Worcestershire sauce
½ teaspoon garlic powder
   Salt and pepper to taste
1 cup peanuts
   * Seasonal

** Make ahead to this point.

Spring Vegetable Toss

Wendy Worrall, Texas

Layer broccoli, cauliflower, carrots, green pepper, celery and olives in glass salad bowl. Drain and slice artichoke hearts. Arrange over top. Combine oil, vinegar, mustard and sugar in small covered jar; shake until sugar dissolves. Pour over layers. Marinate, covered, in refrigerator overnight. ** Add layers of avocado, tomato and mushrooms. Toss lightly just before serving. Yield: 6 servings. 🍎 🥄 🍲

2 cups broccoli flowerets *
2 cups cauliflowerets *
½ cup thinly sliced carrots *
½ cup chopped green pepper
1 cup chopped celery
¼ cup sliced ripe olives
1 small jar marinated artichoke hearts
½ cup oil
¼ cup white wine vinegar
1 tablespoon Dijon mustard
¼ cup sugar
1 avocado, chopped *
1 tomato, cut into wedges *
1 cup sliced fresh mushrooms *
   * Seasonal

** Make ahead to this point.

Pasta Salad with Herb Dressing

Anita Frow, Maryland

2	cups cooked macaroni shells
2	cups cooked spiral-shaped pasta
½	cup green pepper rings
½	cup broccoli flowerets *
½	cup green beans *
½	cup sliced fresh mushrooms *
¼	cup asparagus spears *
¼	cup radish slices *
¼	cup zucchini slices
½	cup cherry tomato halves *
¼	cup small red onion rings
¼	cup sweet red pepper strips
	* Seasonal

Combine pasta, green pepper, broccoli, green beans, mushrooms, asparagus, radish slices, zucchini, cherry tomatoes, onion rings and red pepper in bowl. Chill, covered, in refrigerator. ** Add Herb Dressing; toss gently. Yield: 6 servings.

** *Make ahead to this point.*

Herb Dressing

3	tablespoons olive oil
2	tablespoons red vinegar
1½	teaspoons basil
1	clove of garlic, minced
1	teaspoon grated lemon rind
½	teaspoon minced chives

Combine olive oil, vinegar, basil, garlic, lemon rind and chives in covered jar. Shake to mix well. Let stand for 10 minutes or longer to blend flavors.

Tuna Salad Niçoise

1⅓	cups oil
¼	cup lemon juice
¼	cup tarragon vinegar
2	teaspoons salt
2	teaspoons grated onion
1	teaspoon each dry mustard, basil
¼	teaspoon pepper
2	potatoes, cooked, sliced
8	tomato wedges *
2	cups cooked whole green beans *
1	red onion, sliced
2	7-ounce cans solid-pack tuna
½	cup pitted ripe olives
	Crisp lettuce leaves *
	* Seasonal

Combine first 8 ingredients in covered jar; shake vigorously. Let stand for several minutes. Place potatoes, tomatoes and green beans in bowl. Pour half the dressing over vegetables. Marinate, covered, in refrigerator for 2 hours. ** Arrange potato slices, tomato wedges, green beans, onion rings, tuna chunks and olives on lettuce-lined serving plate. Drizzle remaining dressing over top as desired. Yield: 6 servings.

** *Make ahead to this point.*

Sukiyaki

Vicki Kidd, Oklahoma

Slice tenderloin very thinly cross grain. Stir-fry tenderloin in hot oil in wok for 1 to 2 minutes or until brown. Sprinkle with sugar. Add mixture of stock and soy sauce; mix well. Push beef to side. Add green onions and celery. Stir-fry for 1 minute. Push vegetables to side. Add spinach, drained bean sprouts, mushrooms and drained water chestnuts in order listed, stir-frying for 1 minute after each addition and pushing each to side as cooked. Serve over rice.
Yield: 6 servings.

1	*pound boneless beef tenderloin*
2	*tablespoons oil*
2	*tablespoons sugar*
½	*cup beef stock*
⅓	*cup soy sauce*
2	*cups diagonally sliced green onions* *
2	*cups diagonally sliced celery*
1	*cup small spinach leaves*
1	*16-ounce can bean sprouts*
1	*cup thinly sliced mushrooms* *
1	*5-ounce can sliced water chestnuts*
	Hot cooked rice
	* Seasonal

Veal Audrey

Lisa Wolman, Maryland

Pound veal very thin with meat mallet. Mix eggs, half and half, cheese, parsley and salt and pepper in bowl; mix well. Coat veal lightly with flour. Dip in egg mixture. Coat with seasoned crumbs. Brown in mixture of butter and olive oil in skillet. Place veal on ovenproof platter. Add 1 tablespoon flour, broth, lemon juice and Sherry to pan drippings. Simmer until slightly thickened, stirring constantly. Broil veal until crisp. Pour Sherry sauce over top. Garnish with lemon slices and parsley.
Yield: 8 servings.

Suggestion: Substitute chicken breast filets for veal.

3	*pounds veal scallops* *
3	*eggs*
¼	*cup half and half*
2	*tablespoons Parmesan cheese*
1	*tablespoon chopped parsley*
	Salt and pepper to taste
1	*cup (or more) flour*
	Seasoned bread crumbs
	Equal parts butter and olive oil
1	*tablespoon flour*
1	*10-ounce can chicken broth*
3	*tablespoons lemon juice*
¾	*cup Sherry*
	Lemon slices and parsley for garnish
	* Seasonal

Pork Chops with Orange Rice

Janet Price, Ohio

Brown pork chops on both sides in skillet. Season with salt and pepper. Place rice in 7x12-inch baking dish. Pour orange juice and soup over rice. Arrange pork chops over rice. Bake, covered, at 350 degrees for 45 minutes. Bake, uncovered, for 10 minutes longer.
Yield: 6 servings.

6	*thin pork chops* *
	Salt and pepper to taste
1⅓	*cups minute rice*
1	*cup orange juice*
1	*can chicken with rice soup*
	* Seasonal

Ham and Broccoli Pie

Photograph for this recipe on page 105.

1	**small bunch broccoli, cut into flowerets ***
1	**cup sliced celery**
1	**cup chopped onion**
2	**tablespoons margarine**
2	**tablespoons cornstarch**
2	**teaspoons dry mustard**
¼	**teaspoon dried leaf marjoram, crushed**
¼	**teaspoon grated lemon rind**
⅛	**teaspoon pepper**
2	**cups milk**
2	**tablespoons fresh lemon juice**
2	**cups cubed cooked ham**
1	**recipe pie pastry**
	* Seasonal

Simmer broccoli in ½-inch water in covered saucepan for 5 minutes. Drain; set aside. Sauté celery and onion in margarine in skillet for 3 minutes or until tender. Combine cornstarch, mustard, marjoram, lemon rind and pepper in saucepan. Stir in milk. Add celery and onion mixture. Bring to a boil, stirring constantly. Cook for 1 minute, stirring constantly. Remove from heat. Add lemon juice, ham and broccoli. Pour into 2-quart casserole. Place lattice-woven pie pastry on top; flute edge. Refrigerate if desired. ** Bake at 375 degrees for 35 minutes or until crust is golden brown. Yield: 4 to 6 servings.

*** Make ahead to this point.*

Tahoe Brunch

Carol Hall, California

8	**ounces mushrooms, sliced ***
1⅓	**cups chopped green onions ***
½	**cup butter**
	Salt and pepper to taste
1½	**pounds pork sausage**
12	**slices bread**
2	**tablespoons butter, softened**
1	**pound cheese, grated**
5	**eggs**
2½	**cups milk**
1	**tablespoon Dijon mustard**
1	**teaspoon dry mustard**
½	**teaspoon nutmeg**
	* Seasonal

Sauté mushrooms and green onions in ½ cup butter in skillet over medium heat for 5 to 8 minutes or until tender. Season with salt and pepper. Brown sausage in skillet, stirring until crumbly; drain. Spread bread with butter; trim crusts. Layer bread, sautéed vegetables, sausage and cheese ½ at a time in greased 9x13-inch casserole. Combine eggs, milk, mustard and nutmeg; beat well. Pour over layers. Chill, covered, overnight. ** Bake at 350 degrees for 1 hour. Yield: 12 to 16 servings.

*** Make ahead to this point.*
Suggestion: Substitute crisp-fried bacon or ham for sausage.

Lemon-Broiled Chicken

3	**tablespoons melted butter**
3	**tablespoons lemon juice**
2	**cloves of garlic, minced**
¼	**cup minced parsley**
	Parmesan cheese
1	**chicken, cut up ***
	* Seasonal

Combine butter, lemon juice, minced garlic, parsley and cheese in bowl; mix well. Brush on chicken. Place skin side down on rack in broiler pan. Broil for 15 minutes. Turn chicken over. Brush with butter mixture. Broil for 10 minutes longer. Yield: 4 servings.

Recipes on pages 99, 104 and 131.

Chicken Nuggets
Helen Zurek, California

Combine bread crumbs, cheese, parsley and seasonings; mix well. Cut chicken breasts into bite-sized pieces. Dip chicken nuggets into butter; coat with crumb mixture. Thread onto skewers. Refrigerate for several hours if desired. ** Place on baking sheet. Bake at 350 degrees for 20 to 30 minutes or until tender and brown. Arrange on serving plate. Serve hot. Yield: 4 servings.

** *Make ahead to this point.*
Serving suggestion: Use whole chicken breasts and bake for 1 hour.

½	cup fine bread crumbs
½	cup Parmesan cheese
2	tablespoons chopped parsley
1	teaspoon garlic powder
1	teaspoon salt
¼	teaspoon pepper
4	boned chicken breasts *
¼	cup melted butter
	* Seasonal

Perch Turbans à la Newburg
Melissa Vickers, Texas

Cut fillets into serving-sized portions. Season fillets with salt and pepper. Roll into turbans; secure with toothpicks. Place in greased 8-inch square baking dish. Brush with ¼ cup butter. Bake at 350 degrees for 15 minutes or microwave on High for 10 minutes or until fish flakes easily. Blend flour, ½ teaspoon salt, cayenne pepper and ½ cup butter in saucepan. Stir in half and half gradually. Cook until thickened, stirring constantly. **Stir a small amount of hot sauce into egg yolks; stir egg yolks into hot sauce.** Remove from heat. Blend in Sherry. Spoon rice onto serving plate. Arrange fish on rice. Spoon sauce over fish. Garnish with parsley sprigs. Dust with paprika. Yield: 6 servings.

2	pounds perch fillets *
	Salt and pepper to taste
¼	cup melted butter
¼	cup flour
½	teaspoon salt
⅛	teaspoon cayenne pepper
½	cup melted butter
3	cups half and half
6	egg yolks, beaten
⅓	cup Sherry
2	cups cooked rice
	Parsley sprigs
	Paprika to taste
	* Seasonal

Hot Shrimp Salad
Joy Reagan, Texas

Combine crab meat, shrimp, celery, onion, green pepper, salt, salad dressing and Worcestershire sauce in bowl; mix well. Refrigerate for several hours if desired. ** Spoon into individual baking shells. Sprinkle with mixture of cracker crumbs and butter. Bake at 350 degrees for 30 minutes. Yield: 6 servings.

** *Make ahead to this point.*

1	cup cooked fresh crab meat *
2	pounds uncooked peeled shrimp *
1	cup finely chopped celery
1	medium onion, chopped
1	green pepper, chopped
½	teaspoon salt
1	cup salad dressing
1	teaspoon Worcestershire sauce
1	cup butter cracker crumbs
¼	cup melted butter
	* Seasonal

Recipe on page 101.

Mandarin Casserole
Genevieve Van Epps, Michigan

¼ cup chopped green onions *
1 tablespoon butter
1 cup sliced celery
1 can cream of mushroom soup
1 7-ounce can tuna
½ cup toasted cashews
2 cups chow mein noodles
1 cup mandarin orange sections
   * Seasonal

Sauté green onions in butter in skillet. Add celery. Sauté for several minutes. Add soup, tuna, cashews, half the noodles and ¼ cup water; mix well. Spoon into 1-quart casserole. Chill in refrigerator if desired. ** Sprinkle remaining noodles over top. Bake at 350 degrees for 15 minutes. Garnish with mandarin oranges.
Yield: 4 servings.

** Make ahead to this point.

Easter Brunch Lasagna
Shirley MacNitt, Florida

1 pound bacon
1 cup chopped onion
⅓ cup margarine
⅓ cup flour
½ teaspoon salt
¼ teaspoon pepper
3 cups milk
1 cup sour cream
12 lasagna noodles, cooked
12 hard-boiled eggs, sliced
2 cups shredded Swiss cheese
¼ cup Parmesan cheese
   Chopped parsley

Fry bacon in skillet until crisp or microwave according to manufacturer's instructions. Drain and crumble. Sauté onion in margarine in skillet. Blend in flour, salt and pepper. Add milk gradually, stirring constantly. Cook until thickened, stirring constantly. Blend in sour cream. Spoon a small amount of sauce into 9x13-inch baking dish. Layer noodles, bacon, eggs, Swiss cheese and sauce ⅓ at a time in prepared dish. Sprinkle with Parmesan cheese and parsley. Chill, covered, for several hours if desired. ** Bake at 350 degrees for 30 minutes or until bubbly. Let stand for 10 minutes before serving.
Yield: 8 servings.

** Make ahead to this point.

Asparagus with Three-Cheese Sauce
Eileen Nottingham, California

2 pounds fresh asparagus *
½ cup evaporated milk
3 ounces cream cheese, softened
   Salt and pepper to taste
1 tablespoon Parmesan cheese
½ cup shredded Cheddar cheese
   * Seasonal

Place asparagus in shallow 2-quart glass casserole. Microwave, covered, for 4 minutes or until tender-crisp. Combine evaporated milk and cream cheese in blender container. Process until smooth. Pour into 2-cup glass measure. Microwave on High for 2 minutes, stirring twice. Stir in seasonings and Parmesan cheese. Pour over hot asparagus. Sprinkle with Cheddar cheese.
Yield: 4 servings.

Cabbage Mallum
Beverly Oldaker, Colorado

Sauté onion and garlic in margarine in skillet. Shred cabbage finely. Add cabbage and salt to skillet. Stir-fry until cabbage is tender. Combine coconut, turmeric, pepper and mustard seed in bowl. Add to cabbage. Cook until heated through, stirring constantly. Spoon into serving dish.
Yield: 6 servings.

1 **tablespoon minced onion**
2 **teaspoons garlic flakes**
¼ **cup margarine**
2 **small heads cabbage ***
   Salt to taste
2 **cups shredded coconut**
¼ **teaspoon turmeric**
1 **teaspoon pepper**
¾ **teaspoon crushed mustard seed**
   * Seasonal

Green Beans Tartare

Cook green beans in a small amount of water in saucepan, or microwave on High until tender-crisp; drain well. Place in serving dish. Combine mayonnaise, lemon juice, salt, pickle relish, dillweed and mustard in bowl; mix well. Spoon sauce over green beans. Serve immediately.
Yield: 8 servings.

3 **cups green beans ***
¼ **cup mayonnaise**
¼ **cup lemon juice**
¼ **teaspoon salt**
1 **tablespoon sweet pickle relish**
1 **teaspoon dillweed**
2 **tablespoons prepared mustard**
   * Seasonal

Oriental Mushrooms
Holly Lamberton, Texas

Remove and discard mushroom stems. Combine butter, soy sauce and bouillon in saucepan. Heat until butter melts and bouillon dissolves. Add seasonings and lemon juice; mix well. Add mushrooms, water chestnuts and parsley. Simmer until mushrooms are tender. Pour into serving dish.
Yield: 6 to 8 servings.

2 **pounds fresh mushrooms ***
¼ **cup butter**
¼ **cup soy sauce**
1 **teaspoon instant chicken bouillon**
1 **teaspoon garlic powder**
½ **teaspoon salt**
½ **teaspoon lemon-herb seasoning**
2 **teaspoons lemon-pepper seasoning**
1 **tablespoon lemon juice**
1 **can sliced water chestnuts**
2 **tablespoons parsley flakes**
   * Seasonal

Crispy Cheese Potatoes
Margaret Scholtz, Illinois

6 cups thinly sliced new
   potatoes *
1 teaspoon salt
2 teaspoons melted butter
1 cup grated Cheddar cheese
1½ cups bread crumbs
   * Seasonal

Season potatoes with salt; toss lightly. Arrange in greased 9x13-inch baking dish. Drizzle with butter. Sprinkle with cheese and bread crumbs. Bake at 450 degrees for 20 minutes or until tender.
Yield: 8 servings.

Fresh Vegetable Ghivetch
Hazel T. Ivey, California

8 new potatoes *
2 carrots, peeled, sliced *
2 cups cauliflowerets *
2 stalks celery, chopped
8 ounces mushrooms, sliced *
2 cups chopped green onions *
1 sweet red pepper, chopped
1 clove of garlic, minced
1 13-ounce can chicken broth
2 teaspoons salt
⅛ teaspoon pepper
2 tablespoons chopped fresh
   dillweed
   * Seasonal

Coarsely chop potatoes. Combine potatoes, carrots, cauliflowerets, celery, mushrooms, green onions, red pepper and garlic in greased 2-quart casserole. Add broth, salt, pepper and dillweed; mix lightly. Bake, covered, at 350 degrees for 1 hour, or microwave on High until vegetables are tender.
Yield: 8 servings.

Ham and Cheese Bread
Laurie Fohn, Texas

6 slices bacon, chopped
6 eggs, well beaten
¾ cup milk
1½ cups flour
2½ teaspoons baking powder
½ teaspoon salt
1 cup chopped ham
1 cup cubed Swiss cheese
1 cup cubed Cheddar cheese

Brown bacon in skillet; drain. Combine eggs, milk, flour, baking powder and salt in bowl; mix well. Stir in bacon, ham and cheeses. Pour into greased and floured loaf pan. Bake at 350 degrees for 50 minutes or until bread tests done. Cool in pan on wire rack. Slice thinly. Toast if desired.
Yield: 12 servings.

Pecan Waffles
Christine Shore, Michigan

Combine first 3 ingredients in bowl. Add eggs and milk gradually, mixing well after each addition. Stir in butter and pecans. Bake in hot waffle iron according to manufacturer's instructions. Serve hot with butter and syrup.
Yield: 5 servings. ✓4

2	*cups flour*
4	*teaspoons baking powder*
4	*teaspoons sugar*
2	*eggs*
1¾	*cups milk*
⅓	*cup melted butter*
1	*cup coarsely chopped pecans*

Chocolate-Peppermint Crunchies
Elva Koonig, Iowa

Combine first 3 ingredients in saucepan. Bring to a boil, stirring constantly. Boil for 2 minutes, stirring constantly. Boil for 2 minutes, stirring constantly. Remove from heat. Stir in chocolate chips until melted. Cool for 10 minutes. Stir in candy and nuts. Drop by teaspoonfuls onto waxed paper. Chill for several hours.
Yield: 2 dozen. ✓4 🥘

½	*cup evaporated milk*
½	*cup sugar*
1	*tablespoon light corn syrup*
1	*6-ounce package semisweet chocolate chips*
½	*cup coarsely chopped peppermint stick candy*
1	*cup chopped nuts*

Fruited Cheesecake

Combine graham cracker crumbs, pecans and cinnamon in bowl. Add butter and 2 tablespoons honey; mix well. Press into pie plate. Bake at 350 degrees for 10 minutes. Cool completely. Combine ricotta cheese, yogurt, eggs, lemon juice and vanilla in blender container. Process until smooth. Add bananas, flour and 2 tablespoons honey. Process until smooth. Pour into prepared crust. Bake at 350 degrees for 30 minutes or until set. Chill in refrigerator. ** Arrange kiwifruit and strawberries over cheesecake.
Yield: 6 to 8 servings. 🍎 🥘

** *Make ahead to this point.*

1¼	*cups graham cracker crumbs*
¼	*cup finely chopped pecans*
½	*teaspoon cinnamon*
3	*tablespoons melted butter*
2	*tablespoons honey*
¾	*cup ricotta cheese*
½	*cup yogurt*
2	*eggs*
2	*tablespoons freshly squeezed lemon juice*
1	*teaspoon vanilla extract*
2	*bananas, sliced*
¼	*cup flour*
2	*tablespoons honey*
2	*kiwifruit, peeled, sliced*
1	*cup fresh strawberries* *
	* Seasonal

Strawberry-Rhubarb Soufflé

Photograph for this recipe on page 106.

4   *cups sliced rhubarb* *
¾   *cup sugar*
1   *envelope unflavored gelatin*
3   *egg whites*
¼   *cup sugar*
2   *cups coarsely chopped*
     strawberries *
1   *cup whipping cream, whipped*
     * Seasonal

Combine rhubarb and ¾ cup sugar in 2-quart glass casserole. Cover with SARAN WRAP™, turning back edge to vent. Microwave on High for 8 to 10 minutes or until rhubarb is tender, stirring once. Chill, covered, in refrigerator. Soften gelatin in ¼ cup cold water. Microwave on High for 1 minute, stirring once. Cool to room temperature. Beat egg whites until soft peaks form. Add ¼ cup sugar gradually, beating until stiff peaks form. Add gelatin gradually, beating constantly at medium speed. Combine 1 cup rhubarb mixture and strawberries. Fold in egg whites and half the whipped cream gently. Spoon remaining rhubarb mixture into 4-cup soufflé dish with 2-inch foil collar. Spoon strawberry mixture over top. Chill for 4 hours. Remove collar. Garnish with remaining whipped cream.
Yield: 4 to 6 servings.

Serving suggestion: Serve fluffy soufflé with rhubarb sauce from bottom of soufflé dish in each serving.

Butterscotch Carrot Cake

Bobbi Berry, Indiana

¾   *cup butter, softened*
1¼   *cups sugar*
2   *eggs*
3   *cups sifted flour*
1   *teaspoon each baking powder,*
     soda and salt
1   *teaspoon cinnamon*
½   *teaspoon nutmeg*
¼   *teaspoon ground cloves*
1   *6-ounce package butterscotch*
     chips, melted
1   *cup grated carrots* *
1   *cup raisins*
1   *cup applesauce* *
     * Seasonal

Cream butter and sugar in bowl until light and fluffy. Add eggs 1 at a time, beating well after each addition. Mix flour, baking powder, soda, salt, cinnamon, nutmeg and cloves in small bowl. Add to creamed mixture alternately with butterscotch chips and ½ cup water, mixing well after each addition. Stir in carrots, raisins and applesauce. Pour into 2 greased and waxed paper-lined 8-inch cake pans. Bake at 350 degrees for 35 to 45 minutes or until cake tests done. Cool on wire rack. Frost as desired.
Yield: 16 servings.

Banana Black Bottom Pie

Lisa Anne Hooper, Tennessee

Combine sugar, cornstarch and gelatin in saucepan; mix well. Stir in mixture of beaten egg yolks and milk. Cook over low heat until thickened, stirring constantly, or microwave on Medium-High, stirring twice. Remove from heat. Stir in vanilla. Blend half the hot custard with melted chocolate. Cool. Chill remaining custard, covered, in refrigerator. Arrange ⅔ of the bananas in pie shell. Pour chocolate custard over bananas. Stir orange rind and Brandy into vanilla custard. Fold in stiffly beaten egg whites gently. Spoon over chocolate layer. Chill for several hours or until set. Brush remaining banana slices with lemon juice. Arrange on top of pie. Grate semisweet chocolate. Sprinkle around banana slices. Yield: 6 to 8 servings.

¾	**cup sugar**
1	**tablespoon cornstarch**
1	**envelope unflavored gelatin**
3	**eggs, separated**
1¼	**cups milk**
1	**teaspoon vanilla extract**
4	**squares baking chocolate, melted**
3	**bananas, sliced**
1	**baked 9-inch pie shell**
1	**tablespoon grated orange rind**
2	**tablespoons orange-flavored Brandy**
1	**teaspoon lemon juice**
3	**squares semisweet chocolate**

Strawberry Cream Pie

Judith See, Michigan

Scald milk. Combine sugar, flour and salt in saucepan. Blend in milk gradually. Cook over low heat until thickened, stirring constantly. **Stir a small amount of hot mixture into beaten egg yolks; stir egg yolks into hot mixture.** Cook for 1 minute longer. Stir in butter and vanilla; cool. Slice strawberries; reserve 1 cup for topping. Place remaining strawberries in pie shell. Spread custard over strawberries. Combine egg whites, confectioners' sugar and reserved berries in bowl. Beat until stiff peaks form. Spread over pie. Chill until serving time. Yield: 6 to 8 servings.

2	**cups milk**
⅔	**cup sugar**
½	**cup flour**
½	**teaspoon salt**
2	**eggs, separated**
2	**tablespoons butter**
1	**teaspoon vanilla extract**
1	**quart fresh strawberries ***
1	**baked pie shell**
1	**cup confectioners' sugar**
	* Seasonal

Strawberry-Lemon Spritzer

Purée strawberries with lemon juice in blender container. Add Equal; mix well. Pour strawberry mixture into 4 tall glasses. Add ½ cup club soda to each glass; mix gently. Add enough ice to fill glasses. Yield: 4 servings.

4	**cups strawberries ***
½	**cup lemon juice ***
4	**to 6 packets Equal**
16	**ounces club soda**
	* Seasonal

May

Artichoke Puffs
Ethel Chance, Maryland

1	*loaf thinly sliced white bread*
2	*cups mayonnaise*
1	*teaspoon Dijon mustard*
1½	*cups Parmesan cheese*
1	*clove of garlic, minced*
½	*teaspoon Worcestershire sauce*
2	*teaspoons minced parsley*
2	*14-ounce cans artichoke hearts, cut into quarters* *
	* Seasonal

Cut bread into 2-inch rounds. Toast one side. Combine mayonnaise, mustard, cheese, garlic, Worcestershire sauce and parsley in bowl; mix well. Spread thinly on untoasted side of bread rounds. Place quartered artichoke heart on center of each. Spread mayonnaise mixture generously over top. Place on baking sheet. Broil until puffed and brown. Arrange on serving plate.
Yield: 1½ dozen canapés.

Berry-Yogurt Grapefruit
Kathy Blount, Georgia

½	*cup chopped strawberries* *
½	*cup vanilla yogurt*
4	*grapefruit halves* *
4	*whole strawberries* *
	* Seasonal

Combine strawberries and yogurt in small bowl; mix well. Chill in refrigerator. ** Cut around grapefruit sections to loosen fruit from membrane. Spoon strawberry-yogurt topping over each grapefruit half. Garnish with whole strawberry. Yield: 4 servings.

** *Make ahead to this point.*

May Poles
Donna Guard, Iowa

Wrap bacon around bread sticks. Place in paper towel-lined glass dish; cover with paper towel. Microwave on High for 3 minutes; turn sticks. Microwave for 2 to 4 minutes longer. Cool on wire rack.
Yield: 4 servings.

10	*slices bacon, cut into halves lengthwise*
20	*garlic bread sticks*

Blueberry Freezer Jam
Irene Haas, Michigan

Mash blueberries in mixer bowl. Add mixture of Sure-Jel and 2 tablespoons sugar; mix well. Add remaining ingredients. Beat at low speed for 7 minutes. Pour into freezer jars; seal. Let stand at room temperature overnight. Store in freezer.
Yield: 2 cups.

1	*cup blueberries *
¼	*cup Sure-Jel*
2	*tablespoons sugar*
2	*tablespoons corn syrup*
2	*tablespoons lemon juice*
¾	*cup sugar*
	* Seasonal

Mystery Marmalade
Taryn Rogers, Texas

Combine first 4 ingredients in saucepan; mix well. Add several drops of green food coloring if desired. Bring to a full rolling boil. Boil for exactly 1 minute, stirring constantly. Remove from heat. Stir in pectin. Skim foam. Stir for 5 minutes to cool slightly; skim. **Ladle into hot sterilized jelly glasses, leaving ¼ inch headspace. Seal with 2-piece lids.** Process in boiling water bath for 5 minutes.
Yield: 5 medium jelly glasses.

2	*cups finely chopped cucumbers *
4	*cups sugar*
⅓	*cup lime juice *
2	*tablespoons grated lime rind *
½	*bottle of liquid fruit pectin*
	* Seasonal

No-Cook Pizza Sauce
Darlene Borger, Texas

Combine tomato purée, tomato sauce and oil in 2-quart jar. Add cheese and seasonings. Cover jar; shake vigorously until well mixed. Store in refrigerator for up to 1 month.
Yield: 1½ quarts.

1	*29-ounce can tomato purée*
1	*15-ounce can tomato sauce*
¾	*cup oil*
2	*tablespoons grated cheese*
1	*tablespoon sugar*
1	*tablespoon parsley flakes*
1	*tablespoon oregano*
1	*teaspoon garlic salt*
1	*teaspoon salt*
½	*teaspoon pepper*

Suggestion: Use on ground beef patties or as cooking sauce on chicken breast filets. Top with cheese if desired.

Asparagus Soup Marseilles

1	pound asparagus spears *
2½	cups milk
1	teaspoon instant minced onion
1	teaspoon salt
1	teaspoon dry mustard
½	teaspoon capers
	Pinch of pepper
1	hard-boiled egg, chopped
	Pimento strips
	* Seasonal

Chop asparagus. Cook in a small amount of water in saucepan or microwave until tender. Drain. Combine asparagus, milk, onion, salt, mustard, capers and pepper in blender container. Process until smooth. Refrigerate for several hours if desired. ** Heat in saucepan or microwave on High to serving temperature. Pour into soup bowls. Garnish with chopped egg and pimento.

Yield: 4 servings.

** *Make ahead to this point.*

Spinach-Rice Soup

Jan Abraham, California

6	cups chicken broth
1	can cream of celery soup
¾	soup can milk
1	tablespoon onion flakes
½	teaspoon pepper
2	tablespoons parsley flakes
2	cups minute rice
10	ounces frozen chopped spinach, thawed *
	* Seasonal

Combine broth, soup, milk, onion, pepper and parsley in saucepan. Add rice and thawed spinach. Simmer, covered, for 5 minutes or until rice is tender. Pour into serving bowls.

Yield: 8 to 10 servings.

Preparation suggestion: May substitute 1½ cups cooked rice for minute rice.

Pineapple-Berry Boats

Ann Pinkston, Alabama

3	small pineapples *
2	cups sliced strawberries *
2	cups blueberries *
⅓	cup raspberry preserves
3	ounces cream cheese, softened
1	tablespoon milk
½	teaspoon grated lemon rind
2	teaspoons lemon juice
½	cup whipping cream
	* Seasonal

Cut pineapples into halves through tops. Scoop out pulp, reserving shells. Combine pineapple chunks and berries in bowl. Spoon into reserved shells. Chill until serving time. ** Arrange on serving platter. Combine preserves, cream cheese, milk, lemon rind and juice in bowl. Beat until smooth. Whip cream just until soft peaks form. Fold into cream cheese mixture. Pour into serving bowl. Serve with fruit.

Yield: 6 servings.

** *Make ahead to this point.*

Spring Barley Salad
Lynn Daugherty, Maryland

Combine barley, 1 teaspoon salt and 3 cups boiling water in saucepan. Simmer, covered, for 10 to 12 minutes or until barley is tender, stirring occasionally. Drain and cool. Combine barley, carrots, celery, radishes and green onions in serving bowl. Chill in refrigerator. ** Combine oil, vinegar, mustard, garlic, salt and pepper to taste in bowl; mix well. Pour over salad; toss lightly. Chill until serving time. Yield: 6 to 8 servings. 🍎 🍲

** *Make ahead to this point.*

1 *cup quick-cooking barley*
1 *teaspoon salt*
3 *carrots, sliced ***
¾ *cup chopped celery*
4 *large radishes, sliced ***
3 *green onions with tops, thinly sliced ***
⅓ *cup oil*
3 *tablespoons vinegar*
½ *teaspoon mustard*
1 *clove of garlic*
  Salt and pepper to taste
  * Seasonal

Garden-Style Chicken Salad
Laurie Smith, Texas

Cook chicken with celery, salt and pepper in water to cover in saucepan until chicken is tender. Cool. Bone and chop chicken. Cook broccoli, cauliflower and carrots in boiling water in saucepan for 3 minutes or microwave until tender-crisp; drain. Layer cooked vegetables, tomatoes and chicken in glass bowl. Mix olive oil, wine vinegar, honey and salt and pepper to taste in small bowl; mix well. Pour over layers. Chill for 6 hours, stirring occasionally. ** Drain. Serve on lettuce-lined salad plates. Yield: 4 servings. 🍎 〰 🍲

** *Make ahead to this point.*

1 *3-pound chicken ***
1 *cup chopped celery*
½ *teaspoon each salt and pepper*
1 *cup broccoli flowerets ***
1 *cup cauliflowerets ***
½ *cup diagonally sliced carrots ***
½ *cup cherry tomatoes ***
⅔ *cup olive oil*
⅓ *cup red wine vinegar*
2 *to 3 tablespoons honey*
  * Seasonal

Oriental Meat Loaf
Kathy Kreisel, Maryland

Combine ground beef, egg, bread crumbs, parsley, onion flakes, ginger, 1 tablespoon brown sugar and 1 tablespoon soy sauce in bowl; mix well. Press into glass ring or glass loaf pan. Chill in refrigerator for several hours if desired. ** Microwave on High for 10 to 12 minutes, turning once. Invert onto serving plate. Pour mixture of honey, 1 tablespoon brown sugar and 1 tablespoon soy sauce over meat loaf. Yield: 4 servings. 🔪 🍲 〰 🍲

** *Make ahead to this point.*

1½ *pounds ground beef*
1 *egg, beaten*
1 *cup bread crumbs*
2 *tablespoons chopped parsley*
2 *tablespoons onion flakes*
1 *teaspoon ginger*
1 *tablespoon brown sugar*
1 *tablespoon soy sauce*
1 *tablespoon honey*
1 *tablespoon brown sugar*
1 *tablespoon soy sauce*

Meatballs con Queso

Ann Schroeder, Texas

1½	**pounds ground beef**
1½	**cups bread crumbs**
⅓	**cup chopped onion**
⅓	**cup milk**
3	**tablespoons chopped parsley**
¼	**teaspoon pepper**
1	**egg**
3	**tablespoons oil**
1	**4-ounce can chopped green chilies**
16	**ounces Velveeta cheese**
1	**envelope taco seasoning mix**

Combine ground beef, bread crumbs, onion, milk, parsley, pepper and egg in bowl; mix well. Shape into 1-inch balls. Chill in refrigerator if desired. ** Brown meatballs in oil in skillet. Add chilies, cheese, taco seasoning mix and ¾ cup water to skillet; mix well. Cook over low heat until cheese melts, stirring constantly. Serve with corn bread and red beans. Yield: 4 servings.

** *Make ahead to this point.*

Roast Leg of Lamb

Ken Wahl, Michigan

1	**5 to 6-pound leg of lamb ***
2	**cloves of garlic, sliced**
2	**tablespoons Worcestershire sauce**
3	**tablespoons chopped parsley**
1	**teaspoon thyme**
4	**bay leaves**
2	**medium onions, sliced**
	* Seasonal

Cut 1-inch slits in roast; insert garlic. Sprinkle with Worcestershire sauce, parsley and thyme. Place roast fat side up on rack in roasting pan. Add bay leaves, onions and 2 cups water. Bake at 325 degrees to 130 degrees for very rare, 140 degrees for rare or to desired degree of doneness on meat thermometer. **Remove bay leaves.** Let stand for 15 minutes before slicing. Serve with mint jelly. Yield: 10 servings. ✳

Triple-Crown Roast of Lamb

Joan Dew, Tennessee

1	**medium eggplant, peeled, sliced**
	Salt and freshly ground pepper to taste
1	**crown roast of lamb ***
8	**cloves of garlic, sliced**
1	**medium onion, finely chopped**
2	**tablespoons olive oil**
1	**clove of garlic, minced**
¾	**pound ground lamb ***
¼	**pound ground sausage**
½	**cup fresh bread crumbs**
¼	**cup minced parsley**
1	**egg**
	* Seasonal

Sprinkle eggplant with salt. Place between paper towels. Place heavy plate on top. Let stand for several minutes. Chop finely. Rub roast with salt, pepper and garlic inside and out. Place in shallow roasting pan. Sauté onion in oil in skillet. Add eggplant, minced garlic, ground lamb and sausage. Sauté for several minutes. Remove from heat. Stir in bread crumbs, parsley, egg and salt and pepper to taste. Spoon into center of roast. Brush roast and stuffing with additional olive oil. Cover tips with foil. Roast at 400 degrees for 1 hour or to 128 degrees on meat thermometer. Replace foil with paper frills. Place on serving platter. Carve 2 chops per serving and serve with stuffing.

Note: Crown roast is prepared by having butcher tie rib sections of 2 loins of lamb together.

Ham Rolls with Spinach

Drain spinach and squeeze dry. Combine spinach, crumbled bread, egg and onion in bowl; mix well. Spoon onto ham slices. Roll ham slices from narrow end as for jelly roll. Place seam side down in shallow 1½-quart baking dish. Blend melted butter and flour in saucepan. Cook over medium heat for 1 minute. Stir in milk gradually. Cook until thickened, stirring constantly. Add cheese. Cook until cheese melts. Pour over ham rolls. Cover with foil. Chill in refrigerator if desired. ** Bake at 350 degrees for 25 minutes or until heated through.
Yield: 6 servings. ✔4 🍎 🌰 🍳

** *Make ahead to this point.*

1	cup cooked fresh spinach *
3	slices bread, crumbled
1	egg
2	teaspoons grated onion
2	6-ounce cooked ham slices
1	tablespoon butter
1	tablespoon flour
1½	cups milk
¼	cup shredded Cheddar cheese
	* Seasonal

Stir-Fried Sesame-Lemon Chicken

Danielle Dukowicz, New Mexico

Cut chicken into uniform bite-sized pieces. Marinate in mixture of parsley, lemon rind, garlic, gingerroot, ¼ cup Sherry, 2 teaspoons oil, 2 tablespoons lemon juice and 2 teaspoons cornstarch for 30 minutes to 4 hours. ** Drain chicken. Stir-fry in 2 tablespoons oil in skillet until cooked through. Add snow peas, drained water chestnuts and sesame seed. Stir-fry until heated through. Add mixture of broth, honey, ¼ cup Sherry, lemon juice, soy sauce and 1 tablespoon cornstarch. Cook until slightly thickened, stirring constantly.
Yield: 12 servings. ✔4 🍎

** *Make ahead to this point.*

12	chicken breast filets *
¼	cup minced parsley
1	teaspoon grated lemon rind
1	clove of garlic, minced
1	tablespoon minced gingerroot
¼	cup dry Sherry
2	teaspoons oil
2	tablespoons lemon juice
2	teaspoons cornstarch
2	tablespoons oil
2	cups snow peas *
1	can sliced water chestnuts
¼	cup toasted sesame seed
¼	cup chicken broth
¼	cup honey
¼	cup Sherry
⅓	cup lemon juice
¼	cup soy sauce
1	tablespoon cornstarch
	* Seasonal

Special Chicken Rolls

Phyllis McDuffie, Texas

Place 1 slice ham on each chicken breast filet. Roll up; secure with toothpick. Place in shallow baking dish. Blend soup and Durkee sauce. Spoon over chicken. Bake, covered, at 350 degrees for 45 minutes or until chicken is tender.
Yield: 6 servings. ✔4

6	thin slices ham
6	chicken breast filets
1	can cream of chicken soup
½	cup Durkee Famous Sauce

Orange Spice Duck

Arline Manning, Tennessee

1	**4 to 5-pound duckling ***
	Salt to taste
2	**leeks, sliced**
1	**cup dry Sherry**
¼	**cup soy sauce**
1	**whole star anise**
1	**large piece dried tangerine rind**
1	**tablespoon corn syrup**
1	**tablespoon cornstarch**
2	**oranges, sliced**
	Chinese parsley
	***** Seasonal

Wash duckling; pat dry inside and out. Sprinkle with salt. Place on rack in roasting pan. Add 1-inch water to pan. Roast at 350 degrees until duckling is tender. Prick duckling with fork. Place half the leeks in Dutch oven. Stuff duckling with remaining leeks. Place duckling breast side up in prepared Dutch oven. Add Sherry and soy sauce. Bring to a boil. Add 2½ cups hot water. Simmer for 1 hour, basting frequently. Add anise, tangerine rind and corn syrup. Simmer for 1 hour longer. Remove duckling to serving platter. Skim pan juices; strain. Stir mixture of cornstarch and 1 tablespoon cold water into pan juices. Cook until thickened, stirring constantly. Pour over duckling. Garnish with orange slices and Chinese parsley. Yield: 6 servings.

Turkey Teriyaki

Leslie A. Geris, California

1	**boneless turkey breast**
¾	**to 1 cup teriyaki marinade**
2	**tablespoons oil**
3	**to 4 cups bean sprouts**
5	**stalks celery, chopped**
1	**medium onion, chopped**
16	**ounces mushrooms, sliced ***
1	**sweet red pepper, thinly sliced**
6	**green onions, chopped ***
1	**tablespoon cornstarch**
	Hot cooked rice
	***** Seasonal

Cut turkey breast into 1-inch cubes. Combine turkey and teriyaki marinade in bowl. Marinate, tightly covered, in refrigerator for 8 hours, stirring occasionally. ** Drain turkey, reserving marinade. Stir-fry turkey in hot oil in skillet or wok for 6 to 8 minutes or until cooked through. Add bean sprouts, chopped celery and onion, sliced mushrooms, red pepper and green onions. Stir-fry until vegetables are tender-crisp. Stir in mixture of cornstarch and ¼ cup water. Add reserved marinade to taste. Cook until thickened, stirring constantly. Serve over rice.
Yield: 10 servings.

*** Make ahead to this point.*
Preparation suggestion: Thinly sliced Chinese cabbage, water chestnuts, green pepper or carrot may be substituted for bean sprouts.

Baked Salmon

Barbara Stalick, Oregon

1	**8 to 10-pound salmon ***
	Lemon-pepper seasoning
2	**lemons, sliced**
1	**onion, sliced**
¼	**cup melted butter**
	***** Seasonal

Wash salmon; pat dry inside and out. Rub cavity with lemon-pepper seasoning. Place lemon and onion slices in cavity. Place salmon on large sheet of heavy-duty foil. Drizzle with butter; seal foil. Bake at 350 degrees for 1½ hours or grill over hot coals until salmon flakes easily.
Yield: 10 to 12 servings.

Seafood Cioppino

Violet Imoto, California

Sauté onion, garlic and green peppers in oil in large saucepan for 10 minutes. Add tomatoes, tomato sauce, 2 cups water, bay leaves, oregano and salt and pepper. Simmer for 45 minutes. Add wine and fish fillets. Simmer for 10 minutes. Add crab, shrimp and clams. Simmer for 10 minutes longer. **Remove bay leaf.** Ladle into soup bowls. Serve with crusty French bread.
Yield: 4 to 6 servings.

1	cup chopped onion
4	cloves of garlic, minced
2	green peppers, chopped
¼	cup oil
1	28-ounce can tomatoes
1	8-ounce can tomato sauce
2	bay leaves
1	teaspoon oregano
	Salt and pepper to taste
¼	cup dry white wine
1	pound white fish fillets *
1	crab, cracked *
8	ounces shrimp *
1	cup chopped cooked clams *
	* Seasonal

Shrimp-Glazed Trout

Darlene Fairfax, Maryland

Coat trout with mixture of flour, salt and pepper. Brown on both sides in oil in skillet; drain on paper towels. Arrange on ovenproof serving platter. Bake at 375 degrees for 5 to 10 minutes or until fish flakes easily. Sauté mushrooms in margarine in skillet. Add lemon juice and shrimp. Heat to serving temperature. Spoon over trout. Sprinkle parsley over top. Yield: 6 servings.

6	small trout *
¾	cup flour
¾	teaspoon salt
	Pepper to taste
½	cup peanut oil
3	cups sliced mushrooms *
¼	cup margarine
1½	tablespoons lemon juice
18	medium cooked shrimp *
½	bunch parsley, chopped
	* Seasonal

Easy Egg and Cheese Casserole

Kay Myers, Oregon

Spread croutons over bottom of 6x10-inch casserole. Sprinkle with cheese. Combine eggs, milk and seasonings in bowl; mix well. Pour over cheese. Chill in refrigerator if desired. **
Bake at 350 degrees for 35 minutes or until set. Cut into squares. Yield: 4 servings.

*** Make ahead to this point.*

2	cups croutons
1	cup grated Cheddar cheese
4	eggs, beaten
2	cups milk
	Salt and pepper to taste
	Onion powder to taste

Tofu Lasagna
Beverly L. Quast, California

12	ounces whole wheat lasagna noodles
1	cup sliced mushrooms *
1	green pepper, chopped
1	large onion, chopped
2	small zucchini, chopped *
2	tablespoons margarine
1	cup chopped tofu
½	cup chopped parsley
½	cup Parmesan cheese
3	cups spaghetti sauce
1½	cups shredded Monterey Jack cheese
	* Seasonal

Cook lasagna noodles using package directions. Drain and set aside. Sauté mushrooms, green pepper, onion and zucchini in margarine in skillet. Combine tofu, parsley and Parmesan cheese in bowl. Layer spaghetti sauce, sautéed vegetables, noodles, tofu mixture and Monterey Jack cheese alternately in 9x13-inch baking pan. Refrigerate for several hours if desired. ** Bake at 350 degrees for 45 minutes. Serve with green salad and garlic toast.

Yield: 12 servings.

** *Make ahead to this point.*

Spinach Soufflé
Dee Rosenberg, Maryland

4	cups torn spinach *
½	cup chopped onion
1	cup sliced mushrooms *
1	stick butter
3	eggs, beaten
1	16-ounce carton cottage cheese
1	cup grated Swiss cheese
	Salt and pepper to taste
	Nutmeg and garlic powder to taste
	Tabasco sauce to taste
	* Seasonal

Cook spinach in a small amount of water in saucepan until wilted. Cool slightly. Squeeze dry with paper towels. Sauté onion and mushrooms in butter in skillet until tender. Combine spinach, onion, mushrooms and eggs in bowl; mix well. Add cottage cheese and Swiss cheese; mix well. Season to taste. Spoon into greased soufflé dish. Bake at 350 degrees for 1 hour. Serve immediately.

Yield: 4 servings.

Asparagus Custard
Joan Dew, Tennessee

2	pounds fresh asparagus *
¼	cup butter
	Grated Parmesan cheese
½	cup chopped onion
1	cup light cream
1	teaspoon salt
¼	teaspoon sugar
	Dash of white pepper
	Dash of nutmeg
½	cup fresh bread crumbs
⅓	cup grated Swiss cheese
4	eggs, beaten
	* Seasonal

Cook asparagus in a small amount of water in saucepan until tender. Drain and slice. Butter 8 individual custard cups or one 4½-cup ring mold. Dust with Parmesan cheese. Sauté onion in remaining butter in saucepan for 5 minutes. Add asparagus, cream, salt, sugar, pepper and nutmeg. Heat just to boiling point. Combine bread crumbs, cheese and eggs in bowl. Stir in asparagus mixture gradually. Pour into prepared cups or mold. Place in baking pan or oven rack. Add 1½ inches hot water. Cover with waxed paper. Bake in preheated 350-degree oven for 25 to 35 minutes or until knife inserted in center comes out clean. Loosen custard with knife. Invert onto serving plate. Serve immediately.

Yield: 8 servings.

Sesame Asparagus

S. Mouton, Tennessee

Cut asparagus diagonally into bite-sized pieces. Cook in boiling salted water in saucepan for 3 to 4 minutes, or microwave on High until tender-crisp; drain. Rinse with cold water; pat dry. ** Combine melted butter, lemon juice, sesame seed, oil and seasonings in saucepan. Add asparagus; toss to coat. Heat to serving temperature. Spoon into heated serving dish. Yield: 4 servings.

1 *pound fresh asparagus* *
¼ *cup unsalted butter*
2 *tablespoons lemon juice*
2 *tablespoons toasted sesame seed*
2 *teaspoons sesame oil*
   Salt and pepper to taste
   * Seasonal

** *Make ahead to this point.*

Cheesy Green Beans

Mary Arndt, Michigan

Cook green beans in a small amount of water in saucepan or microwave on High until tender-crisp; drain. Combine milk, cream cheese, seasonings and Parmesan cheese in saucepan. Cook over low heat until cream cheese is melted, stirring constantly. Add green beans. Heat to serving temperature. Spoon into serving dish. Yield: 8 servings.

4 *cups cut green beans* *
¾ *cup milk*
8 *ounces cream cheese*
½ *teaspoon salt*
1 *teaspoon garlic salt*
½ *cup Parmesan cheese*
   * Seasonal

Nutty Broccoli Casserole

Betty Lou Fisher, Kansas

Trim broccoli; separate stalks. Cook in a small amount of water on stovetop or in microwave until tender-crisp; drain. Arrange broccoli in buttered 9x13-inch baking dish. Combine margarine, soup mix, pecans and water chestnuts in bowl; mix lightly. Sprinkle over broccoli. Chill, covered, if desired. ** Sprinkle bread crumbs over casserole. Bake at 300 degrees for 1 hour. Yield: 8 to 10 servings.

2 *large bunches broccoli* *
2 *sticks margarine*
1 *envelope dry onion soup mix*
1 *cup chopped pecans*
1 *cup sliced water chestnuts*
1 *cup bread crumbs*
   * Seasonal

** *Make ahead to this point.*

Crock•Pot Au Gratin Potatoes

June Graf, Ohio

Combine milk, margarine and 4 cups boiling water in Crock•Pot. Stir in cheese packets from potatoes. Add potatoes; mix well. Cook on Low for 3 to 3½ hours or until potatoes are tender. Yield: 8 servings.

1½ *cups milk*
¼   *cup margarine*
2   *packages au gratin potatoes*

Gourmet Potatoes

Areva Haldeman, Ohio

2	**pounds new potatoes ***
3	**cups shredded Cheddar cheese**
¼	**cup butter**
2	**cups sour cream**
⅓	**cup chopped green onions ***
¼	**teaspoon each salt and pepper**
2	**tablespoons butter**
	* Seasonal

Cook potatoes in boiling salted water in saucepan until tender. Drain and cool. ** Peel and coarsely shred potatoes. Melt cheese and ¼ cup butter in saucepan, stirring constantly. Remove from heat. Stir in sour cream, green onions and seasonings. Add potatoes; mix well. Spoon into greased 2-quart casserole. Dot with 2 tablespoons butter. Refrigerate for several hours. ** Bake at 350 degrees for 30 minutes. Yield: 6 servings.

** *Make ahead to this point.*

Peas Orléans

Bernice Williams, Missouri

2	**cups peas ***
2	**tablespoons butter**
2	**tablespoons chopped mint ***
	Coarsely grated rind and juice of ½ orange *
2	**teaspoons sugar**
	Pinch of salt
	Juice of ½ orange *
	* Seasonal

Cook peas in a small amount of water in saucepan or microwave on High until tender. Combine butter, mint and orange rind in skillet. Cook over low heat for 3 to 4 minutes. Stir in orange juice, sugar, salt and peas. Heat to serving temperature. Pour into serving dish. Yield: 4 to 6 servings.

Spring Rice Ring

Frances Hutchison, Tennessee

3	**cups cooked rice**
2	**eggs, beaten**
1	**cup milk**
¼	**cup melted butter**
¼	**cup grated sharp cheese**
1½	**teaspoons grated onion**
¾	**cup chopped fresh spinach ***
⅓	**cup minced parsley**
1	**teaspoon Worcestershire sauce**
	Salt to taste
	* Seasonal

Combine rice, eggs, milk, butter and cheese in bowl; mix well. Add onion, spinach, parsley and seasonings; mix well. Pack into greased and floured 2-quart ring mold. Chill in refrigerator for several hours if desired. ** Bake at 325 degrees for 45 minutes. Unmold onto serving plate. Yield: 6 servings.

** *Make ahead to this point.*

Lemon-Spice Loaf

Gertrude Shockley, Maryland

Blend gingerbread and cake mixes with ½ cup water in mixer bowl. Beat at medium speed for 2 minutes. Add ½ cup water, blending until smooth. Beat for 1 minute. Fold in raisins. Pour into greased and floured loaf pan. Sprinkle with nuts. Bake at 375 degrees for 20 to 25 minutes. Cool in pan for 10 minutes. Remove to wire rack to cool completely. Yield: 12 servings.

1	*7-ounce package gingerbread mix*
½	*2-layer package lemon cake mix*
¾	*cup raisins*
¾	*cup chopped nuts*

Fresh Orange Muffins

Lisa Dobbins, Michigan

Sift first 6 ingredients into bowl. Cut in shortening until crumbly. Add mixture of egg and milk; mix just until moistened. Batter will be thick. Fold in oranges. Fill greased muffin cups ¾ full. Bake at 350 degrees for 20 to 25 minutes or until muffins test done. Dip hot muffin tops into butter. Coat with mixture of ¼ cup sugar and cinnamon. Yield: 1 dozen.

1½	*cups flour*
½	*cup sugar*
1¾	*teaspoons baking powder*
½	*teaspoon salt*
¼	*teaspoon allspice*
½	*teaspoon nutmeg*
⅓	*cup shortening*
1	*egg, slightly beaten*
¼	*cup milk*
2	*oranges, peeled, chopped* *
¼	*cup melted butter*
¼	*cup sugar*
½	*teaspoon cinnamon*
	* Seasonal

Fiesta Fruit Cups

Donita Massey, New Mexico

Place tortillas 1 at a time in several inches deep hot oil in skillet. Form cup by pressing down in center with empty can with holes punched in bottom. Fry until crisp and golden; drain on paper towels. Store in airtight container. ** Place on serving plates. Fill with sherbet and fruit. Yield: 6 servings.

** Make ahead to this point.

6	*flour tortillas*
	Oil for deep frying
6	*scoops lime sherbet*
1	*cup sliced banana*
2	*cups fresh strawberries* *
1	*cup sliced kiwifruit* *
2	*cups fresh orange sections* *
	* Seasonal

Lemon Cream and Berries

Margaret Koonce, Tennessee

4	**egg yolks**
½	**cup sugar**
¼	**cup lemon juice** *
1	**tablespoon cornstarch**
½	**cup sugar**
1	**teaspoon vanilla extract**
2	**tablespoons grated lemon rind** *
1	**cup whipping cream, whipped**
4	**cups fresh blueberries, blackberries or strawberries** *
	* Seasonal

Beat egg yolks, ½ cup sugar and lemon juice in bowl until light. Combine cornstarch and ½ cup sugar in saucepan. Stir in ½ cup cold water. Cook over medium heat until thickened, stirring constantly. Remove from heat. Stir a small amount of hot mixture into egg yolks; stir egg yolks into hot mixture. Cook over very low heat until slightly thickened, stirring constantly. Remove from heat. Stir in vanilla and lemon rind. Cool completely. Fold in whipped cream gently. Spoon into serving bowl. Chill in refrigerator. ** Serve over berries in chilled dessert glasses.
Yield: 4 servings.

** *Make ahead to this point.*

Cherry Angel Torte

4	**cups fresh cherries** *
½	**cup sugar**
3	**tablespoons flour**
2	**tablespoons cornstarch**
½	**teaspoon salt**
1¾	**cups milk**
2	**egg yolks**
1	**teaspoon vanilla extract**
1	**cup whipping cream, whipped**
1	**10-inch angel food cake**
	* Seasonal

Cut 2 cups cherries into halves; chop remaining 2 cups cherries. Combine sugar, flour, cornstarch and salt in saucepan. Blend in milk gradually. Cook over medium heat until thickened, stirring constantly. Stir a small amount of hot mixture into beaten egg yolks; stir egg yolks into hot mixture. Bring just to the boiling point, stirring constantly. Cool. Stir in vanilla. Chill in refrigerator. Beat chilled custard until smooth. Fold in half the stiffly whipped cream gently. Fold in chopped cherries. Split cake into 3 layers. Spread cherry mixture between layers. Sweeten remaining whipped cream to taste. Spread over top of cake. Arrange cherry halves cut side down over top. Chill until serving time.
Yield: 16 servings.

Strawberry Tango

Marilyn Wilkinson, Ontario, Canada

2	**cups sour cream**
1½	**cups packed brown sugar**
¾	**cup Amaretto**
6	**cups sliced fresh strawberries** *
6	**whole strawberries** *
	* Seasonal

Combine sour cream, brown sugar and Amaretto in bowl; mix well. Fold in sliced strawberries. Spoon into serving dishes. Garnish with whole strawberries.
Yield: 6 servings.

Straw-Ba-Nut Ice Cream

Peggy O. Munter, Oklahoma

Beat sugar and eggs in large mixer bowl until thick and lemon-colored. Add remaining ingredients; mix well. Pour into ice cream freezer container. Freeze according to manufacturer's instructions. Remove dasher; cover top with foil. Pack with ice and salt. Let ripen for 1 to 3 hours or until of desired consistency.
Yield: 2 quarts.

2 cups sugar
6 eggs, beaten
1 can sweetened condensed milk
½ teaspoon vanilla extract
2 cups sliced fresh strawberries *
2 bananas, mashed
1 cup chopped pecans
8 ounces whipped topping
* Seasonal

Mocha Mousse

Combine egg, gelatin, cornstarch and 1 tablespoon cold water in blender container. Process until mixed. Add 1 cup boiling water. Process until gelatin dissolves. Add coffee powder, ricotta cheese, milk, cocoa, salt and Equal. Process until smooth. Pour into bowl. Chill until set. ** Beat until smooth. Pour into dessert dishes. Serve immediately.
Yield: 4 servings.

** *Make ahead to this point.*

1 egg
1 envelope unflavored gelatin
1 tablespoon cornstarch
2 tablespoons instant coffee powder
½ cup ricotta cheese
½ cup skim milk
2 tablespoons cocoa
⅛ teaspoon salt
9 packets Equal

Chocolate-Cream Cheese Pie

Deborah J. Dewart, California

Melt chocolate chips in double boiler over hot water or in microwave. Cool for 10 minutes. Beat cream cheese with salt in bowl until fluffy. Add ½ cup brown sugar. Beat well. Add egg yolks 1 at a time, beating well after each addition. Blend in chocolate and vanilla. Beat egg whites until stiff peaks form. Add ¼ cup brown sugar, beating until very stiff peaks form. Fold chocolate mixture gently into egg whites. Fold in stiffly whipped cream gently. Spoon into pie shell. Chill until firm. Yield: 6 to 8 servings.

Note: May substitute peanut butter or butterscotch chips for chocolate chips if desired.

1 cup chocolate chips
6 ounces cream cheese, softened
⅛ teaspoon salt
½ cup packed brown sugar
2 egg yolks
1 teaspoon vanilla extract
2 egg whites
¼ cup packed brown sugar
1 cup whipping cream, whipped
1 9-inch graham cracker pie shell

June

Crab Mousse

Naomi Hirst, Connecticut

1	**tablespoon unflavored gelatin**
1	**can cream of mushroom soup**
8	**ounces cream cheese, chopped**
1	**cup mayonnaise**
1	**small onion, grated**
1	**cup minced celery**
8	**ounces cooked crab meat ***
	Dash of Worcestershire sauce
	Assorted crackers
	* Seasonal

Soften gelatin in 3 tablespoons cold water in saucepan. Heat over low heat or microwave until gelatin dissolves. Add soup and cream cheese. Heat or microwave until blended, stirring frequently. Add onion, celery, crab meat and Worcestershire sauce; mix well. Spoon into 6-cup mold. Chill until firm. ** Unmold onto serving plate. Serve with assorted crackers. Yield: 6 cups.

** Make ahead to this point.

Fluffy Ginger Dip

Kathleen Hammer, Virginia

8	**ounces cream cheese, softened**
1	**7-ounce jar marshmallow creme**
1	**tablespoon orange juice**
1	**tablespoon grated orange rind**
	Grated gingerroot to taste
	Grapes, pineapple spears,
	strawberries and other bite-
	sized fruit for dipping *
	* Seasonal

Combine cream cheese, marshmallow creme, orange juice and rind in bowl; blend well. Add gingerroot; mix well. Chill, covered, for several hours to overnight. ** Spoon dip into serving dish. Place on serving plate. Arrange small grape clusters, pineapple spears, strawberries with stems and other fresh fruit as desired around dip. Yield: 3 cups.

** Make ahead to this point.

Cucumber Sauce

Peel and shred cucumber; drain well. Blend mayonnaise, sour cream, onion powder and lemon juice in bowl. Add cucumber; mix well. Store in covered container in refrigerator. Serve over vegetables or meats.
Yield: 3½ cups.

1	*medium cucumber* *
½	*cup mayonnaise*
2	*cups sour cream*
1	*teaspoon onion powder*
1	*tablespoon lemon juice* *
	* Seasonal

Fruity Sauce

Garlene Knight, Iowa

Combine pineapple, pears, peaches and pie filling in 2-quart baking dish; mix well. Bake at 300 degrees until fruits are tender and sauce is of desired consistency. Store in refrigerator. ** Serve hot or cold as accompaniment with baked ham or ham loaf.
Yield: 8 cups.

2	*cups chopped pineapple* *
2	*cups chopped pears* *
2	*cups chopped peaches* *
1	*can cherry pie filling*
	* Seasonal

Cool Curried Soup

Emma Bischoff, Kentucky

Combine soup, evaporated milk, lemon juice and curry powder in blender container. Process until smooth. Chill in refrigerator. ** Pour into soup bowls.
Yield: 3 servings.

*** Make ahead to this point.*

1	*can chicken and rice soup*
1	*small can evaporated milk*
	Juice of ½ lemon
1	*teaspoon curry powder*

Minted Melon Ring Salad

Betty A. Armacost, Maryland

Soften gelatin in 1 cup orange juice in saucepan or glass cup. Add sugar and mint. Bring to a boil over low heat or in microwave, stirring frequently. Remove from heat. Add lemon juice, 1 cup orange juice and 12 to 15 ice cubes; stir until mixture thickens. Discard unmelted ice cubes and mint leaves. Fold in melon balls and grapes. Pour into 6-cup mold. Chill until firm. ** Unmold onto lettuce-lined plate. Garnish with additional melon balls.
Yield: 8 servings.

*** Make ahead to this point.*

2	*envelopes unflavored gelatin*
1	*cup orange juice* *
⅔	*cup sugar*
¼	*cup fresh mint leaves, bruised* *
½	*cup lemon juice* *
1	*cup orange juice* *
3	*cups mixed cantaloupe, watermelon and honeydew balls* *
½	*cup green grape halves* *
	* Seasonal

Spring Vegetables Vinaigrette

Anne Wilson, North Carolina

8   ounces asparagus *
2   cups snow peas *
1   bunch baby carrots *
8   to 12 small new potatoes *
¼   cup tarragon vinegar
¼   cup Dijon mustard
6   tablespoons oil
6   tablespoons olive oil
    Salt and pepper to taste
3   shallots, chopped
    Chervil and dillweed to taste
    * Seasonal

Blanch vegetables in boiling water; drain. Chill in refrigerator. Whisk vinegar and mustard together in bowl. Add oils gradually, whisking constantly. Add seasonings, shallots and herbs to taste. Chill in refrigerator. ** Arrange vegetables on serving plate. Whisk vinaigrette to blend. Drizzle over vegetables.
Yield: 4 servings.

** Make ahead to this point.

Fresh Mushroom Salad

Rosemary Arnold, Florida

8   ounces fresh mushrooms *
2   to 3 teaspoons lemon juice
¼   cup minced green onion tops *
3   tablespoons olive oil
    Salt to taste
    * Seasonal

Thinly slice mushrooms. Sprinkle with lemon juice. Add green onion tops, olive oil and salt; toss lightly. Chill until serving time.
Yield: 4 servings.

Dandelion and Duck Salad

Joan Dew, Tennessee

6   duck breast filets *
6   cups fresh dandelion greens,
    washed, patted dry *
1   small head radicchio, torn
¼   cup fresh orange juice *
3   tablespoons white wine vinegar
    Finely grated zest of 1 orange
    Salt and freshly ground pepper
    to taste
    * Seasonal

Roast duck breast filets in roasting pan at 350 degrees for 25 minutes or until medium-rare. Drain, reserving ¾ cup drippings. Remove skin. Place skin in roasting pan. Bake at 350 degrees until very crisp. Chop finely; reserve for garnish. Slice duck thinly at an angle. Arrange dandelion leaves in circles on 6 salad plates. Arrange radicchio leaves around edge of plates. Arrange duck slices in circle on dandelion leaves. Sprinkle with reserved garnish. Combine reserved drippings, orange juice, vinegar, orange zest and seasonings in saucepan. Heat over medium heat. Pour over salads. Serve immediately. Yield: 6 servings.

Note: May substitute tender mustard greens or the inner leaves of Boston lettuce for dandelion greens.

Oriental Crab Salad

Trim asparagus; cut into diagonal pieces. Cook in a small amount of water in saucepan or microwave on High until tender-crisp. Cool. Combine crab meat, asparagus, green onions and water chestnuts in bowl. Add Yogurt Dressing; toss gently. Chill for several hours. ** Spoon into lettuce cups. Garnish with parsley.
Yield: 4 servings. ✔4 🍎 〰 🛢

8	ounces fresh asparagus *
8	ounces cooked crab meat *
¼	cup sliced green onions *
⅓	cup sliced water chestnuts
4	lettuce leaf cups
	Parsley sprigs
	* Seasonal

Yogurt Dressing

Combine yogurt, mustard, mayonnaise, Equal, soy sauce and Worcestershire sauce in bowl; mix well.

** *Make ahead to this point.*

½	cup low-fat yogurt
2	tablespoons horseradish mustard
1	tablespoon reduced-calorie mayonnaise
2	packets Equal
2	teaspoons soy sauce
1	teaspoon Worcestershire sauce
	* Seasonal

Tofu Salad

Drain tofu in colander for 20 minutes. Pat dry with paper towels. Crumble into salad bowl. Add carrots, celery, green onions and walnuts; mix gently. Combine lemon juice, mustard, basil, garlic, salt, vinegar and Tabasco sauce in small bowl; mix well. Pour over tofu mixture; mix gently. Chill for 4 hours or longer.
Yield: 4 to 6 servings. 🍎 🥜 🛢

Serving suggestion: Serve as a sandwich filling on toasted whole grain bread or in whole grain pita pockets.

1	16-ounce package tofu
½	cup shredded carrots *
½	cup chopped celery
½	cup sliced green onions *
½	cup chopped walnuts
⅓	cup lemon juice *
2	tablespoons Dijon mustard
1	tablespoon basil
1	clove of garlic, minced
¼	teaspoon salt
2	tablespoons vinegar
	Tabasco sauce to taste
	* Seasonal

Shoestring Tuna Salad

Betty Paul, California

Combine tuna, carrots, celery and onion in bowl. Add enough mayonnaise to moisten; mix lightly. Chill until serving. **Add potatoes just before serving.
Yield: 4 servings. ✔4 🛢

** *Make ahead to this point.*

1	6-ounce can tuna, drained
1	cup shredded carrots *
1	cup chopped celery
¼	cup minced onion
¾	cup mayonnaise
1	4-ounce can shoestring potatoes
	* Seasonal

Gazpacho Dressing
Laura Brittingham, Maryland

1	**large tomato ***
5	**tablespoons oil**
1	**tablespoon olive oil**
1½	**tablespoons vinegar**
1	**clove of garlic**
½	**teaspoon each salt, oregano**
¼	**teaspoon sugar**
	Freshly ground pepper to taste
	* Seasonal

Peel, seed and chop tomato. Combine tomato, oil, vinegar, garlic, salt, oregano, sugar and pepper in blender or food processor container. Process until smooth. Chill in refrigerator if desired.
Yield: 1 cup.

Roquefort Salad Dressing
Patti Meyer, California

1¼	**ounces Roquefort cheese**
3	**ounces cream cheese, softened**
1	**cup mayonnaise**
1	**cup yogurt**
1	**clove of garlic, pressed**
½	**cup buttermilk**

Cream first 2 ingredients in bowl. Stir in mayonnaise, yogurt, garlic juice and enough buttermilk to make of desired consistency. Yield: 3 cups.

Fruit Salad Pitas
Denise Deeke, Oregon

½	**cup whipping cream**
¼	**cup mayonnaise**
1	**tablespoon honey**
1	**red apple, chopped**
1	**tablespoon chopped walnuts**
1	**banana, cut into chunks**
1	**cup fresh pineapple chunks ***
3	**pita bread rounds**
3	**frilly lettuce leaves ***
	* Seasonal

Whip cream in large bowl until thickened. Blend in mayonnaise and honey. Fold in apple, walnuts, banana and drained pineapple. Cut pitas into halves; open to form pockets. Line pockets with lettuce; fill with fruit mixture.
Yield: 3 servings.

Tortilla Roll-Ups

6	**12-inch flour tortillas**
1	**8-ounce carton sour cream with bacon and horseradish dip**
12	**ounces thinly sliced roast beef**
1	**head Boston lettuce ***
	* Seasonal

Soften tortillas using package directions. Spread with sour cream dip. Layer roast beef and lettuce on top. Spread with remaining dip. Roll up to enclose filling. Cut into halves or thirds. Place on serving plate.
Yield: 6 servings.

Beef Burgundy for Two

Photograph for this recipe on page 71.

Wrap steaks with bacon; secure with string. Brown steaks in butter in skillet for 2 minutes on each side. Add mushrooms. Cook until mushrooms are tender. Blend flour with ½ cup water. Add with soup mix, parsley, Burgundy, lemon juice and Worcestershire sauce to skillet. Simmer for 8 minutes or until tender, turning steaks occasionally. Serve with hot cooked julienne-style vegetables.
Yield: 2 servings.

2	*beef tenderloin steaks*
2	*slices bacon*
2	*tablespoons butter, melted*
½	*cup sliced mushrooms*
1½	*teaspoons flour*
1	*envelope dry onion soup mix*
1	*tablespoon finely chopped parsley*
¼	*cup dry red Burgundy*
1	*teaspoon lemon juice*
1	*teaspoon Worcestershire sauce*

Marinated Brisket

Bill Crowl, Texas

Marinate brisket in mixture of vinegar, wine, chili sauce, Worcestershire sauce and seasonings in bowl for 24 hours. Turn occasionally. Place in shallow baking dish. Pour marinade over top. Bake, covered, at 275 degrees for 8 hours or until tender. Place on serving plate. Slice thinly.
Yield: 8 servings.

1	*3 to 4-pound brisket*
¼	*cup cider vinegar*
¼	*cup red wine*
3	*tablespoons chili sauce*
¼	*cup Worcestershire sauce*
1	*tablespoon salt*
1½	*teaspoons pepper*
½	*teaspoon garlic salt*

Shepherd's Pie

Mrs. Ronald Peters, California

Sauté onion and sliced mushrooms in butter in skillet until golden. Add lamb, gravy and seasonings; mix well. Spoon into greased 2-quart casserole. Combine potatoes and beaten egg in mixer bowl; beat until smooth and creamy. Spread over lamb mixture; swirl into decorative pattern. Chill for several hours if desired. ** Bake at 425 degrees for 20 minutes or until potatoes are tipped with brown.
Yield: 6 to 8 servings.

** *Make ahead to this point.*

1	*onion, chopped*
4	*ounces fresh mushrooms, sliced **
¼	*cup butter*
3	*cups ground cooked lamb **
1½	*cups gravy*
2	*teaspoons Worcestershire sauce* *Salt and pepper to taste*
2	*cups seasoned mashed potatoes*
1	*egg, beaten* ** Seasonal*

Sweet and Sour Pork

4	**pork steaks ***
	Salt and pepper to taste
1	**cup barbecue sauce**
⅓	**cup vinegar**
1	**green pepper, chopped**
1	**12-ounce jar pineapple preserves ***
	* Seasonal

Cut pork into bite-sized pieces. Brown on all sides in skillet. Season with salt and pepper. Add mixture of barbecue sauce, vinegar and ½ cup water. Simmer for 45 minutes or until pork is tender. Add green pepper and preserves. Simmer for 15 minutes longer. Serve over rice.
Yield: 4 servings.

Stir-Fried Chicken and Broccoli

Adeline Smith, Louisiana

8	**chicken thighs ***
¼	**teaspoon ginger**
	Pepper to taste
1	**bunch broccoli ***
1	**cup chopped scallions**
½	**teaspoon sugar**
1	**teaspoon salt**
1	**cup chicken broth**
1	**tablespoon cornstarch**
¼	**cup Parmesan cheese**
3	**cups hot cooked rice**
	* Seasonal

Skin and bone chicken thighs; cut into bite-sized pieces. Sprinkle with ginger and pepper. Slice broccoli thinly. Stir-fry chicken in hot oil in wok for 3 minutes or until golden brown; push to side. Add broccoli and scallions. Stir-fry for 3 minutes. Add mixture of sugar, salt and ⅔ cup broth. Simmer, covered, for 2 minutes. Add mixture of ⅓ cup broth and cornstarch. Cook for 1 minute, stirring constantly. Add cheese; mix well. Serve over rice.
Yield: 6 servings.

Chicken Piccata

Amy Wood, Texas

4	**chicken breast filets ***
3	**tablespoons flour**
	Salt and pepper to taste
¼	**cup butter**
2	**tablespoons oil**
⅓	**cup chicken broth**
2	**teaspoons lemon juice ***
8	**lemon slices ***
	Chopped parsley
	* Seasonal

Flatten chicken filets slightly with meat mallet. Coat with mixture of flour, salt and pepper. Cook in mixture of butter and oil in 340-degree electric skillet for 3 minutes on each side or until light brown. Keep warm in small casserole. Deglaze skillet with broth. Add lemon juice and lemon slices. Cook for 2 minutes or until slightly thickened, stirring constantly. Spoon over chicken. Garnish with chopped parsley. Yield: 4 servings.

Flounder in Sour Cream Sauce

Mary Busch, Maryland

Arrange fillets in buttered shallow baking dish. Spread mixture of sour cream and seasonings over fillets. Bake at 400 degrees for 25 minutes, or microwave on High until fish flakes easily. Garnish with parsley sprigs and lemon wedges. Yield: 4 servings.

1	*pound flounder fillets* *
1	*cup sour cream*
1½	*teaspoons Beau Monde seasoning*
⅛	*teaspoon mustard*
⅛	*teaspoon ginger*
¼	*teaspoon salad herbs*
	Parsley sprigs
	Lemon wedges
	* Seasonal

Linguine with Smoked Salmon Sauce

Mary Helen Pope, Idaho

Sauté ¼ cup green onions in ¼ cup olive oil in skillet for 1 minute. Add salmon, cream and pepper. Simmer until reduced by ⅓. Bring 4 quarts salted water and 2 tablespoons olive oil to a boil. Add linguine. Cook just until tender; drain. Add 2 tablespoons olive oil; toss to coat. Place on serving plates. Top with salmon sauce, Parmesan cheese, 2 tablespoons green onions and parsley. Yield: 6 servings.

¼	*cup diagonally sliced green onions* *
¼	*cup olive oil*
1	*cup flaked smoked salmon* *
2	*cups cream*
	Pepper to taste
2	*tablespoons olive oil*
2	*pounds fresh linguine*
2	*tablespoons olive oil*
½	*cup Parmesan cheese*
2	*tablespoons diagonally sliced green onions* *
2	*tablespoons minced parsley*
	* Seasonal

Basque Tuna Casserole

Photograph for this recipe on page 72.

Sauté onion and garlic in olive oil in skillet until tender. Combine toast, eggs, wine, hot pepper sauce and 1 cup water in blender container. Process on High for 1 minute or until smooth. Combine tuna, blended mixture, sautéed vegetables, chopped almonds and parsley, olives and ¼ cup cheese in bowl; mix well. Spoon into 1-quart casserole. Sprinkle ¼ cup cheese over top. Refrigerate, covered, if desired. ** Bake at 350 degrees for 30 minutes or until heated through. Garnish with whole almonds and parsley sprigs. Yield: 6 servings.

** *Make ahead to this point.*

1	*cup chopped onion*
1	*clove of garlic, minced*
2	*tablespoons olive oil*
4	*slices white bread, toasted*
2	*hard-boiled eggs, chopped*
⅓	*cup dry white wine*
⅛	*teaspoon hot pepper sauce*
2	*7-ounce cans oil-pack tuna, drained*
¼	*cup chopped almonds*
2	*tablespoons chopped parsley*
¼	*cup pimento-stuffed olives*
½	*cup grated Gruyère cheese*
	Whole almonds and parsley sprigs

Omelet Roll
Barbara Gawron, Michigan

½ cup mayonnaise
2 tablespoons flour
1 cup milk
12 eggs, separated
½ teaspoon salt
⅛ teaspoon pepper
1½ cups chopped ham
1 cup shredded Swiss cheese

Line 10x15-inch baking pan with waxed paper. Grease with mayonnaise. Blend ½ cup mayonnaise and flour in saucepan. Stir in milk and beaten egg yolks gradually. Cook over low heat until thickened, stirring constantly. Cool for 20 minutes, stirring occasionally. Fold in stiffly beaten egg whites, salt and pepper gently. Spread batter in prepared pan. Bake at 425 degrees for 20 minutes. Invert onto towel; peel off waxed paper. Sprinkle with mixture of ham and cheese. Roll as for jelly roll from narrow end. Place on serving plate. Cut into slices. Serve with favorite cheese sauce. Yield: 6 servings.

Spinach Fettucini

4 cups torn fresh spinach *
1 cup fresh parsley
¾ cup Parmesan cheese
½ cup walnuts
½ cup olive oil
1 clove of garlic
½ teaspoon salt
¼ teaspoon pepper
12 ounces fettucini
Parmesan cheese
* Seasonal

Combine spinach, parsley, ¾ cup Parmesan cheese, walnuts, olive oil, garlic and seasonings in blender container. Process until smooth. Cook fettucini according to package directions just until tender; drain. Place in large serving bowl. Add spinach mixture; toss until coated. Serve immediately with additional Parmesan cheese. Yield: 4 to 6 servings.

Dilly Beans and Carrots

1 pound fresh whole green beans *
1 pound baby carrots *
2 teaspoons dried dillweed
1 teaspoon mustard seed
4 cloves of garlic
1 cup vinegar
½ cup sugar
* Seasonal

Trim ends from beans. Cook green beans in a small amount of water in saucepan for 5 minutes, or microwave on High in glass casserole until tender-crisp. Rinse with cold water; drain well. Cut carrots into strips. Cook carrots in a small amount of water for 3 minutes or microwave until tender-crisp. Rinse with cold water; drain well. Combine beans, carrots and seasonings in glass bowl. Bring mixture of vinegar, sugar and 2½ cups water to a boil in saucepan or microwave. Pour over vegetables. Store in refrigerator for up to 2 weeks. Yield: 8 cups.

Cauliflower Parmesan
Artes Proctor, Kansas

Separate cauliflower into flowerets. Cook in water to cover in saucepan with 1 teaspoon salt and lemon juice for 10 minutes or until tender-crisp; drain well. Sauté garlic in olive oil in skillet until brown. Add cauliflowerets. Sauté lightly. Add tomatoes and remaining ½ teaspoon salt; mix gently. Steam, covered, for 2 to 3 minutes. Spoon into serving dish. Top with parsley and cheese.
Yield: 6 servings.

1	head cauliflower *
1	teaspoon salt
1	teaspoon lemon juice
1	clove of garlic, minced
2	tablespoons olive oil
8	to 10 tomato wedges
½	teaspoon salt
1	teaspoon chopped parsley
2	tablespoons grated Parmesan cheese

* Seasonal

Baked Swiss Chard
Mrs. Lyle Abel, California

Rinse chard well; chop into bite-sized pieces. Cook in a small amount of water in saucepan until tender; drain. Sauté onion in butter in skillet until tender. Combine with chard in casserole. Add egg; mix well. Spread mayonnaise over top. Sprinkle with cheese. Bake at 350 degrees for 15 minutes or until golden brown.
Yield: 6 servings.

1	bunch red or green Swiss chard *
1	onion, chopped
1	tablespoon butter
1	egg, beaten
½	cup mayonnaise
¼	cup Parmesan cheese

* Seasonal

Fried Vidalia Onion Rings
Viola DeMoss, California

Slice onions ¼ inch thick; separate into rings. Dip in milk; coat with flour. Dip in buttermilk; coat with mixture of cracker crumbs and a small amount of flour. Deep-fry until golden brown; drain on paper towels.
Yield: 4 servings.

4	large Vidalia onions *
1	cup milk
2	cups flour
1	cup buttermilk
2	cups cracker crumbs
	Oil for deep frying

* Seasonal

Italian Potatoes
Mary Bailey, Texas

Slice potatoes 1 inch thick. Place in 2-quart casserole. Add salad dressing and butter. Sprinkle with salt, pepper and parsley. Bake at 350 degrees for 45 minutes or until potatoes are tender. Yield: 5 servings.

5	potatoes, peeled
½	cup Italian salad dressing
3	tablespoons melted butter
	Salt and pepper to taste
	Minced parsley

Orange-Dilled Summer Squash

2 **pounds squash** *
¼ **cup butter**
2 **tablespoons orange juice concentrate**
1 **onion, sliced**
1 **teaspoon dried dillweed**
1 **teaspoon salt**
* Seasonal

Slice unpeeled squash ½ inch thick. Melt butter in skillet. Blend in orange juice concentrate. Add squash and onion. Sprinkle with dillweed and salt. Cook, covered, over medium heat for 10 minutes or until tender. Spoon into serving dish. Yield: 4 servings.

Fresh Vegetables in Cheese Sauce

8 **ounces fresh green beans** *
1 **medium head cauliflower** *
2 **carrots** *
4 **ounces mushrooms** *
8 **ounces small onions** *
2 **tablespoons butter**
3 **tablespoons flour**
¼ **teaspoon dry mustard**
1 **teaspoon salt**
Dash of pepper
3 **tablespoons melted butter**
2 **cups milk**
1 **cup shredded sharp Cheddar cheese**
* Seasonal

Trim vegetables. Cut green beans in half. Separate cauliflower into flowerets. Cut carrots into julienne strips. Slice mushrooms. Combine green beans and onions with a small amount of water in saucepan. Cook, covered, for 5 minutes. Add cauliflower and carrots. Cook, covered, until vegetables are tender-crisp; drain. Sauté mushrooms in 2 tablespoons butter in skillet for 5 minutes. Add to vegetable mixture. Blend flour, dry mustard, salt and pepper with 3 tablespoons butter in skillet. Stir in milk gradually. Cook over medium heat until thickened, stirring constantly. Stir in cheese until melted. Pour over vegetables in serving dish. Yield: 8 servings.

Spring Pilaf
Photograph for this recipe on page 71.

½ **cup rice**
⅓ **cup sliced green onion tops** *
⅓ **cup sliced celery**
2 **teaspoons butter**
Salt and pepper to taste
1 **teaspoon grated lemon rind**
Lemon slices
Parsley sprigs
* Seasonal

Cook rice using package directions. Sauté onions and celery in butter in skillet until tender but not brown. Add seasonings and cooked rice. Heat to serving temperature. Spoon into serving dish. Garnish with twisted lemon slices and parsley sprigs. Yield: 2 servings.

Recipe on page 70.

Sprouted Herb Loaf
Joey Newsom, Texas

Combine milk, shortening, honey and salt in saucepan. Heat to 115 to 120 degrees. Pour over mixture of yeast and 1 cup flour in mixer bowl; mix well. Add egg. Beat at low speed for 30 seconds, scraping bowl constantly. Beat at high speed for 3 minutes. Add remaining ingredients; mix until smooth. Place in greased bowl, turning to grease surface. Let rise, covered, for 1 hour or until doubled in bulk. Stir dough down with wooden spoon. Let rest, covered, for 10 minutes. Place in greased loaf pan. Let rise, covered, for 20 minutes or until doubled in bulk. Bake at 375 degrees for 20 minutes. Cover with foil. Bake for 20 minutes longer or until loaf tests done. Remove loaf to wire rack. Cool completely before slicing. Serve with whipped cream cheese.
Yield: 12 servings.

¾ cup milk
2 tablespoons shortening
1 tablespoon honey
½ teaspoon salt
1 package or 1 tablespoon dry yeast
1 cup flour
1 egg
1 cup snipped alfalfa sprouts
½ cup toasted wheat germ
½ teaspoon basil
1 cup flour

Butterscotch Breakfast Rolls
Merlene Jensen, Idaho

Sprinkle walnuts in greased bundt pan. Arrange rolls in pan. Sprinkle mixture of brown sugar and pudding mix over rolls. Drizzle with butter. Let rise, covered, in refrigerator overnight. ** Bake at 350 degrees for 30 minutes. Invert onto serving plate.
Yield: 10 servings.

** *Make ahead to this point.*
Note: Do not use instant pudding mix.

1 cup chopped walnuts
25 frozen rolls
1 cup packed brown sugar
1 package butterscotch pudding and pie filling mix
½ cup melted butter

Herb-Buttered Bread
Julee Nordin, Michigan

Combine softened butter and next 8 ingredients in bowl; mix well. Slice bread diagonally. Spread slices with butter mixture. Wrap in foil. Store in refrigerator or freezer if desired. ** Place slices buttered side up on baking sheet. Bake at 350 degrees for 15 minutes or until heated through.
Yield: 8 servings.

** *Make ahead to this point.*

1 cup butter, softened
2 teaspoons finely chopped green onion
2 teaspoons finely chopped ripe olives
2 teaspoons finely chopped parsley
1 teaspoon basil
½ teaspoon each thyme, marjoram and tarragon
1 teaspoon garlic powder
1 long loaf French bread

Recipe on page 78.

Pear-Bran Muffins

Melissa Lowe, Indiana

2	pears, peeled, chopped *
1¼	cups whole bran cereal
½	cup milk
¼	cup oil
1	egg
1	cup flour
½	cup sugar
2½	teaspoons baking powder
½	teaspoon salt
	* Seasonal

Combine pears with cereal and milk in bowl. Let stand for 5 minutes. Stir in oil and egg. Add mixture of dry ingredients; stir just until mixed. Fill greased muffin cups ¾ full. Bake at 400 degrees for 18 minutes or until muffins test done.

Yield: 1 dozen.

Frozen Fruit Cups

Ivy Subacz, Michigan

1	quart strawberries *
1	pineapple *
6	bananas *
3	oranges *
12	ounces frozen orange juice concentrate, thawed
⅓	cup lemon juice *
	* Seasonal

Stem and slice strawberries. Peel and chop pineapple. Slice bananas. Peel and section oranges. Combine fruit, orange juice concentrate and lemon juice in bowl; mix well. Spoon into fluted foil cups. Freeze. ** Thaw at room temperature for 30 to 60 minutes. Remove foil cups if desired. Place on dessert plates.

Yield: 25 servings.

** *Make ahead to this point.*

Red Raspberry Pudding

Ruth Wallace, Tennessee

1	cup sugar
⅓	cup margarine, softened
2	cups flour, sifted
2	teaspoons baking powder
1	teaspoon salt
1	cup milk
2	cups red raspberries *
1	cup sugar
	* Seasonal

Cream 1 cup sugar and margarine in mixer bowl until light and fluffy. Add flour, baking powder, salt and milk; mix well. Pour into 9x13-inch baking pan. Sprinkle raspberries over top. Sprinkle with 1 cup sugar. Pour 2 cups boiling water over pudding. Bake at 350 degrees until golden brown. Serve warm or cold.

Yield: 10 servings.

Easy Rhubarb Dessert

B.J. Scheid, California

Combine rhubarb and sugar in 1-quart glass baking dish; mix well. Microwave on High for 2½ to 3 minutes, stirring once. Combine butter, brown sugar, flour, oats and cinnamon in bowl; mix until crumbly. Add walnuts. Sprinkle evenly over rhubarb. Microwave on Medium for 6 minutes. Let stand for 4 to 6 hours to improve flavor. Serve at room temperature with ice cream.
Yield: 4 servings.

2	*cups chopped rhubarb* *
⅓	*cup sugar*
2	*tablespoons butter*
¼	*cup packed brown sugar*
¼	*cup whole wheat flour*
¼	*cup quick-cooking oats*
¼	*teaspoon cinnamon*
¼	*cup chopped walnuts*

* Seasonal

Strawberries and Yogurt San Remo

Mary Harvey, California

Stem strawberries; cut into halves. Mix with 3 tablespoons sugar in bowl. Let stand, covered, for 5 minutes. Combine egg yolks, ⅓ cup sugar, vanilla, nutmeg and Brandy in bowl; beat until smooth. Fold in yogurt. Spoon strawberries into 4 dessert dishes. Top with yogurt mixture. Sprinkle with almonds. Garnish with shaved chocolate.
Yield: 4 servings.

2	*cups strawberries* *
3	*tablespoons sugar*
3	*egg yolks*
⅓	*cup sugar*
1	*teaspoon vanilla extract*
	Dash of nutmeg
1	*tablespoon Brandy*
2	*cups yogurt*
2	*tablespoons sliced almonds*
	Shaved chocolate

* Seasonal

Coconut-Strawberry Sherbet Mold

Photograph for this recipe on page 2.

Soften gelatin in orange juice in saucepan for 1 minute. Cook over medium heat for 3 minutes, stirring constantly. Remove from heat. Stir in strawberry purée and rum. Pour into freezer tray. Freeze until partially frozen. Beat egg whites until foamy. Add sugar gradually, beating until stiff peaks form. Beat frozen mixture in mixer bowl until smooth. Fold in egg whites gently. Pour into 5-cup mold. Freeze until firm. Unmold onto serving plate. Garnish with sliced strawberries.
Yield: 8 to 10 servings.

1	*envelope unflavored gelatin*
⅔	*cup orange juice*
1½	*cups strawberry purée* *
¾	*cup Coco Ribe coconut rum*
2	*egg whites*
¼	*cup sugar*

* Seasonal

Cherry-Chocolate Chip Cake

Karlon Blythe, New Mexico

1 **2-layer package devil's food cake mix**
1 **can cherry pie filling**
2 **eggs**
⅓ **cup oil**
1 **teaspoon almond extract**
1 **cup sugar**
5 **tablespoons margarine**
⅓ **cup milk**
1 **cup chocolate chips**

Combine cake mix, pie filling, eggs, oil and flavoring in bowl; mix well by hand. Pour into greased and floured 9x13-inch cake pan. Bake at 350 degrees for 25 to 30 minutes or until cake tests done. Cool for 10 minutes. Combine sugar, margarine and milk in saucepan. Bring to a boil. Stir in chocolate chips. Spread over warm cake.
Yield: 16 servings.

Garden Cookies

Margaret Conn, California

2 **cups sugar**
2½ **cups shortening**
2 **eggs**
6 **cups sifted flour**
1 **teaspoon each allspice, cloves, nutmeg and cinnamon**
½ **teaspoon salt**
1 **cup tomato juice**
1 **cup grated carrots ***
1 **cup chopped spinach ***
1 **cup raisins**
½ **cup chopped nuts**
* Seasonal

Cream sugar and shortening in mixer bowl until light and fluffy. Add eggs; mix well. Add sifted dry ingredients alternately with tomato juice, mixing well after each addition. Stir in carrots, spinach, raisins and nuts. Drop by spoonfuls onto greased cookie sheet. Bake at 375 degrees for 15 to 20 minutes or until brown. Cool on wire rack.
Yield: 8 dozen.

Cottage Cheese Crêpes

Mary Sheidler, Michigan

1 **cup flour**
1½ **cups milk**
2 **eggs**
1 **tablespoon oil**
2 **tablespoons sugar**
¼ **teaspoon baking powder**
¼ **teaspoon salt**
2 **cups large curd cottage cheese**
½ **cup sugar**
1 **egg**
1 **cup sour cream**

Combine first 7 ingredients in bowl. Beat with rotary beater until smooth. **Spoon a small amount at a time into hot, lightly greased skillet, tilting to coat bottom.** Bake until light brown on both sides. Repeat with remaining batter. ** Combine cottage cheese, ½ cup sugar and egg in bowl; mix well. Spread 1½ tablespoons on each crêpe; roll to enclose filling. Place in single layer in 9x13-inch baking pan. Spread sour cream over top. Chill in refrigerator if desired. ** Bake at 350 degrees for 20 minutes. Serve with fresh fruit.
Yield: 6 servings.

** *Make ahead to this point.*

Rocky Road Ice Cream

Treas Koyama, California

Soften ice cream slightly. Spread half the ice cream in 8-inch square dish. Combine nuts, chocolate and marshmallows. Sprinkle ⅔ of the mixture over ice cream. Spread remaining ice cream on top. Sprinkle with remaining nut mixture. Freeze, covered, until firm.
Yield: 8 servings.

3	*pints chocolate ice cream*
1	*cup chopped nuts*
1	*cup chocolate chips*
2	*cups miniature marshmallows*

Special Blueberry Pie

Tammy Knox, Texas

Combine blueberries, sugar, cornstarch and nutmeg in bowl; mix gently. Spoon into pie plate lined with Walnut-Orange Pastry. Dot with butter. Top with remaining pastry; flute edge and cut vents. Bake at 375 degrees until brown. Cool on wire rack. Sprinkle with confectioners' sugar.
Yield: 6 to 8 servings.

4	*cups fresh blueberries* *
1	*cup sugar*
¼	*cup cornstarch*
½	*teaspoon nutmeg*
1	*recipe Walnut-Orange Pastry*
2	*tablespoons butter*
	Confectioners' sugar
	* Seasonal

Walnut-Orange Pastry

Cut shortening into mixture of flour, salt and sugar in bowl until crumbly. Stir in orange rind and walnuts. Sprinkle 5 tablespoons water, 1 tablespoon at a time over mixture, mixing lightly until dough forms ball. Chill for 1 hour. ** Divide into 2 portions. Roll on floured surface.

** *Make ahead to this point.*

¾	*cup shortening*
2	*cups flour*
¼	*teaspoon salt*
2	*teaspoons sugar*
1	*teaspoon grated orange rind*
⅓	*cup chopped walnuts*

Fruit Medley Punch

Rhonda Hammond, Tennessee

Purée strawberries in blender container. Combine strawberries, chilled apricot nectar, 3 cups water, lemon juice, orange juice concentrate and sugar in large container; stir until sugar dissolves. Chill in refrigerator if desired. ** Pour into punch bowl. Add chilled ginger ale. Garnish with ice ring. Yield: 14 cups.

** *Make ahead to this point.*

2	*10-ounce packages frozen strawberries* *
3	*cups apricot nectar, chilled* *
1	*cup lemon juice* *
6	*ounces frozen orange juice concentrate, thawed*
1	*cup sugar*
1	*liter ginger ale, chilled*
	* Seasonal

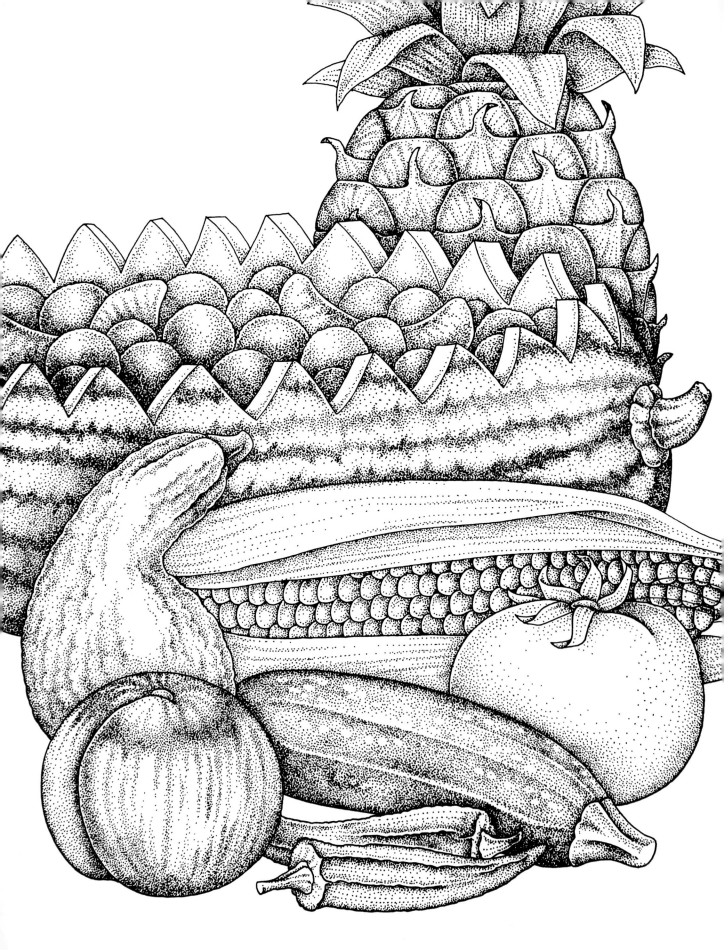

Summer

S ummertime—and the livin' is easy. Humid afternoons, lazy sunsets, warm nights with flickering fireflies and sweet-smelling jasmine. Neighborhood games of softball; lounging by the pool in search of the perfect tan; picnics; fireworks; having the kids underfoot for a couple of months— these are the sights, sounds, and sensations of Summer. None are more clearly etched in our minds than fresh Summer foods and cool frosty drinks.

In Summer we not only want to eat out of doors, we want to cook there as well. Patio or back yard grilling has come a long way from my childhood when it consisted mainly of hamburgers and hot dogs and an occasional steak. Nowadays everything goes on the grill—meats, poultry, fish, vegetables, even fruit. At my house hot dogs are often replaced with thick Polish or Italian sausages, and the burgers are fancier than the ones Dad used to make. We like beef burgers stuffed with bleu cheese or smoked mozzarella; we love patties made from a mixture of ground veal, ground pork, and sausage; and spicy Cajun burgers are a family favorite.

Swordfish or salmon steaks with lime-butter or jumbo shrimp with lemon-dill sauce make grilled Summer meals as grand as any prepared over a hot stove, especially when accompanied by vegetable kabobs of green and red peppers, corn, squash, baby red potatoes, and cherry tomatoes. A cooling dish of rich homemade peach ice cream is the perfect finish.

Barbecue, that old Summer stand-by, is more popular than ever, with contests now held annually around the country to determine whose sauce is the best. In the North or Far West when you see *barbecue* on a restaurant menu, it means a method of cooking, as in barbecued chicken or beef. On a menu in the Deep South, barbecue refers to a specific dish of shredded (or pulled) pork served with a sauce on the side. Western sauces have a tomato base; traditional Southern sauces are vinegar-based with lots of spices and peppers.

Entertaining is never more relaxing, spontaneous, and *fun* than it is in Summer. Whether it's a family reunion picnic or dinner on the deck under the stars, the secret is serving foods that can be prepared well ahead of time and stored in the freezer or refrigerator. Since foods are most appealing in hot weather when served chilled or at room temperature, this is not difficult to do. Summer soups like chilled avocado with coriander sauce, spicy *gazpacho*, or cucumber soup with buttermilk make perfect starters for dinner parties. And a buffet table laden with colorful Summer salads of seafood, vegetables, beef, chicken, pasta, potatoes, rice, and fruit are as appealing to the eye as to the palate.

The intense flavors of mid-Summer's vegetables make them delicious eaten raw, whether in salads or attractively presented with sauces and dips. I know of no better taste in the world than a vine-ripened, just-picked tomato, eaten whole like an apple. But the abundance of fresh vegetables this time of year encourages us to use them in as many ways as possible. As entrées, vegetable dishes rate star billing. The selectivity and economy afforded by Summer's bounty make it a fine time to heed the gastronomic calendar and enliven one's menus with seasonal stuffed vegetables. Zucchini, tomato, eggplant, green pepper, and cucumber all lend themselves splendidly to savory stuffings.

Summer fruits are no less appealing than the vegetables. From the luscious coolness of a freshly cut watermelon to the fragrance of an abundant blueberry bush, the pleasures abound. This is the season to savor perfectly ripened peaches; sweet but slightly tart raspberries; plump green grapes and juicy Bing cherries; ripe figs; lemons, limes, and mangos; and melons of all types.

At no other time of the year are fruit desserts so welcome: scrumptious strawberry shortcake, lemon meringue pie, peach melba, blueberry cobbler with vanilla ice cream, Key lime pie, Cherries Jubilee, fig and raspberry tart, mango and lime sorbet. Have a dessert party, and serve them all!

On the Fourth of July, America celebrates its birthday with fireworks and picnics. All-day barbecues are the tradition in many parts of the country; lavish picnics spread on the banks of a river or lake are popular in other areas. But wherever Americans gather to celebrate the Fourth, the food is good and plentiful. Given our "melting-pot" heritage, food for Fourth of July gatherings is more fun when it includes ethnic dishes such as Italian pasta salad; Jewish cream cheese and lox (smoked salmon); English roast beef; African couscous salad; Indian corn pudding; Mexican nachos; German potato salad; Spanish shrimp and rice; Scottish shortbread cookies and French pastries.

One Fourth of July dish that never fails to show up at our house is called Grandma Schmitt's Baked Beans. Grandma Schmitt came to America from Germany as a young bride back in the early 1900's. Whether she brought this recipe with her or created it here isn't known, but by the time her children were grown, her baked beans had become so famous in Brooklyn, where she lived, that restaurants had offered to buy the recipe. Grandma wouldn't sell, but she was more than willing to pass the recipe on to her children and grandchildren. In the world of pork and beans, this dish is without peer. Once you've tasted it, all other baked bean dishes seem like poor substitutes.

Summer's outdoor life puts us back in touch with nature. The best dishes are ones that capitalize on the peak of ripeness of every growing thing. It is a time for foods shared in the open air, for foods eaten for no other reason than the freshness of their taste.

Summer Foods

*S*ummer brings an abundance of beautiful, naturally perfect vegetables and fruits, never better than when harvested as close to the table as possible. This is the season to indulge one's tastes, to preserve the wealth for less generous months, and to celebrate the joys of the garden.

Apricots: Choose plump, firm, evenly golden apricots which yield to gentle pressure and are free from very soft spots. Store in refrigerator. Use as soon as possible.

Cherries: Choose plump, bright, glossy sweet or sour cherries with fresh stems and good color for the variety. Very deep color may mask imperfections. Store in plastic bag in refrigerator. Use as soon as possible. Rinse just before serving.

Melons: Choose firm, plump Cantaloupe, Persian, Crenshaw, Casaba, Honeydew, or Honeyball melons which yield to slight pressure, have fragrant aroma, and are free from punctures or soft spots. Store in refrigerator.

Peaches: Choose firm-tender, fragrant peaches without greenish spots which are free from blemishes and bruises. Ripen at room temperature. Store in refrigerator.

Corn: Choose iced corn in bright-green, snug fitting husks with bright, plump, milky kernels. Store husked corn, uncovered, in refrigerator. Use as soon as possible.

Eggplant: Choose firm, heavy, smooth eggplant which are evenly deep-purple and are free from scars, shriveling and flabbiness. Store in cool place or in refrigerator.

Peppers: Choose bright, firm, well-shaped peppers with thick flesh which are free from watery spots or shriveling. Store in vegetable crisper in refrigerator.

Tomatoes: Choose firm, well-shaped, plump tomatoes with bright color and good fragrance which are free from wrinkling and blemishes. Ripen in paper bag. Store in refrigerator.

Fish and Poultry: Fish should have firm flesh, clear eyes, pink or red gills, and a fresh, clean aroma. Store, tightly wrapped in foil, in freezer. Poultry should be plump and well-formed with soft skin. Store, loosely wrapped, in refrigerator for 2 days or tightly wrapped in freezer.

Menus

BREAKFASTS

Omelet Brunch

Omelets with Spanish Sauce	127
Easy Mix Cinnamon Rolls	154
Chilled Cantaloupe Halves	
Iced Coffee	

A Summer Brunch for Six

Sun Porch Breakfast

Peaches-and-Cream French Toast	143
Peach Butter and Maple Syrup	
Bacon Curls	
Sparkling Fruit	144

An Easy Breakfast for Three to Four

LUNCHES

Firecracker Lunch

Independence Burgers	122
Sesame Buns	
Relishes and Accompaniments	
Old Glory Dessert Pizza	132

A Fourth of July Lunch for Eight

Hot Weather Soup Lunch

Make-Ahead Gazpacho	120
Crusty French Rolls	
Fresh Fruit with Dessert Cheese	155
Minted Iced Tea	

A Cool Lunch for Four

Summer Picnic

Nectarine Soup	135
Cold Lemon Chicken	139
Sicilian Tomato Salad	136
French Peach Tartlets	145

An Elegant Picnic For Two

DINNERS

126	Marinated Chicken Kabobs	*Easy-Does-It*
129	Zucchini-Stuffed Tomatoes	*Grillout*
118	Crisp Vegetables with Garlic-Cheese Dip	
159	Fresh Pear Tart	*A Grilled Dinner for Six*

149	Fruited Ham Slice	*Clock-Watcher's*
	Hot Fluffy Rice	*Dinner*
136	Confetti Salad	
131	Quick Chocolate Mousse	*A Thirty-Minute Dinner for Five*

127	Grilled Marinated Salmon Steaks	*Catch-of-the-Day*
141	Corny Peppers	*Barbecue*
143	Sourdough Bread with Garlic Spread	
159	Layered Fruit Compote	*A Seafood Dinner for Four*

SUPPERS

121	Greek Tomato Salad	*Garden Bounty*
	Fresh Melon Platter	*Supper*
128	Garden Pasta	
	Garlic Toast	
145	Zucchini Crisp	*A Vegetable Supper for Six*

144	Apricot-Grapefruit Ice Cream	*New-Fashioned*
156	Frozen Colada Yogurt	*Ice Cream*
133	Peach Praline Ice Cream	*Social*
	Sugar Cookies	
	Brownies	*A Frosty Dessert Party*

July

Garlic-Cheese Vegetable Dip

Donna Johnson, Michigan

⅔	*cup salad dressing*
1	*cup sour cream*
1	*tablespoon onion flakes*
1	*teaspoon seasoned salt*
1	*tablespoon parsley flakes*
1	*teaspoon dillweed*
½	*teaspoon chives*
½	*envelope dry garlic-cheese salad dressing mix*

Combine salad dressing, sour cream, seasonings and salad dressing mix in bowl; mix well. Chill, covered, in refrigerator. ** Spoon into individual serving dishes. Serve with crisp carrot and celery sticks.
Yield: 2 cups. ✓4 🍶 📦

** *Make ahead to this point.*

Paradise Jelly

Rosa Shultz, Ohio

2½	*cups apple juice*
2½	*cups quince juice* *
2	*cups cranberry juice*
1	*box Sure-Jel*
9	*cups sugar*
	* Seasonal

Combine juices and Sure-Jel in saucepan. Bring to a rolling boil. Add sugar; mix well. Cook until mixture thickens and sheets from spoon. **Pour into hot sterilized jelly jars, leaving ½-inch headspace. Seal with 2-piece lids.** Process in boiling water bath for 5 minutes.
Yield: 4 to 5 cups. ✓4 📦 ✳

Peach Pickles

Peel peaches. Bring sugar and vinegar to the simmering point in saucepan, stirring until sugar dissolves. Add peaches. Simmer for 10 minutes. **Place ¼ teaspoon pickling spices, 2 cloves and 1 cinnamon stick in each of 5 sterilized 1-quart jars. Pack hot peaches into jars. Cover with hot syrup, leaving ½-inch headspace. Seal with 2-piece lids.** Process in boiling water bath for 25 minutes. Let stand for 1 week before serving. Yield: 5 quarts.

5	quarts peaches *
6½	cups sugar
1	quart cider vinegar
1½	teaspoons mixed pickling spices
10	whole cloves
5	small cinnamon sticks
	* Seasonal

Tomato-Apple Chutney

Peel and chop tomatoes and apples. Combine with raisins, onions, green pepper and cucumbers in stockpot. Add brown sugar, vinegar, salt and ginger; mix well. Tie pickling spices in cheesecloth bag. Add to stockpot. Bring to a boil, stirring frequently; reduce heat. Simmer for 1 hour or until of desired consistency, stirring frequently. **Discard spice bag. Ladle into hot sterilized pint jars, leaving ½-inch headspace; seal with 2-piece lids.** Process in boiling water bath for 10 minutes.
Yield: 10 to 12 pints.

3	quarts whole ripe tomatoes *
3	quarts whole apples
1	cup raisins
2	cups chopped onions
1	cup chopped green pepper
2	cups chopped cucumbers *
2	pounds brown sugar
1	quart white vinegar
4	teaspoons salt
1	teaspoon ground ginger
¼	cup pickling spices
	* Seasonal

Danish-Style Cucumber Soup
Zunny McLellan, Alberta, Canada

Peel and slice cucumbers and leek thinly. Sauté with bay leaves in butter in skillet until tender. Stir in flour and salt. Cook for 1 minute or until bubbly, stirring constantly. Stir in broth gradually. Simmer for 20 minutes, stirring occasionally. **Discard bay leaf.** Press through sieve or process in blender. Chill until serving time. ** Grate 1 cucumber. Add grated cucumber, cream, lemon juice and dill to soup; mix well. Adjust seasonings if necessary. Serve in chilled soup cups. Garnish with sour cream and additional dill.
Yield: 6 servings.

*** Make ahead to this point.*

2	cucumbers, peeled *
1	medium leek
2	bay leaves
2	tablespoons butter
1	tablespoon flour
1	teaspoon salt
3	cups chicken broth
1	cucumber, peeled, seeded *
1	cup light cream
1½	tablespoons lemon juice
	Minced fresh dill to taste
	Sour cream
	* Seasonal

Make-Ahead Gazpacho

R.C. Deal, Texas

2	cucumbers, peeled *
4	stalks celery *
1	green pepper *
1	yellow onion *
2	cloves of garlic
3	large tomatoes, peeled *
8	green onions *
½	cup olive oil
2	tablespoons vinegar
	Juice of 3 lemons *
¼	teaspoon garlic salt
	Salt to taste
2	teaspoons pepper
2½	cups (or more) V-8 juice
2½	cups spicy hot V-8 juice
¾	cup tomato juice
1	cup clamato juice
1	tablespoon Worcestershire sauce
¼	teaspoon Tabasco sauce
	* Seasonal

Chop cucumbers, celery, green pepper, onion, garlic, tomatoes and green onions coarsely in food processor. Place in glass bowl. Add olive oil, vinegar, lemon juice, garlic salt, salt and pepper; mix well. Let stand for 15 minutes. Stir in juices, Worcestershire and Tabasco sauces and enough additional V-8 juice to make of desired consistency. Chill for 24 hours or longer. Pour into chilled serving bowls. Garnish as desired. Yield: 4 servings.

Peaches and Cream Salad

Marcie Hill, Texas

1	cup chopped fresh peaches *
1	cup chopped fresh pineapple *
1	cup shredded coconut *
1	cup miniature marshmallows
1	cup sour cream
1	tablespoon vanilla extract
8	lettuce cups
16	peach slices *
8	mint sprigs *
	* Seasonal

Combine peaches, pineapple, coconut, marshmallows, sour cream and vanilla in bowl; mix gently. Spoon into crisp lettuce cups. Garnish with peach slices and mint sprigs. Serve immediately. Yield: 8 servings.

Serving suggestion: Serve salad in orange cups.

Hominy Salad

Combine hominy with vegetables in serving bowl. Blend sour cream, mayonnaise, vinegar and mustard in small bowl. Add to hominy mixture; mix well. Chill overnight.
Yield: 8 servings. ✔4 🥄 🍲

Serving suggestion: Use this salad as a substitute for potato or macaroni salad.

2 *cans hominy, drained*
¼ *cup chopped celery* *
¼ *cup chopped green pepper* *
¼ *cup shredded carrot* *
¼ *cup chopped green onions* *
½ *cup sour cream*
¼ *cup mayonnaise*
2 *tablespoons vinegar*
1 *tablespoon mustard*
   * Seasonal

Greek Tomato Salad

Photograph for this recipe on page 123.

Combine olive oil, lemon juice, garlic, oregano, salt and pepper in small bowl; mix well. Let stand for 10 minutes. Combine tomatoes, cheese and olives in bowl. Drizzle dressing over top; toss gently. Serve immediately.
Yield: 6 servings. ✔4 🍎

3   *tablespoons olive oil*
1½ *tablespoons lemon juice*
1   *clove of garlic, crushed*
1½ *teaspoons oregano*
½   *teaspoon salt*
⅛   *teaspoon pepper*
6   *medium tomatoes, chopped* *
8   *ounces feta cheese, cubed*
½   *cup ripe olives*
    * Seasonal

Aegean Shrimp Salad

Dorothy Wentzel, California

Combine shrimp with water to cover in saucepan. Bring to a boil; cover. Remove from heat. Let stand for 4 minutes. Drain shrimp; rinse and peel. Chop tomatoes, cucumber, and scallions. Slice radishes and celery. Cut feta cheese into ½-inch cubes. Combine spinach, romaine, tomatoes, cucumbers, scallions, radishes, celery and cheese in salad bowl; toss lightly. Combine egg yolks, oils, vinegar, lemon juice and seasonings in jar; shake well. Chill shrimp, salad and dressing until serving time if desired. ** Reserve ¼ cup dressing. Pour remaining dressing over salad; toss lightly. Arrange shrimp over top. Drizzle with reserved dressing.
Yield: 6 servings. ✔4 🍎 🍲

*** Make ahead to this point.*

1½ *pounds medium shrimp*
2   *cups torn spinach* *
2   *cups torn romaine* *
2   *tomatoes* *
½   *cucumber* *
1   *bunch scallions* *
2   *large radishes* *
2   *stalks celery* *
8   *ounces feta cheese*
2   *hard-boiled egg yolks, mashed*
¼   *cup olive oil*
¼   *cup salad oil*
1½ *teaspoons white wine vinegar*
    Juice of ½ lemon
¼   *teaspoon each salt and pepper*
1   *teaspoon minced dillweed*
    * Seasonal

Independence Burgers
Betty Vetter, California

2	**pounds ground chuck**
1	**cup grated sharp Cheddar cheese**
1½	**tablespoons chopped green chilies ***
1	**cup drained crushed pineapple**
⅓	**cup fine bread crumbs**
2	**teaspoons garlic salt**
½	**teaspoon oregano**
2½	**tablespoons chopped parsley**
	Dash of pepper
8	**sesame seed buns**
	* Seasonal

Combine ground chuck, cheese, chilies, pineapple and bread crumbs in bowl; mix well. Add garlic salt, oregano, parsley and pepper; mix lightly. Shape into 8 patties. Chill, wrapped in plastic wrap, for several hours if desired. ** Grill 4 inches from hot coals for 4 minutes on each side or to desired degree of doneness. Serve on buns with desired relishes and accompaniments.
Yield: 8 servings.

** *Make ahead to this point.*

Marinated Flank Steak
Rose Marie Hurdle, Maryland

¼	**cup soy sauce**
½	**cup oil**
3	**tablespoons honey**
1	**tablespoon minced onion**
½	**teaspoon garlic powder**
½	**teaspoon ginger**
1	**flank steak**

Combine first 6 ingredients in shallow dish; mix well. Pierce steak with fork. Place in marinade. Marinate, covered, in refrigerator for 24 hours, turning several times. ** Drain, reserving marinade. Grill over hot coals for 15 minutes on each side or to desired degree of doneness, basting occasionally with reserved marinade. Place on serving plate. Slice thinly cross grain.
Yield: 4 servings.

** *Make ahead to this point.*

Baked Cavatini
Cindy Hardy, Ohio

16	**ounces macaroni**
1	**pound ground beef**
8	**ounces mushrooms, sliced ***
1	**package pepperoni, chopped**
2	**green peppers, chopped ***
1	**onion, chopped**
1	**medium can tomato sauce**
2	**jars pizza sauce**
4	**cups shredded mozzarella cheese**
	* Seasonal

Cook macaroni according to package directions; drain. Brown ground beef in skillet, stirring until crumbly. Add mushrooms. Sauté until tender-crisp; drain. Add pepperoni, green peppers and onion. Stir in tomato sauce, pizza sauce, macaroni and half the cheese. Spoon into 11x15-inch baking dish. Top with remaining cheese. Chill, covered, for several hours if desired. ** Bake at 350 degrees for 30 minutes or until bubbly.
Yield: 10 servings.

** *Make ahead to this point.*

Recipes on pages 121, 136 and 148.

Veal Scallopini

Amy Sklar, Texas

Cut veal into serving-sized pieces. Pound with meat mallet. Coat with mixture of flour, salt, pepper and paprika. Brown on both sides in 1 tablespoon oil in skillet. Place in 9-inch baking dish. Deglaze skillet with ½ cup water. Blend in gravy base. Pour over veal. Bake, covered, at 350 degrees for 30 minutes. Slice mushrooms. Sauté in 1 tablespoon oil in skillet. Add tomato sauce and green pepper; mix well. Pour over veal. Bake, uncovered, for 15 minutes. Serve over hot noodles. Garnish with Parmesan cheese.
Yield: 4 servings. 🍎

1½ *pounds veal round steak*
½ *cup flour*
1 *teaspoon salt*
Dash of pepper
2 *teaspoons paprika*
1 *tablespoon oil*
1 *teaspoon beef-flavored gravy base*
8 *ounces mushrooms* *
1 *tablespoon oil*
1 *8-ounce can tomato sauce*
2 *tablespoons chopped green pepper* *
Parmesan cheese
* *Seasonal*

Fruited Chicken

Donna Poto, Florida

Season chicken with salt and pepper. Brown in butter in skillet. Place chicken in baking dish; reserve drippings. Combine raisins, cherry juice, mint, sugar, vinegar and orange juice concentrate in saucepan. Bring to a boil. Stir in reserved drippings and cornstarch dissolved in ¼ cup cold water. Cook until thickened, stirring constantly. Pour over chicken. Bake at 350 degrees for 25 minutes. Add mango, litchi nuts, pineapple and cherries; stir lightly. Cook for 10 minutes longer. Turn off oven. Let stand in warm oven for 10 to 15 minutes. Serve with rice.
Yield: 6 servings.

2 *pounds chicken breast filets* *
Salt and pepper to taste
¼ *cup butter*
2 *tablespoons raisins*
2 *tablespoons cherry juice* *
3 *sprigs of fresh mint*
3 *tablespoons sugar*
3 *tablespoons vinegar*
¼ *cup orange juice concentrate*
1 *to 2 tablespoons cornstarch*
1 *mango, sliced*
12 *litchi nuts*
½ *cup pineapple chunks*
1 *cup fresh pitted cherries* *
Hot cooked rice
* *Seasonal*

Recipes on pages 133, 144 and 155.

Chicken-Calabasa Stew

Betty Rice, Texas

2	**pounds boned chicken**
	Salt and pepper to taste
3	**cloves of garlic**
½	**cup butter**
1	**large green pepper, chopped ***
2	**medium onions, chopped ***
4	**tomatoes, chopped ***
1½	**cups corn ***
1	**teaspoon comino seed**
½	**teaspoon pepper**
½	**teaspoon oregano**
2	**or 3 calabasa, chopped ***
	* Seasonal

Cut chicken into small pieces; sprinkle with salt and pepper. Sauté chicken and minced garlic in butter in saucepan for several minutes. Add green pepper, onions, tomatoes and corn and seasonings; mix well. Add enough water to cover; mix well. Simmer, covered, for 45 minutes to 1½ hours or until chicken is tender, stirring occasionally. Add calabasa. Cook until tender. Ladle into soup bowls.

Yield: 8 servings.

Note: May substitute 1 pound beef or pork cubes for chicken and/or 10 zucchini for calabasa.

Marinated Chicken Kabobs

David Dent, Maryland

⅓	**cup peanut oil**
⅔	**cup reduced-sodium soy sauce**
⅓	**cup dry Sherry**
	Juice of ½ lemon *
2	**cloves of garlic, crushed**
1	**tablespoon grated orange rind**
1	**tablespoon grated gingerroot**
1	**tablespoon coriander seed**
	Salt and pepper to taste
6	**chicken breast filets ***
3	**green peppers ***
1	**pound mushrooms ***
3	**onions**
	* Seasonal

Combine peanut oil, soy sauce, Sherry, lemon juice, garlic, orange rind, gingerroot, coriander seed, salt and pepper in glass bowl; mix well. Cut chicken into 1-inch pieces; add to marinade. Marinate in refrigerator for 3 hours or longer; stir several times. ** Cut green peppers into 1-inch pieces. Stem mushrooms. Cut onions into quarters. Thread chicken and vegetables alternately onto skewers; brush with marinade. Grill over hot coals for 5 to 8 minutes or until chicken is tender. Yield: 6 servings.

** Make ahead to this point.

Fillet of Sole with Dill Sauce

1	**pound sole fillets**
1	**medium carrot ***
1	**small zucchini ***
2	**green onions ***
½	**teaspoon salt**
2	**teaspoons cornstarch**
¼	**cup sour cream**
¼	**teaspoon dillweed**
	* Seasonal

Cut fillets into serving-size pieces. Arrange in shallow baking dish. Bake at 400 degrees for 10 minutes or until fish flakes easily. Drain, reserving juice. Cut vegetables into julienne strips. Spray skillet with nonstick cooking spray. Stir-fry vegetables with salt for 2 minutes. Add 1 cup water. Simmer, covered, for 5 minutes. Remove vegetables to warm bowl with slotted spoon. Blend cornstarch with 1 tablespoon water; stir into pan juices. Cook until thickened, stirring constantly; remove from heat. Stir in sour cream and dillweed. Spoon half the dill sauce into serving plate; arrange sole over sauce. Top with vegetables. Blend fish pan juices into remaining dill sauce. Serve with sole.

Yield: 4 servings.

Grilled Marinated Salmon Steaks

Debra Richer, Michigan

Arrange salmon steaks in shallow dish. Combine remaining ingredients in bowl; mix well. Pour over salmon. Marinate at room temperature for 2 hours or in refrigerator for 4 to 6 hours, turning occasionally. ** Drain, reserving marinade. Grill salmon steaks over medium-hot coals for 8 minutes or until light brown. Baste with reserved marinade; turn steaks over. Grill for 8 to 10 minutes or until fish flakes easily. Bring reserved marinade to a boil in saucepan. Place salmon steaks on serving plate. Drizzle hot marinade over top.
Yield: 4 servings.

** *Make ahead to this point.*

4	*1-inch thick salmon steaks* *
⅓	*cup orange juice*
⅓	*cup soy sauce*
2	*tablespoons chopped parsley*
2	*tablespoons oil*
1	*clove of garlic, crushed*
½	*teaspoon basil*
	* Seasonal

Green Peppers Stuffed with Shrimp

Edna Clements, Georgia

Sauté minced celery and green pepper in butter in skillet for 3 minutes. Mix shrimp with eggs, bread crumbs, milk, Worcestershire sauce, salt and pepper. Stir in sautéed vegetables. Cut off and reserve green pepper tops; discard seed. Spoon shrimp mixture into green peppers; replace tops. Place in deep baking dish. Chill in refrigerator if desired. ** Sprinkle with oil. Bake, covered, at 350 degrees for 50 minutes or until peppers are tender.
Yield: 4 servings.

** *Make ahead to this point.*

3	*tablespoons minced celery* *
1	*tablespoon minced green pepper* *
3	*tablespoons butter*
2	*cups chopped shrimp*
2	*eggs, beaten*
1	*cup bread crumbs*
½	*cup milk*
1	*tablespoon Worcestershire sauce*
1	*teaspoon salt*
¼	*teaspoon pepper*
4	*medium green peppers* *
2	*tablespoons oil*
	* Seasonal

Omelets with Spanish Sauce

Clint Kuchan, New Mexico

Peel and chop tomatoes. Chop green pepper and onion. Sauté green pepper and onion in 3 tablespoons butter in skillet. Add tomatoes, celery, mushrooms, ham and seasonings. Simmer for 10 minutes. Keep warm. Melt ¾ tablespoon margarine in omelet pan. Pour in ½ cup eggs. Cook over medium heat until set, shaking pan and lifting side of set eggs occasionally. Fold over; place on heated plates. Spoon vegetable sauce over top. Repeat with remaining eggs and sauce.
Yield: 6 servings.

6	*tomatoes* *
1	*green pepper* *
1	*onion* *
3	*tablespoons butter*
1	*cup chopped celery* *
1	*cup chopped mushrooms* *
1	*cup chopped ham*
	Salt and pepper to taste
¼	*cup margarine*
12	*eggs, beaten*
	* Seasonal

Garden Pasta

8	medium carrots *
16	ounces mushrooms *
4	medium zucchini *
10	green onions *
2	large bunches broccoli *
3	tablespoons margarine
1⅓	cups nonfat dry milk powder
1	cup chicken stock
1	tablespoon basil, garlic salt and pepper to taste
4	medium tomatoes *
2	cups peas *
16	ounces pasta, cooked
	* Seasonal

Slice carrots, mushrooms, zucchini and green onions. Cut broccoli into flowerets. Stir-fry broccoli and sliced vegetables in margarine in wok. Dissolve milk powder in 1 cup water. Stir into wok with chicken stock and seasonings. Cook for 3 minutes, stirring constantly. Cut tomatoes into thin wedges. Add tomatoes and peas to wok. Cook for 2 minutes. Combine with pasta in serving bowl; toss lightly. Serve immediately. Yield: 8 servings. ✔ ● ◗

Note: May add 2 cups chopped cooked ham, chicken or shrimp.

Italian Green Beans

Kathleen Shafer, Colorado

2	pounds fresh green beans *
¼	cup crumbled crisp-fried bacon
1	cup Italian salad dressing
	* Seasonal

Trim and snap green beans. Cook in a small amount of water in saucepan or microwave until tender; drain. Stir in bacon and salad dressing; toss to coat well. Spoon into serving dish. Yield: 6 servings. ✔ ◗

Nippy Beets

2	cups chopped beets *
3	tablespoons melted butter
1	tablespoon honey
1	teaspoon Worcestershire sauce
	Salt to taste
	* Seasonal

Cook beets in a small amount of water in saucepan or microwave until tender; drain. Blend butter, honey, Worcestershire sauce and salt in saucepan. Cook just until heated through. Add beets; stir gently until glazed. Spoon into serving dish. Yield: 4 servings. ✔ ◗ ≋

Fresh Corn Pudding

2	eggs
2	tablespoons sugar
1	teaspoon salt
	Dash of red pepper
2	cups scraped corn *
1	tablespoon flour
1	cup milk
¼	cup melted butter
	* Seasonal

Combine eggs, sugar, salt and red pepper in bowl; beat until smooth. Mix corn with flour and milk in bowl. Stir into egg mixture. Stir in butter. Pour into greased baking dish. Bake at 375 degrees for 30 minutes. Yield: 4 servings. ✔ ◗

Okra Italiano
Nancy Watson, California

Cut tomatoes into wedges. Chop green peppers. Slice onion and okra. Combine tomatoes, green peppers, onion, okra and seasonings in saucepan. Simmer for 15 minutes or until onion and peppers are tender-crisp, stirring frequently. **Remove bay leaf.** Spoon into serving dish; sprinkle with croutons. Yield: 6 servings.

4	plum tomatoes, peeled *
2	green peppers, chopped *
1	large onion, sliced *
1	pound okra, sliced *
1	bay leaf
½	teaspoon basil, oregano and garlic powder to taste
1½	cups croutons

* Seasonal

Baked Sliced Potatoes
Lorna Polasck, California

Slice unpeeled potatoes ¼ inch thick. Place overlapping slices in buttered baking dish. Brush slices with mixture of butter and oil. Pour remaining mixture over top. Sprinkle with garlic, salt and thyme. Bake at 400 degrees for 25 minutes or until potatoes are tender and brown at edges. Yield: 6 servings.

4	large baking potatoes
¼	cup melted butter
¼	cup oil
2	cloves of garlic, minced
½	teaspoon salt
½	teaspoon thyme

Zucchini-Stuffed Tomatoes
Jeanie Crumley, Tennessee

Slice stem ends from tomatoes. Scoop out centers; reserve shells and chop pulp. Sprinkle shells with salt; invert on paper towel. Drain for 30 minutes. Pat dry. Place on squares of heavy foil or in baking dish. Combine tomato pulp, salt, zucchini, onion, cheese, pepper and basil in bowl; mix lightly. Spoon into shells. Chill for several hours if desired. ** Grill or bake at 350 degrees for 10 minutes. Yield: 6 servings.

** *Make ahead to this point.*

6	medium tomatoes *
	Salt to taste
2	zucchini, grated *
½	cup chopped onion
1½	cups grated Swiss cheese
¼	teaspoon pepper
¼	teaspoon basil

* Seasonal

Microwave Curried Rice
Donna Wilterink, California

Microwave onion and butter in 2-quart glass casserole on High for 1 minute. Add rice and curry powder. Microwave for 2 minutes, stirring once. Stir in hot chicken stock and salt. Microwave, covered, for 11 minutes, stirring once. Let stand for 10 minutes. Add sesame seed; toss lightly. Yield: 4 servings.

1	tablespoon minced onion
3	tablespoons butter
1	cup rice
1	teaspoon curry powder
2	cups hot chicken stock
1	teaspoon salt
2	tablespoons toasted sesame seed

Tomato and Basil Fettucini

¼	cup chopped onion
1	clove of garlic, minced
¼	cup olive oil
4	cups chopped peeled tomatoes *
1	teaspoon salt
½	teaspoon pepper
6	to 8 fresh basil leaves, chopped
12	ounces fettucini
	Parmesan cheese
	* Seasonal

Sauté onion and garlic in olive oil in skillet until tender; do not brown. Add tomatoes and seasonings. Simmer for 15 minutes or until of desired consistency, stirring occasionally. Cook fettucini according to package directions just until tender; drain. Combine fettucini and sauce in large bowl; toss until coated. Serve immediately with Parmesan cheese. Yield: 4 to 6 servings.

Blueberry-Ice Cream Muffins

Karina Stanaland, Texas

1	cup vanilla ice cream
1	cup self-rising flour
1	teaspoon cinnamon
1	cup blueberries *
	* Seasonal

Let ice cream stand until soft but not melted. Add flour and cinnamon; mix well. Stir in blueberries gently. Fill greased miniature muffin cups ⅔ full. Bake at 350 degrees for 20 minutes or until brown. Yield: 2 dozen.

Corn Bread Olé

½	cup butter, softened
¼	cup sugar
4	eggs
2	cups cooked whole kernel corn *
½	cup chopped onion
1	4-ounce can chopped green chilies
1	cup shredded sharp Cheddar cheese
⅓	cup milk
1½	cups flour
1	cup yellow cornmeal
4	teaspoons baking powder
¼	teaspoon salt
	* Seasonal

Cream butter and sugar in mixer bowl until light and fluffy. Add eggs 1 at a time, beating well after each addition. Add corn, onion, green chilies, cheese and milk; mix well. Add mixture of flour, cornmeal, baking powder and salt; mix well. Pour into greased 9x13-inch baking pan. Bake at 300 degrees for 1¼ hours or until golden brown. Yield: 12 servings.

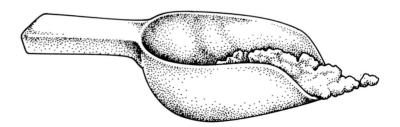

Cheesy Tomato Crescents
Traci Wilson, Texas

Dissolve yeast and sugar in lukewarm tomato juice in mixer bowl. Add salt, 3 tablespoons melted butter and half the flour; beat until smooth. Add remaining flour; mix well. Place in greased bowl, turning to grease surface. Let rise, covered, for 1½ hours or until doubled in bulk. Knead on lightly floured surface for 3 to 5 minutes. Roll ¼ inch thick. Spread with softened butter; sprinkle with mixture of cheese and celery seed. Cut into 16 wedges; roll each from wide end. Shape into crescents on greased baking sheet. Brush with 2 tablespoons melted butter. Let rise, covered, until doubled in bulk. Bake at 325 degrees for 15 minutes.
Yield: 16 servings.

1	package dry yeast
1	tablespoon sugar
¾	cup tomato juice
1	teaspoon salt
3	tablespoons melted butter
2¼	cups flour
2	tablespoons butter, softened
¾	cup grated sharp Cheddar cheese
1	tablespoon celery seed
2	tablespoons melted butter

Variation: Substitute vegetable juice cocktail for tomato juice and Parmesan cheese for Cheddar.
Preparation note: Check microwave manufacturer's instructions for letting dough rise in microwave.

Squash Bread
Cherry Couley, Oklahoma

Combine eggs and sugar in bowl; beat until thick and lemon-colored. Add oil, vanilla and squash; mix well. Add mixture of flour, baking powder, soda, salt and cinnamon; mix well. Pour into greased loaf pan. Bake at 350 degrees for 40 minutes or until bread tests done. Cool in pan for 10 minutes. Remove to wire rack to cool completely.
Yield: 12 servings.

2	eggs
¾	cup sugar
½	cup oil
2	teaspoons vanilla extract
1⅓	cups coarsely shredded yellow squash *
1½	cups flour
1	teaspoon baking powder
½	teaspoon soda
¼	teaspoon salt
2	teaspoons cinnamon
	* Seasonal

Quick Chocolate Mousse
Photograph for this recipe on page 71.

Bring half and half to the simmering point in saucepan. Combine with chocolate chips, egg, Crème de Menthe and salt in blender container. Process at high speed for 1 minute or until smooth. Pour into serving dishes. Chill until set. Top with stiffly whipped cream.
Yield: 5 servings.

1	cup half and half
1	cup chocolate chips
1	egg
1	tablespoon Crème de Menthe
	Pinch of salt
1	cup whipping cream

Angel Shortcake

Adeline Hoffman, New Jersey

1	*package angel food cake mix*
1½	*cups orange juice*
¾	*cup sugar*
2	*tablespoons cornstarch*
¼	*teaspoon salt*
1	*teaspoon each orange, lemon rind*
3	*peaches, peeled, sliced* *
1	*cup blueberries* *
1	*cup pitted cherries* *
	* Seasonal

Prepare cake mix according to package directions. Spread in 10x15-inch baking pan lined with greased waxed paper. Bake at 375 degrees for 20 minutes. Loosen from pan sides; invert onto waxed paper-lined wire rack. Peel off waxed paper. Cool completely. ** Combine orange juice, sugar, cornstarch, salt and orange and lemon rinds in glass bowl; mix well. Microwave, covered, on High for 6 minutes or until thickened, stirring every 2 minutes. Chill for 1 hour. **Invert cake onto serving tray. Brush with half the sauce. Arrange fruit in decorative pattern. Brush with remaining sauce. Yield: 12 to 15 servings.

** *Make ahead to this point.*

Old Glory Dessert Pizza

Shawn Coffey, Texas

2	*cups buttermilk baking mix*
¼	*cup sugar*
¼	*cup margarine, softened*
3	*ounces cream cheese, softened*
⅓	*cup sugar*
1	*teaspoon vanilla extract*
1	*cup whipping cream*
2	*cups raspberries* *
14	*apricot halves* *
1	*cup blueberries* *
½	*cup apple jelly, melted*
	* Seasonal

Combine baking mix and ¼ cup sugar in bowl. Cut in margarine until crumbly. Press over bottom and side of 12-inch pizza pan. Bake for 12 minutes or until light brown. Cool. Beat cream cheese, ⅓ cup sugar and vanilla in small mixer bowl until light and fluffy. Add whipping cream. Beat at medium speed until stiff peaks form. Spread over crust, leaving ¼-inch border. Arrange fruit in circular pattern over top. Brush jelly over fruit. Chill for 2 hours or longer. Yield: 8 servings.

Poached Peaches with Rum Custard

Joan Stockman, Colorado

1¼	*cups sugar*
2	*teaspoons rum extract*
8	*medium peaches, peeled* *
¼	*cup sugar*
¼	*teaspoon salt*
1	*tablespoon cornstarch*
2	*egg yolks, beaten*
2	*cups milk*
1	*teaspoon rum extract*
	* Seasonal

Dissolve 1¼ cups sugar in 6 cups water in skillet. Bring to a boil. Add 2 teaspoons rum flavoring and peaches. Simmer, covered, for 10 minutes, turning peaches and basting occasionally. Remove peaches to dessert dishes. Chill until serving time. ** Mix ¼ cup sugar, salt and cornstarch in saucepan. Add egg yolks; mix well. Stir in milk gradually. Cook over medium heat until thickened, stirring constantly; remove from heat. Add 1 teaspoon rum flavoring. Cover surface with plastic wrap. Cool to room temperature. Serve custard over peaches. Yield: 8 servings.

** *Make ahead to this point.*

Peach-Praline Ice Cream

Photograph for this recipe on page 124.

Combine peaches, 1 cup sugar and lemon juice in large bowl; toss gently. Let stand for 15 minutes. Soften gelatin in ¼ cup cold water in double boiler. Heat over hot water until gelatin dissolves. Add scalded milk; mix well. Remove from heat. Add 1 cup sugar and salt; stir until sugar dissolves. Cool. Purée half the peaches in blender. Chop remaining peaches. Combine chopped and puréed peaches, 1½ cups whipping cream, flavorings and gelatin mixture in bowl. Chill for 2 hours. Pour into 9x13-inch metal pan. Freeze for 1 hour or until partially frozen. Pour into chilled mixer bowl. Beat until smooth. Fold in Praline and whipped cream. Pour into pan. Freeze for 4 hours or until firm, stirring several times. Yield: 8 cups.

2	*16-ounce packages frozen sliced peaches*
1	*cup sugar*
2	*tablespoons lemon juice*
2	*envelopes unflavored gelatin*
3	*cups milk, scalded*
1	*cup sugar*
¼	*teaspoon salt*
1½	*cups whipping cream*
1	*teaspoon almond extract*
½	*teaspoon vanilla extract*
1½	*cups whipping cream, whipped*

Praline

Combine all ingredients and 1 tablespoon water in saucepan. **Cook to 300 degrees on candy thermometer, hard-crack stage.** Pour onto buttered cookie sheet, spreading as thin as possible. Cool completely. Pulverize in blender.

¼	*cup margarine*
6	*tablespoons packed light brown sugar*
½	*cup light corn syrup*
⅓	*cup pecans*

Fresh Raspberry Cake

Kirsten Bancroft, Michigan

Cream butter and 1¼ cups sugar in mixer bowl until light and fluffy. Add egg yolks and vanilla; beat until smooth. Add mixture of 2¾ cups flour, baking powder and salt alternately with milk, mixing well after each addition. Sprinkle 1 tablespoon flour over raspberries; toss lightly. Stir into batter. Beat egg whites until soft peaks form. Add ¼ cup sugar gradually, beating constantly until stiff. Fold gently into batter. Pour into greased and floured bundt pan. Bake at 350 degrees for 50 minutes or until cake tests done. Cool on wire rack. Invert onto cake plate. Blend confectioners' sugar and raspberry juice in bowl. Drizzle over cake. Yield: 16 servings.

¾	*cup butter, softened*
1¼	*cups sugar*
3	*eggs, separated*
1½	*teaspoons vanilla extract*
2¾	*cups flour*
2	*teaspoons baking powder*
½	*teaspoon salt*
½	*cup milk*
1	*tablespoon flour*
2	*cups fresh raspberries* *
¼	*cup sugar*
1½	*cups confectioners' sugar*
3	*tablespoons raspberry juice* *
	* Seasonal

August

Salmon Spread

Lois Lawler, Iowa

---

8   *ounces cream cheese, softened*
1   *16-ounce can salmon*
1   *teaspoon liquid smoke*
1   *teaspoon lemon juice*
    Onion flakes to taste
    Assorted crackers

Beat cream cheese in bowl until smooth. Drain and flake salmon. Add to cream cheese with liquid smoke, lemon juice and onion flakes; mix well. Spoon into serving bowl. Chill if desired. ** Let stand at room temperature for 30 minutes or until of spreading consistency. Serve with crackers.
Yield: 3 cups.

** *Make ahead to this point.*

Pickled Okra

June Dodson, California

---

2   *pounds fresh okra ***
5   *hot peppers ***
5   *cloves of garlic*
4   *cups white vinegar*
6   *tablespoons salt*
1   *tablespoon celery seed*
    * *Seasonal*

Pack whole or sliced okra into 5 hot sterilized 1-pint jars. Add 1 pepper and 1 clove of garlic to each jar. Combine vinegar, salt, celery seed and ½ cup water in saucepan. Bring to a boil. **Pour over okra, leaving ½-inch headspace; seal with 2-piece lids.** Process in boiling water bath for 15 minutes. Let stand for 8 weeks before serving.
Yield: 5 pints.

Vinegar-Based Barbecue Basting Sauce

Joan Dew, Tennessee

Combine cider, vinegar, green onions, butter, steak sauce, honey and seasonings in saucepan. Bring to a boil. Simmer for 20 minutes, stirring occasionally. Use as marinade or basting sauce for chicken, beef, pork or fish during last 15 to 20 minutes of barbecuing. Serve barbecued foods with heated sauce.
Yield: 2 cups.

- ½ cup apple cider
- ¼ cup vinegar
- ¼ cup sliced green onions
- 2 tablespoons butter
- 2 tablespoons steak sauce
- 2 tablespoons honey
- 1 teaspoon tarragon
- 1 teaspoon salt
- ½ teaspoon pepper

Avocado Soup

Place avocados, broth, lime juice, salt and garlic powder in blender container. Process until smooth. Stir in chilled cream. Chill in refrigerator. ** Pour into soup bowls. Garnish with lemon slices. Yield: 6 servings.

** Make ahead to this point.

- 4 ripe avocados, sliced *
- 3 cups chilled chicken broth
- 2 teaspoons lime juice
- ½ teaspoon salt
- ⅛ teaspoon garlic powder
- 2 cups cream
- 6 lemon slices *
   * Seasonal

Nectarine Soup

Patti Filbert, Maryland

Combine all ingredients in blender container. Process until puréed. Chill in refrigerator. ** Serve in frosted bowls.
Yield: 2 servings.

** Make ahead to this point.

- 2 cups sliced nectarines *
- ½ cup sour cream
- ½ cup Rosé wine
   * Seasonal

Mixed Fruit Salad

Michelle Davis, Texas

Peel, seed and chop papayas. Peel and slice kiwifruit. Combine papayas, kiwifruit and blueberries in bowl. Combine salad dressing, honey and poppy seed in covered jar; shake to mix well. Pour over fruit; mix gently. Spoon onto serving plates lined with crisp salad greens. Sprinkle with almonds.
Yield: 6 servings.

- 2 papayas *
- 2 kiwifruit *
- 2 cups blueberries *
- ½ cup red wine vinegar and oil salad dressing
- 2 tablespoons honey
- ½ teaspoon poppy seed
   Crisp salad greens
- ½ cup toasted almonds
   * Seasonal

Confetti Salad

Sarah Peterson, New Mexico

½   **cup grated peeled carrot ***
1   **tomato, peeled, chopped ***
⅓   **cup chopped cucumber ***
⅓   **cup chopped celery ***
2   **tablespoons chopped green pepper ***
2   **tablespoons chopped green onion ***
2   **cups small curd cream-style cottage cheese**
1   **teaspoon salt**
    * Seasonal

Combine carrot, tomato, cucumber, celery, green pepper and green onion in bowl; mix well. Add cottage cheese and salt; toss gently. Chill for several hours if desired. ** Spoon onto lettuce-lined serving plate.
Yield: 5 servings.

** *Make ahead to this point.*

Secret Potato Salad

Mary Bearee, California

4   **medium potatoes**
3   **green onions, chopped**
6   **hard-boiled eggs, chopped**
1   **2-ounce jar chopped pimento**
3   **tablespoons Durkee Famous Sauce**
¼   **cup buttermilk**
    Salt and pepper to taste
    Mayonnaise

Cook potatoes in water to cover in saucepan or microwave until tender; drain. Peel and chop potatoes; place in salad bowl. Cool. Add onions, eggs and drained pimento. Combine Durkee sauce, buttermilk and seasonings in small bowl. Add enough mayonnaise to make of desired consistency; blend well. Pour over salad; mix gently. Chill until serving time.
Yield: 6 servings.

Sicilian Tomato Salad

Photograph for this recipe on page 123.

4   **medium Florida tomatoes, sliced ***
1   **red onion, sliced**
½   **cup shredded mozzarella cheese**
    Crisp lettuce leaves
3   **tablespoons olive oil**
1   **tablespoon red wine vinegar**
1¼   **teaspoons basil**
1   **clove of garlic, crushed**
1   **anchovy fillet, crushed**
    * Seasonal

Layer tomatoes, onion and cheese on lettuce-lined serving plate. Combine olive oil, vinegar, basil, garlic and anchovy in small bowl; mix well. Drizzle over layers. Let stand for 15 minutes or longer before serving.
Yield: 4 servings.

Picnic Pita Sandwiches

Photograph for this recipe on page 157.

Combine apples, chicken, lettuce, bean sprouts and carrot in bowl. Combine yogurt, onion and seasonings in small bowl; mix well. Chill chicken mixture and dressing until serving time. ** Cut pita bread into halves; open to form pockets. Spoon chicken mixture and dressing into pockets.
Yield: 3 servings.

** *Make ahead to this point.*

1½ **cups thinly sliced Granny Smith apples ***
1 **cup chopped cooked chicken breast ***
1 **cup shredded lettuce ***
½ **cup fresh bean sprouts**
½ **cup shredded carrot ***
¼ **cup yogurt**
1 **teaspoon grated onion**
½ **teaspoon coriander**
   Cumin and pepper to taste
3 **pita bread rounds**
   * Seasonal

Stir-Fry Beef and Vegetables

Photograph for this recipe on page 158.

Stir-fry broccoli and mushrooms in oil in skillet for 1 minute or until tender-crisp. Remove from skillet. Add steak. Stir-fry for 1 to 2 minutes. Add broccoli mixture and Oriental Sauce Mix. Bring to a boil, stirring constantly. Cook for 1 minute. Add tomatoes. Cook until heated through.
Yield: 1 serving.

½ **cup broccoli flowerets**
¼ **cup sliced mushrooms ***
1 **tablespoon oil**
¼ **pound diagonally sliced steak**
⅓ **cup Oriental Sauce Mix**
4 **cherry tomato halves ***
   * Seasonal

Oriental Sauce Mix

Combine cornstarch, brown sugar, ginger, garlic powder and pepper in jar. Add soy sauce and vinegar. Cover and shake well. Add bouillon and Sherry. Store, covered, in refrigerator for 1 to 2 weeks. Shake before using.
Yield: 1 cup.

1½ **tablespoons cornstarch**
1 **tablespoon brown sugar**
½ **teaspoon minced fresh ginger**
¼ **teaspoon garlic powder**
   Dash of pepper
2 **tablespoons soy sauce**
1 **tablespoon white vinegar**
¾ **cup beef bouillon**
2 **tablespoons dry Sherry**

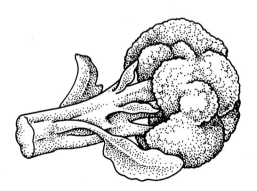

Coronado Casserole

Shirley Griffin, Louisiana

2	*pounds zucchini, sliced* *
1	*pound lean ground beef*
1	*teaspoon salt*
¼	*teaspoon each pepper, garlic powder*
1	*cup chopped onion*
3	*cups cooked rice*
½	*cup chopped green chilies* *
2	*eggs, beaten*
1½	*cups cottage cheese*
2	*tablespoons Parmesan cheese*
2	*cups grated Cheddar cheese*
	* Seasonal

Cook zucchini in a small amount of water or microwave on High for 3 minutes or until tender-crisp; drain. Cook ground beef with seasonings and onion in skillet or microwave until brown and crumbly, stirring frequently; drain. Add rice, chilies, zucchini and mixture of eggs, cottage cheese and Parmesan cheese; mix well. Spoon into 2 greased shallow 1-quart baking dishes. Top with Cheddar cheese. Chill in refrigerator or store, tightly wrapped, in freezer. ** Thaw before baking. Bake at 350 degrees for 30 minutes or until heated through.
Yield: Two 4 to 6 serving casseroles.

** *Make ahead to this point.*

Spit-Barbecued Pork Roast

2	*cups finely chopped onions*
1	*12-ounce can beer*
½	*cup soy sauce*
	Tabasco sauce to taste
1	*5-pound pork roast*

Combine onions, beer, soy sauce, Tabasco sauce and 4 cups water in shallow foil pan. Place in center of grill. Place roast on rotisserie; center over drip pan. Add water-soaked hickory chips to coals. Cook roast over low heat in closed grill for 3½ hours or to 185 degrees on meat thermometer, basting frequently with beer mixture.
Yield: 10 servings.

Chicken Lienz in Cornmeal Shell

Shellie Solomon, Texas

1¾	*cups flour*
½	*cup cornmeal*
½	*teaspoon salt*
¾	*cup shortening*
6	*chicken breasts* *
¼	*cup flour*
¼	*cup butter*
3	*carrots, chopped* *
1	*green pepper, chopped* *
½	*onion, chopped*
10	*mushrooms, sliced* *
3	*tomatoes, chopped* *
1	*teaspoon salt*
1	*teaspoon paprika*
¼	*cup flour*
¾	*cup sour cream*
	Parsley sprigs
	Lemon slices
	* Seasonal

Mix 1¾ cups flour, cornmeal and ½ teaspoon salt in bowl. Cut in shortening, until crumbly. Add 5 to 6 tablespoons cold water gradually, mixing with fork until mixture forms ball. Chill in refrigerator. ** Coat chicken with ¼ cup flour. Brown in butter in skillet. Add vegetables with 1 teaspoon salt and paprika. Simmer for 1 hour or until chicken is tender. ** Roll dough on floured surface. Fit into 7x12-inch baking dish; trim edge and prick with fork. Bake at 450 degrees for 15 to 18 minutes. Bone chicken. Arrange chicken and vegetables in pastry shell. Skim pan juices. Stir mixture of ¼ cup flour and sour cream into pan juices. Cook until thickened, stirring constantly. Spoon over chicken and vegetables. Garnish with parsley and lemon slices.
Yield: 6 servings.

** *Make ahead to this point.*

Cold Lemon Chicken
Scott McGhee, Florida

Melt butter with olive oil in shallow baking dish. Arrange chicken in prepared dish. Sprinkle with salt, pepper, paprika, oregano, garlic and lemon juice. Bake at 375 degrees for 1 hour or until tender, basting frequently. Cool. Chill in refrigerator. Yield: 2 servings.

2 tablespoons butter
1 tablespoon olive oil
2 chicken breasts *
  Salt, pepper and paprika
  to taste
1 teaspoon oregano
1 teaspoon minced garlic
1 tablespoon lemon juice
  * Seasonal

Seafood Lasagna
Mrs. Delbert Larrick, Ohio

Sauté onion in butter in saucepan until tender. Add cream cheese, cottage cheese, egg and seasonings; mix well. Combine soup, milk and wine in bowl. Reserve several shrimp for garnish. Stir in shrimp and crab meat. Layer noodles, cottage cheese mixture and shrimp mixture ½ at a time in greased 9x13-inch baking dish. Chill in refrigerator if desired. ** Sprinkle with Parmesan cheese. Bake at 350 degrees for 45 minutes or until bubbly. Top with Cheddar cheese. Bake for 2 to 3 minutes longer or until cheese melts. Let stand for 15 minutes before serving. Garnish with tomato wedges and reserved shrimp.
Yield: 12 servings.

** *Make ahead to this point.*

1 cup chopped onion
2 tablespoons butter
8 ounces cream cheese, chopped
1½ cups cottage cheese
1 egg, beaten
2 teaspoons basil
  Salt and pepper to taste
2 cans mushroom soup
⅓ cup milk
⅓ cup dry white wine
1 pound peeled shrimp, cooked *
½ pound crab meat
8 lasagna noodles, cooked
¼ cup Parmesan cheese
½ cup grated Cheddar cheese
  Tomato wedges
  * Seasonal

Stuffed Sole
Esther Ferguson, New York

Sauté onion in margarine in skillet. Add rice, cucumber, parsley, eggs, milk, salt and pepper; mix well. Spoon mixture onto fillets. Roll to enclose filling; secure with toothpicks. Arrange rolls in shallow baking dish. Drizzle with butter. Bake at 400 degrees for 45 minutes or until fish flakes easily. Yield: 8 servings.

2 cups chopped onion
1 tablespoon margarine
2 cups cooked rice
½ cup chopped cucumber *
¼ cup chopped parsley
2 hard-boiled eggs, chopped
3 tablespoons milk
2 teaspoons salt
½ teaspoon pepper
4 pounds fresh sole fillets *
½ cup melted butter
  * Seasonal

Zucchini-Tomato Quiche

Sandra Overman, Tennessee

2 cups sliced zucchini *
½ cup chopped onion *
1 tablespoon butter
½ cup shredded Swiss cheese
1 tablespoon flour
1 9-inch pie shell,
   partially baked
1 medium tomato *
6 eggs
1 cup light cream
½ teaspoon each oregano, salt
⅛ teaspoon pepper
   * Seasonal

Sauté zucchini and onion in butter in skillet for 5 minutes or until light brown. Layer zucchini mixture, cheese and flour in pie shell. Chop and seed tomato; drain. Sprinkle over flour. Combine eggs, cream and seasonings in mixer bowl; beat until smooth. Pour over layers. Bake at 375 degrees for 30 minutes or until set. Let stand for 5 minutes. Cut into wedges. Yield: 6 servings.

Green Beans with Tomatoes

Anna Compagnoni, California

1 pound green beans *
1 medium onion, sliced
2 tablespoons oil
3 tomatoes, chopped *
½ teaspoon salt
   Pepper to taste
¼ cup stock
1 teaspoon chopped parsley
   * Seasonal

Trim beans and snap into 1½-inch pieces. Sauté onion in oil in skillet. Add tomatoes, beans, salt and pepper. Cook, covered, over low heat for 40 minutes or until tender, adding stock as necessary. Spoon into serving dish. Sprinkle with parsley. Yield: 4 servings.

Microwave Calabasitas

2 green peppers *
4 small zucchini *
4 ounces mushrooms *
1 tablespoon butter
¾ teaspoon salt
4 green onions, chopped *
1 tomato, chopped *
2 avocados, chopped *
1 teaspoon chili powder
3 cups shredded Swiss cheese
   * Seasonal

Cut green peppers into thin strips. Slice zucchini and mushrooms thinly. Combine with butter in 3-quart glass dish. Microwave on High for 5 to 7 minutes or until tender-crisp. Mix in salt. Combine green onions, tomato and avocados with chili powder and 2 cups cheese; toss to mix well. Add to warm vegetables; mix well. Spoon into serving dish. Sprinkle with remaining cheese.
Yield: 6 servings.

Fried Cucumbers
Barbara White, California

Slice cucumbers and onion. Sauté in shortening in skillet until light brown. Sprinkle with salt and pepper. Cook over medium heat until tender. Add vinegar and sugar. Simmer for several minutes. Stir in sour cream. Simmer for several minutes longer. Mix in flour. Cook until thickened, stirring constantly. Spoon into serving dish. Garnish with crumbled bacon. Yield: 4 servings. ✔4 🐷

4 *medium cucumbers* *
1 *large onion* *
1 *tablespoon shortening*
½ *teaspoon salt*
¼ *teaspoon pepper*
3 *tablespoons vinegar*
1 *tablepoon sugar*
3 *tablespoons sour cream*
1 *teaspoon flour*
6 *slices crisp-fried bacon*
   * Seasonal

Corny Peppers
Jane Phillips, Missouri

Slice tops from green peppers; remove seed. Parboil in boiling salted water to cover for 5 minutes; drain. Combine corn, tomatoes and remaining ingredients in bowl; mix well. Spoon into green peppers. Place stuffed green peppers on foil squares; seal foil. Bake at 375 degrees in baking pan for 35 minutes or grill over hot coals until peppers are tender. Yield: 6 servings. ✔4 🍎 🐷 〰

6 *green peppers* *
½ *teaspoon salt*
3 *cups corn* *
1 *cup chopped tomatoes* *
½ *teaspoon instant minced onion*
¾ *teaspoon salt*
¼ *teaspoon pepper*
⅛ *teaspoon garlic powder*
1 *teaspoon chili powder*
3 *tablespoons flour*
2 *tablespoons butter, melted*
   * Seasonal

Hasselback Potatoes
Irene Cool, California

Slice unpeeled potatoes ¾ through at ⅛-inch intervals. Place each on foil square; separate slices to resemble fan. Drizzle with butter; sprinkle with seasonings. Wrap tightly. ** Bake at 350 degrees or grill over hot coals for 45 minutes. Open foil; shape into cup around potato. Sprinkle with mixture of crumbs and cheese. Bake or grill for 15 minutes longer. Yield: 8 servings. ✔4 🍎 🐷 〰

8 *small baking potatoes*
½ *cup melted butter*
¼ *teaspoon onion salt*
½ *teaspoon paprika*
½ *teaspoon salt*
2 *tablespoons bread crumbs*
½ *cup shredded Cheddar cheese*

** *Make ahead to this point.*

Baked Stuffed Tomatoes

6	large Florida tomatoes *
8	ounces fresh spinach, chopped
3	carrots, chopped *
½	cup chopped onion
1	cup chopped parsley
¼	cup butter
	Salt and pepper to taste
½	teaspoon nutmeg
	* Seasonal

Slice stem ends from tomatoes. Scoop out pulp, reserving shells. Invert on paper towel to drain. Sauté spinach, carrots, onion and parsley in butter in skillet for 2 minutes. Add seasonings. Spoon into tomato shells. Chill in refrigerator if desired. ** Place in shallow baking pan. Add ¼-inch hot water. Bake at 350 degrees for 15 minutes or until heated through. Yield: 6 servings.

** Make ahead to this point.

Ratatouille Savannah

2	cloves of garlic, minced
⅓	cup olive oil
½	teaspoon marjoram
½	teaspoon oregano
¼	teaspoon dillweed
2	teaspoons salt
⅛	teaspoon pepper
	Dash of Tabasco sauce
1¼	pounds yellow squash, sliced *
1	onion, sliced
4	medium tomatoes, sliced *
1	medium eggplant, chopped *
2	green peppers, slivered *
	Freshly cracked pepper
	* Seasonal

Combine garlic, olive oil, herbs, salt, pepper and Tabasco sauce in small bowl; mix well. Let stand until flavors are blended. Layer vegetables alternately in buttered 3-quart casserole, sprinkling each layer with garlic sauce. Chill in refrigerator if desired. ** Bake, covered, at 350 degrees for 1 hour. Sprinkle with pepper. Bake, uncovered, for 15 minutes longer. Serve hot or cold. Yield: 6 to 8 servings.

** Make ahead to this point.

Risotto

Elizabeth Nichols, Oregon

2½	cups beef consommé
1	cup rice
½	cup chopped green pepper *
½	cup chopped onion *
½	cup sliced mushrooms *
½	cup sliced pepperoni
1	tablespoon oil
3½	cups chopped tomatoes *
1	teaspoon salt
6	ounces mozzarella cheese, grated
	* Seasonal

Bring consommé to a boil in saucepan. Add rice. Cook, covered, over low heat for 25 minutes or until liquid is absorbed. Sauté green pepper, onion, mushrooms and pepperoni in oil in skillet. Add tomatoes and salt. Layer rice and vegetables in casserole. Top with cheese. Chill, covered, in refrigerator if desired. ** Bake at 350 degrees for 20 minutes or until bubbly.
Yield: 4 to 6 servings.

** Make ahead to this point.

Sourdough Bread with Garlic Spread

Marve Handley, California

Combine mayonnaise, margarine, cheese, garlic, seasonings and poppy seed in bowl; mix well. Slice bread to but not through bottom. Spread slices with garlic mixture. Wrap in foil. Chill for several hours if desired. ** Bake over hot coals or at 400 degrees until heated through.
Yield: 4 servings.

** *Make ahead to this point.*

¼	cup mayonnaise
¼	cup margarine, softened
1	tablespoon Romano cheese
1	clove of garlic, minced
¼	teaspoon Italian seasoning
⅛	teaspoon paprika
⅛	teaspoon poppy seed
1	loaf sourdough French bread

Blueberry-Cheese Pancakes

Elaine Hillyer, Washington

Combine cottage cheese, eggs, sugar, flour and butter in bowl; mix well. Stir in vanilla and blueberries. Pour ⅓ cup batter at a time onto hot greased griddle. Cook until light brown on both sides, turning once. Remove to serving plates. Serve with butter and syrup.
Yield: 4 servings.

1½	cups cottage cheese
4	eggs
¼	cup sugar
½	cup flour
2	tablespoons melted butter
2	teaspoons vanilla extract
1	cup blueberries *
	* Seasonal

Peaches-and-Cream French Toast

Paula Bennett, Michigan

Combine cream cheese, chopped peach and peach Brandy in bowl; mix well. Cut pockets in bread slices. Stuff with cream cheese mixture. Place in single layer in 7x11-inch baking dish. Mix eggs, 3 tablespoons preserves and half and half in bowl. Pour over bread. Chill, covered, overnight. ** Brown on both sides in mixture of 2 tablespoons butter and oil in skillet. Beat ⅓ cup preserves and ¼ cup butter in mixer bowl until light and fluffy. Arrange French toast on heated serving plate. Arrange sliced peaches on top. Sprinkle with confectioners' sugar and almonds. Serve with peach preserve-butter and maple syrup. Yield: 3 servings.

** *Make ahead to this point.*

8	ounces cream cheese, softened
1	peach, chopped *
3	tablespoons peach Brandy
6	1-inch thick slices French bread
3	eggs
3	tablespoons peach preserves *
¾	cup half and half
2	tablespoons butter
1½	tablespoons oil
⅓	cup peach preserves *
¼	cup butter, softened
2	peaches, sliced *
¼	cup confectioners' sugar
¼	cup chopped toasted almonds
	* Seasonal

Peach Upside-Down Muffins
Frank Bogedain, Michigan

2	cups flour
1½	cups sugar
1	tablespoon baking powder
½	teaspoon salt
¼	cup melted shortening
2	eggs
1	cup milk
6	tablespoons butter
18	tablespoons brown sugar
6	peaches, sliced *
	* Seasonal

Sift flour, sugar, baking powder and salt together 3 times. Add to mixture of shortening, eggs and milk in mixer bowl, gradually; beat until smooth. Place 1 teaspoon butter and 1 tablespoon brown sugar in each of 18 muffins cups. Heat in 375-degree oven until melted. Arrange peach slices in cups. Spoon in batter. Bake at 375 degrees for 25 minutes. Invert onto serving plate.
Yield: 18 muffins.

Serving suggestion: Serve hot or cold with ice cream for dessert.

Apricot-Grapefruit Ice Cream
Photograph for this recipe on page 124.

6	ounces dried apricots
1¾	cups Ocean Spray Indian River grapefruit juice
1	cup sugar
4	egg whites
¼	teaspoon salt
1	cup mashed bananas
2	cups whipping cream, whipped

Combine apricots and 1 cup grapefruit juice in saucepan. Bring to a boil. Remove from heat. Let stand, covered, for 1 hour. Purée in blender. Combine remaining ¾ cup juice and sugar in saucepan. Boil for 5 minutes or until syrupy. Beat egg whites with salt in mixer bowl until soft peaks form. Add hot syrup gradually, beating until very stiff peaks form. Fold gently into mixture of apricot purée and bananas. Fold in half the whipped cream gently, blending well. Pour into 9x13-inch metal dish. Freeze for 1 hour or until partially frozen. Spoon into chilled mixer bowl. Beat until smooth. Fold in remaining whipped cream. Pour into dish. Freeze, covered, for 4 hours or until firm, stirring several times. Yield: 6 servings.

Sparkling Fruit
Cheryl Hassett, Australia

1	peach, peeled, chopped *
1	pear, peeled, chopped *
1	kiwifruit, peeled, sliced
½	cup green grape halves *
½	cup purple grape halves *
1	cup strawberries
½	cup fresh pineapple chunks
1	tablespoon sugar
	Champagne
	* Seasonal

Combine peach, pear, kiwifruit, grapes, strawberries and pineapple in bowl. Sprinkle with sugar. Chill in refrigerator for several hours. ** Spoon into Champagne glasses. Fill with Champagne. Yield: 3 servings.

Suggestion: Substitute sparkling white grape juice for Champagne.

Zucchini Crisp

Doris Burns, Michigan

Mix flour, 2 cups sugar and salt in bowl. Cut in margarine until crumbly. Press half the mixture over bottom of greased 9x13-inch baking pan. Bake at 375 degrees for 10 minutes. Peel, seed and slice enough zucchini to yield 8 cups. Mix with lemon juice in saucepan. Cook until tender. Add 1 cup sugar, nutmeg and 1 teaspoon cinnamon. Simmer for 1 minute. Stir in ½ cup crumb mixture. Cook for 1 minute, stirring constantly. Cool. Pour into greased pan. Sprinkle mixture of ½ teaspoon cinnamon and remaining crumb mixture over zucchini. Bake at 375 degrees for 35 minutes or until light brown. Yield: 10 to 15 servings.

4	*cups flour*
2	*cups sugar*
½	*teaspoon salt*
3	*sticks margarine*
3	*or 4 zucchini**
⅔	*cup lemon juice*
1	*cup sugar*
¼	*teaspoon nutmeg*
1½	*teaspoons cinnamon*
	Seasonal

Note: This dessert tastes like apple crisp.

Lemon Ribbon Alaska Pie

Catherine Eburg, Maryland

Blend first 5 ingredients in double boiler. Add eggs and egg yolks; mix well. Cook over boiling water until thickened and smooth, beating constantly. Cool. Layer half the softened ice cream and half the sauce in pie shell. Freeze until firm. Repeat layers with remaining ice cream and sauce. Freeze until firm. ** Beat egg whites until soft peaks form. Add 6 tablespoons sugar gradually, beating until stiff peaks form. Spread over pie, sealing to edge. Bake at 375 degrees until light brown. Serve immediately.
Yield: 6 to 8 servings.

6	*tablespoons butter*
	Grated rind of 1 lemon
⅓	*cup lemon juice*
⅛	*teaspoon salt*
1	*cup sugar*
2	*eggs*
2	*egg yolks*
1	*quart vanilla ice cream*
1	*baked 9-inch pie shell*
2	*egg whites*
6	*tablespoons sugar*

*** Make ahead to this point.*

French Peach Tartlets

Arrange peach slices in tartlet shells. Combine flour and sugar in bowl. Add lemon juice and egg; mix well. Spoon over peaches. Combine vanilla wafer crumbs, almonds and butter in bowl; mix well. Sprinkle over peaches. Bake at 400 degrees for 5 minutes. Reduce temperature to 375 degrees. Bake for 15 minutes longer or until set and brown. Cool on wire rack. Yield: 8 tartlets.

6	*peaches, peeled, sliced**
8	*unbaked tartlet shells*
1	*tablespoon flour*
1	*cup sugar*
1	*tablespoon lemon juice**
1	*egg*
1	*cup vanilla wafer crumbs*
½	*cup toasted chopped almonds*
¼	*cup melted butter*
	Seasonal

September

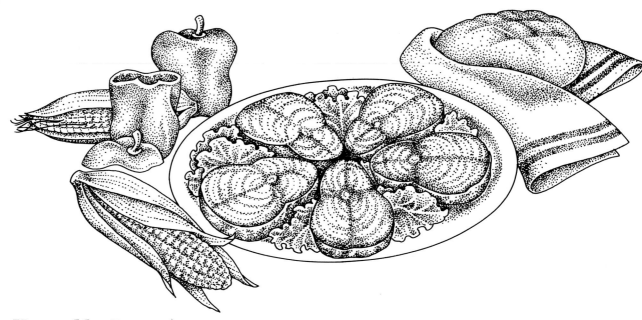

Vegetable Canapés

Elizabeth Sutton, Indiana

1	*envelope unflavored gelatin*
1	*large tomato, peeled, minced **
1	*cup minced celery **
1	*cup minced cucumber **
1	*cup minced green pepper **
½	*cup minced carrot*
1	*to 1½ cups mayonnaise*
1	*teaspoon salt*
1	*loaf thin-sliced bread*
	* Seasonal

Soften gelatin in ¼ cup cold water. Heat on stovetop or in microwave until gelatin dissolves. Cool. Combine vegetables, mayonnaise and salt in bowl; mix well. Mix in gelatin. Chill overnight. ** Cut bread into desired shapes with cookie cutter. Spread with vegetable mixture. Arrange on serving plate. Yield: 3 to 4 dozen canapés.

** Make ahead to this point.

Pineapple-Zucchini Jam

Betty Goeringer, Georgia

6	*cups grated peeled zucchini **
¼	*cup lemon juice **
1	*cup drained crushed pineapple*
1	*package pectin*
6	*cups sugar*
1	*6-ounce package apricot gelatin*
	* Seasonal

Combine zucchini and lemon juice in saucepan. Cook for 1 hour, stirring occasionally. Add pineapple, pectin and sugar. Cook for 6 minutes, stirring constantly. Add gelatin; stir until dissolved. **Pour into hot sterilized 8-ounce jars, leaving ½-inch headspace. Seal with 2-piece lids.** Process in boiling water bath for 5 minutes.
Yield: 8 to 10 cups.

Microwave Nutrition Snacks

Patrick Esper, Michigan

Microwave margarine in large glass bowl on High for 1 minute or until melted. Add brown sugar, honey and cinnamon; mix well. Add mixture of oats, coconut, walnuts, raisins, wheat germ, sunflower seed and sesame seed; mix well. Microwave on High for 6 minutes, stirring every 2 minutes. Shape into small balls; place on waxed paper. Let stand until cool. Store in airtight container.
Yield: 50 snacks.

1	*stick margarine*
¾	*cup packed brown sugar*
⅓	*cup honey*
1	*teaspoon cinnamon*
1½	*cups oats*
1	*cup coconut*
1	*cup chopped walnuts*
½	*cup raisins*
½	*cup each wheat germ, sunflower seed*
⅓	*cup sesame seed*

Cold Lemon Soup

Combine chicken stock and cream in saucepan. Cook over low heat just until heated through. Blend cornstarch with a small amount of water in bowl; stir into soup. Cook over low heat until thickened, stirring constantly. Do not boil. **Stir a small amount of hot mixture into beaten egg yolks; stir egg yolks into hot mixture.** Chill for several hours. ** Whisk in lemon juice and seasonings gradually just before serving. Serve in chilled bowls.
Yield: 6 servings.

** Make ahead to this point.

4	*cups chicken stock*
2	*cups light cream*
2	*tablespoons cornstarch*
6	*egg yolks*
	Juice of 8 lemons *
1	*teaspoon MSG*
	Salt and red pepper to taste
	* Seasonal

Chilled Zucchini Soup

Combine chicken broth, zucchini, onion, minced garlic, basil, salt and Tabasco sauce in large saucepan. Simmer for 15 minutes or until vegetables are tender. Process ¼ at a time in blender until smooth. Process milk and cottage cheese in blender until smooth. Stir milk mixture into zucchini mixture. Chill until serving time.
Yield: 7 cups.

3½	*cups chicken broth*
8	*cups sliced zucchini **
1	*cup chopped onion*
1	*clove of garlic, minced*
1	*teaspoon basil*
½	*teaspoon salt*
½	*teaspoon Tabasco sauce*
½	*cup low-fat milk*
½	*cup low-fat cottage cheese*
	* Seasonal

Della Robbia Fruit Salad

Janet Williams, Tennessee

8	ounces cream cheese, softened
¼	cup milk
2	tablespoons honey
¼	teaspoon almond extract
3	peaches, sliced *
4	nectarines, sliced *
1	cantaloupe, sliced *
3	apples, sliced *
	Red, blue and white grapes *
1	cup blueberries *
1	cup fresh cherries
1	bunch watercress
	* Seasonal

Combine cream cheese, milk, honey and flavoring in mixer bowl; beat at low speed until smooth. Spoon into small serving bowl. Place in center of serving platter. Arrange peaches, nectarines, cantaloupe, apples, small grape clusters, blueberries and cherries around dressing. Garnish with watercress. Yield: 8 servings.

Tomatoes à la Russe

Photograph for this recipe on page 123.

1	10-ounce package frozen mixed vegetables
4	tomatoes *
3	tablespoons mayonnaise
3	tablespoons sour cream
1	teaspoon lemon juice
½	teaspoon tarragon
½	teaspoon salt
	Dash of pepper
	Shredded lettuce
	Parsley sprigs
	* Seasonal

Cook mixed vegetables on stovetop or in microwave according to package directions; drain. Chill in refrigerator. ** Cut thin slice from stem end of each tomato. Scoop out pulp, reserving shells; invert shells on paper towels to drain. Combine chilled vegetables with mayonnaise, sour cream, lemon juice and seasonings; mix lightly. Spoon into tomato shells. Arrange on lettuce-lined serving plate. Garnish with parsley.
Yield: 4 servings.

** *Make ahead to this point.*

Lobster Salad

18	ounces rock lobster tails *
1	pound cabbage, shredded *
1	carrot, shredded *
1	green pepper, chopped *
¼	cup chopped parsley
¾	cup mayonnaise
¼	cup light cream
1	tablespoon chopped pimento
2	tablespoons pickle relish
	Lettuce leaves *
	* Seasonal

Cook lobster tails in boiling salted water for 2 to 3 minutes; drain and rinse with cold water. Remove meat from shells; cut into ½-inch slices. Combine lobster, vegetables, mayonnaise, cream, pimento and relish in bowl; mix well. Chill until serving time. ** Serve on lettuce-lined serving platter. Yield: 6 servings.

** *Make ahead to this point.*

Marinated T-Bones

Brett Bowen, Texas

Place steaks in shallow dish. Combine remaining ingredients in bowl; mix well. Pour over steaks. Marinate in refrigerator for 3 hours, turning steaks frequently. ** Drain, reserving marinade. Grill over hot mesquite coals to desired degree of doneness, basting frequently with reserved marinade or favorite basting sauce.
Yield: 6 servings.

** *Make ahead to this point.*

6	*1 to 1½-inch thick T-bone steaks*
¾	*teaspoon each seasoned salt, lemon-pepper Dash of garlic salt*
⅓	*cup each Worcestershire sauce, liquid smoke*
3	*cups strained jalapēno juice*

Working Girl's Meat Loaf

Combine ground beef and soup in bowl; mix well. Add enough stuffing mix to make of desired consistency. Shape into loaf; place in loaf pan. Bake at 350 degrees for 1 hour. Remove to serving plate. Let stand for several minutes before slicing. Yield: 4 to 6 servings.

1½	*pounds ground beef*
1	*can onion soup*
1	*cup (or more) stuffing mix*

Fruited Ham Slice

Janet Price, Ohio

Trim ham slice. Place in glass baking dish. Drain oranges and pineapple, reserving juice. Arrange fruit and raisins on ham slice. Microwave on High for 10 minutes. Mix reserved juice, brown sugar, cornstarch and cloves in small bowl. Pour over ham slice carefully. Rotate dish ½ turn. Microwave for 8 to 10 minutes longer, basting once.
Yield: 5 servings.

1	*fully cooked 1-inch thick ham slice*
1	*11-ounce can mandarin oranges*
1	*can pineapple chunks*
¼	*cup raisins*
2	*tablespoons brown sugar*
1	*tablespoon cornstarch*
¼	*teaspoon ground cloves*

Barbecued Chicken Mexicana

Thelma Langston, California

Combine tomato sauce, corn syrup, Worcestershire sauce, pepper, garlic and salt in saucepan; mix well. Bring to a boil over medium heat, stirring constantly. Simmer for 5 minutes, stirring frequently. Chill in refrigerator if desired. ** Grill chicken 6 inches from hot coals for 30 minutes, turning several times. Brush with prepared sauce. Grill for 15 minutes longer or until tender, turning and basting frequently.
Yield: 4 servings.

** *Make ahead to this point.*

1	*8-ounce can tomato sauce*
½	*cup corn syrup*
1	*teaspoon Worcestershire sauce*
1	*to 2 tablespoons minced jalapeño pepper*
1	*clove of garlic, minced*
½	*teaspoon salt*
1	*chicken, cut up * *
	* *Seasonal*

Chicken Breasts in Yogurt-Mustard Sauce
Sister Barbara Marie Kleck, Maryland

4	*6-ounce chicken breast filets * *
¼	*teaspoon salt*
⅛	*teaspoon pepper*
2	*tablespoons unsalted butter*
1	*tablespoon oil*
2	*tablespoons chopped shallots*
1	*cup sliced mushrooms * *
⅓	*cup dry white wine*
½	*cup plain yogurt*
1	*teaspoon Pommery mustard*
1	*teaspoon Dijon mustard*
2	*tablespoons chopped parsley*
	* Seasonal

Sprinkle chicken with salt and pepper. Sauté in butter and oil in skillet for 10 minutes or until golden brown on both sides, turning once. Cook, covered, for 2 minutes. Drain, reserving 2 tablespoons drippings; place chicken on warm platter. Sauté shallots in drippings for 30 seconds. Add mushrooms. Cook for 1 minute. Stir in wine. Bring to a boil, stirring to deglaze pan. Add yogurt. Cook for 3 minutes or until thickened. Stir in remaining ingredients. Pour over chicken. Yield: 4 servings.

Turkey and Spinach Lasagna

20	*ounces frozen chopped spinach*
2½	*cups skim milk*
3	*tablespoons flour*
	Salt, pepper and nutmeg to taste
8	*lasagna noodles, cooked*
7½	*ounces ricotta cheese*
1½	*cups chopped cooked turkey*
3	*tablespoons Parmesan cheese*
3	*tablespoons Italian-seasoned bread crumbs*

Cook spinach according to package directions; drain well. Blend milk and flour in saucepan. Cook over low heat until thickened, stirring constantly. Season to taste. Mix half the sauce with spinach; set aside. Pour a small amount of remaining sauce into shallow baking dish. Alternate layers of noodles, spinach mixture, ricotta cheese, turkey and white sauce until all ingredients are used, ending with sauce. Sprinkle with Parmesan cheese and crumbs. Bake at 375 degrees for 30 minutes or until bubbly. Yield: 6 servings.

Shrimp Ratatouille Stir-Fry
Lisa Mutchler, Texas

½	*onion, chopped*
¼	*cup olive oil*
1	*eggplant, peeled, chopped * *
1	*zucchini, sliced * *
1	*green pepper, sliced * *
1	*sweet red pepper, sliced * *
2¼	*cups peeled shrimp*
4	*ounces mushrooms, sliced * *
1	*tomato, chopped * *
1	*tablespoon chopped parsley*
1	*teaspoon basil*
1½	*teaspoons garlic salt*
¼	*teaspoon pepper*
6	*servings hot cooked rice*
	* Seasonal

Stir-fry onion in olive oil in skillet or wok. Add eggplant, zucchini and peppers. Stir-fry until tender-crisp. Add shrimp. Stir-fry for 2 minutes. Add mushrooms, tomato, parsley and seasonings. Cook, covered, for 5 minutes. Serve over rice. Yield: 6 servings.

Preparation suggestion: This is a colorful dish for tabletop cooking. Carry arranged tray of prepared ingredients to the table. Cook and serve in minutes.

Cheesy Tuna Moussaka

Merry Elliott, Texas

Peel and slice eggplant. Cook in boiling water to cover in saucepan for 3 to 4 minutes; drain. Simmer onion in wine in covered saucepan for 5 minutes. Blend in mixture of cornstarch and ¼ cup milk. Stir in remaining milk and seasonings. Cook until thickened, stirring constantly. Combine half the sauce with drained tuna in bowl; mix well. Add cottage cheese and eggs to remaining sauce. Arrange half the eggplant slices in 8-inch square baking dish. Add layers of tuna mixture, half the Parmesan cheese, remaining eggplant, cottage cheese mixture and remaining Parmesan cheese. Chill in refrigerator if desired. ** Bake at 350 degrees for 50 minutes or until set. Let stand for 10 minutes before serving. Yield: 4 servings.

*** Make ahead to this point.*

1	*medium eggplant *
⅓	*cup chopped onion*
3	*tablespoons dry white wine*
2	*tablespoons cornstarch*
2	*cups skim milk*
¼	*teaspoon cinnamon*
	Salt and pepper to taste
	Pinch of nutmeg
1	*7-ounce can tuna*
1	*cup cottage cheese*
2	*eggs, beaten*
½	*cup Parmesan cheese*
	* Seasonal*

Garden Medley

Donna Frischolz, Florida

Cut broccoli and cauliflower into flowerets. Combine rice, butter, broth, soy sauce and half the onions in 3-quart casserole. Bake, covered, at 350 degrees for 20 minutes. Stir in thyme and salt. Sauté remaining onions, garlic, broccoli, cauliflower and peppers in peanut oil in skillet for 5 minutes. Spoon over rice mixture. Bake, covered, for 10 minutes or until rice is tender. Sprinkle cashews in center and cheese around edge. Bake for 5 minutes longer or until cheese melts. Yield: 6 to 8 servings.

1	*bunch broccoli *
1	*head cauliflower *
1½	*cups brown rice *
2	*tablespoons melted butter*
3	*cups vegetable broth*
3	*tablespoons soy sauce*
2	*large onions, chopped*
½	*teaspoon each thyme, salt*
2	*cloves of garlic, minced*
2	*sweet red peppers, slivered *
3	*tablespoons peanut oil*
1	*cup cashews*
2	*cups shredded Cheddar cheese*
	* Seasonal*

Grandma Schmitt's Baked Beans

Joan Dew, Tennessee

Cube pork roast; trim excess fat. Brown pork with onion in a small amount of oil in Dutch oven. Add water to cover and salt and pepper. Cook, covered, over low heat for 1 hour or until tender. Drain, reserving liquid. Add beans, tomato sauce, corn syrup, sugar and salt and pepper; mix well. Place bacon slices on top. Bake, uncovered, at 325 degrees for 5 hours or at 275 degrees overnight. Add reserved liquid as necessary to prevent drying. Yield: 12 servings.

1	*whole pork shoulder roast*
1	*large onion, chopped*
	Salt and pepper to taste
2	*large cans baked beans*
1	*16-ounce can tomato sauce*
1	*tablespoon white corn syrup*
1	*tablespoon sugar*
8	*ounces bacon*

Green Bean Casserole

3	cups small green beans *
1	clove of garlic, chopped
1	onion, chopped
1	green pepper, chopped
¼	cup chopped pimento
3	tablespoons butter
1	8-ounce can tomato sauce
1	teaspoon Tabasco sauce
1	cup shredded Cheddar cheese
	* Seasonal

Cook green beans in a small amount of water in saucepan, or microwave on High until tender-crisp; drain. Sauté garlic, onion, green pepper and pimento in butter in skillet for 5 minutes. Stir in tomato sauce, Tabasco sauce and beans. Spoon into 1-quart casserole; sprinkle with cheese. Refrigerate for several hours if desired. ** Bake at 350 degrees for 25 minutes.

Yield: 4 servings.

** Make ahead to this point.

Monterey Corn Bake

Lynn Buchanan, California

2	cups fresh corn *
1	tablespoon chopped celery *
1	tablespoon chopped pimento
1	4-ounce can chopped green chilies *
2	eggs, beaten
2	cups sour cream
½	cup cornmeal
½	cup melted margarine
1	cup grated Monterey Jack cheese
	Salt to taste
	* Seasonal

Combine corn, celery, pimento and chilies in bowl; mix well. Add eggs, sour cream, cornmeal, margarine, cheese and salt; mix well. Spoon into greased 2-quart casserole. Refrigerate for several hours if desired. ** Bake, covered, at 350 degrees for 45 minutes or until brown.

Yield: 8 servings.

** Make ahead to this point.

Eggplant au Gratin

Ruth White, Maryland

1	eggplant *
1	green pepper, chopped *
2	stalks celery, chopped *
1	onion, chopped
1	clove of garlic, minced
1	tablespoon butter
1	cup buttered bread crumbs
2	tomatoes, chopped *
1	cup grated sharp cheese
1	egg, beaten
½	cup cracker crumbs
⅓	cup grated sharp cheese
	* Seasonal

Cut eggplant in half lengthwise; scoop out pulp, reserving ½-inch thick shells. Cook shells in boiling salted water in saucepan until tender-crisp; drain. ** Sauté green pepper, celery, onion and garlic in butter in skillet. Add crumbs. Sauté for several minutes; remove from heat. Stir in tomatoes, 1 cup cheese and egg. Spoon into eggplant shells. Sprinkle with mixture of cracker crumbs and ⅓ cup cheese. Place in baking dish. Bake at 400 degrees for 40 minutes or until brown.

Yield: 4 servings.

** Make ahead to this point.

Party Potatoes

Cook potatoes in water in saucepan until tender. Drain, peel and mash. Combine mashed potatoes, orange juice, mashed pimento, butter and seasonings in bowl; mix well. Cut peppers lengthwise into halves; discard seed and membranes. Blanch in boiling water for 2 minutes; drain and rinse with cold water. Spoon potatoes or pipe through pastry tube into well-drained pepper shells. Refrigerate for several hours if desired. ** Place on baking sheet. Bake at 400 degrees for 20 minutes or until potatoes are golden brown. Yield: 6 servings.

** *Make ahead to this point.*

6	*medium potatoes*
¾	*cup orange juice*
1	*2-ounce jar pimento*
3	*tablespoons butter, melted*
	Salt and pepper to taste
6	*small green peppers* *
	* Seasonal

Spaghetti Squash Italiano
Richard Aten, Texas

Bake squash at 350 degrees for 1 hour or until tender. Sauté onion, mushrooms, green pepper and garlic powder in ¼ cup margarine in skillet. Stir in spaghetti sauce. Simmer until hot and bubbly. Cut squash in half lengthwise; discard seed. Remove pulp with fork, separating into strands. Combine with ¼ cup margarine, salt and pepper in bowl; toss to mix well. Mound spaghetti squash on serving plate. Spoon spaghetti sauce over top. Sprinkle with Parmesan cheese. Yield: 6 servings.

1	*medium spaghetti squash* *
1	*medium onion, sliced* *
8	*ounces mushrooms, sliced* *
1	*cup chopped green pepper* *
¼	*teaspoon garlic powder*
¼	*cup margarine*
2	*cups prepared spaghetti sauce*
¼	*cup margarine*
1	*teaspoon salt*
½	*teaspoon pepper*
¼	*cup Parmesan cheese*
	* Seasonal

Dilled Zucchini-Rice Bake
Mary Helen Pope, Illinois

Cook zucchini in a small amount of water in saucepan for 5 minutes or until tender-crisp; drain. Combine onion, rice, cottage cheese, eggs and seasonings in bowl; mix well. Layer zucchini and rice mixture ½ at a time in buttered 2-quart casserole. Top with Parmesan cheese. Chill in refrigerator if desired. ** Bake at 350 degrees for 45 minutes or until brown and bubbly. Yield: 6 servings.

** *Make ahead to this point.*

4	*medium zucchini, sliced* *
1	*medium onion, chopped*
2	*cups cooked brown rice*
16	*ounces cottage cheese*
2	*eggs, beaten*
	Salt and pepper to taste
1	*tablespoon dillweed*
¼	*cup Parmesan cheese*
	* Seasonal

Cheddar Bread

Mary Miller, Michigan

2	*tablespoons sugar*
1	*teaspoon salt*
⅓	*cup butter, softened*
1	*teaspoon dry yeast*
2⅓	*cups flour*
2	*tablespoons nonfat dry milk powder*
⅓	*cup butter, softened*
2	*teaspoons minced onion*
¼	*teaspoon dry mustard*
1	*teaspoon Worcestershire sauce*
2	*cups shredded Cheddar cheese*

Combine 1⅓ cups warm water, sugar, salt and ⅓ cup butter in mixer bowl. Stir in yeast. Let stand for 10 minutes. Add flour and dry milk powder. Beat with dough hook until well mixed. Pat evenly onto 13x18-inch baking sheet. Combine ⅓ cup softened butter, onion, dry mustard and Worcestershire sauce in mixer bowl; beat until well blended. Spread over dough. Sprinkle with shredded cheese. Bake at 400 degrees for 25 minutes. Cut into squares.
Yield: 24 servings.

Easy-Mix Cinnamon Rolls

Brenda Oney, Oklahoma

1	*1-layer package yellow cake mix*
1	*package or 1 tablespoon dry yeast*
½	*tablespoon salt*
2½	*cups flour*
½	*cup melted butter*
6	*tablespoons sugar*
1	*tablespoon cinnamon*
2	*cups confectioners' sugar*
2	*to 4 tablespoons milk*

Combine cake mix, yeast, salt and 1¼ cups warm water in bowl; mix well. Stir in flour. Let rise, covered, in warm place for 45 minutes or until doubled in bulk. Roll into rectangle on floured surface. Brush with butter. Sprinkle with mixture of sugar and cinnamon. Roll as for jelly roll. Cut into ½-inch slices. Place in greased baking pan. Let rise for 45 minutes. Bake at 350 degrees for 15 minutes or until brown. Combine confectioners' sugar and enough milk to make of spreading consistency. Spread over warm rolls.
Yield: 12 to 16 rolls.

Note: Do not use pudding-recipe cake mix.
Preparation suggestion: Check microwave manufacturer's instructions for letting dough rise in microwave.

Chocolate Waffles

Kathy Callahan, Wyoming

1	*cup flour*
¾	*cup sugar*
½	*cup cocoa*
½	*teaspoon baking powder*
½	*teaspoon soda*
¼	*teaspoon salt*
2	*eggs, beaten*
1	*cup buttermilk*
¼	*cup butter, melted*
1	*teaspoon vanilla extract*

Combine flour, sugar, cocoa, baking powder, soda and salt in bowl; mix well. Add eggs and buttermilk; mix just until blended. Add butter gradually, beating constantly. Stir in vanilla. Bake in waffle iron according to manufacturer's instructions. Yield: 6 servings.

Serving suggestions: Serve with fresh fruit, sprinkle of confectioners' sugar or with ice cream.

Blueberry-Sour Cream Torte

Sharon Bryan, California

Combine flour, ½ cup sugar and baking powder in bowl. Cut in butter until crumbly. Add egg and vanilla; mix well. Press over bottom of buttered 10-inch springform pan. Spread blueberries in prepared pan. Combine sour cream, egg yolks, ½ cup sugar and 1 teaspoon vanilla in bowl; mix until smooth. Pour over blueberries. Place on center rack in 350-degree oven. Bake for 1 hour or until edge is light brown. Cool on wire rack. Place on serving plate; remove side of pan. Yield: 8 to 10 servings.

1½   *cups flour*
½   *cup sugar*
1½   *teaspoons baking powder*
1   *stick butter*
1   *egg, beaten*
1   *teaspoon vanilla extract*
4   *cups fresh blueberries* *
2   *cups sour cream*
2   *egg yolks*
½   *cup sugar*
1   *teaspoon vanilla extract*
   * Seasonal

Fresh Fruit with Dessert Cheese

Sue Hughs, Texas

Blend cream cheese with confectioners' sugar and curry powder in bowl. Stir in coconut and half the pecans. Spoon into small round bowl lined with plastic wrap. Chill until firm. ** Unmold on serving tray; sprinkle with remaining pecans. Arrange fruit around cheese. Spread cheese on fruit. Yield: 4 servings.

** *Make ahead to this point.*

8   *ounces cream cheese, softened*
2   *tablespoons confectioners' sugar*
½   *teaspoon curry powder*
⅓   *cup flaked coconut*
⅓   *cup chopped pecans*
   Pear and apple wedges *
   Green grapes *
   * Seasonal

Ginger Peachy Cranberry Ice Cream

Photograph for this recipe on page 124.

Thaw peaches slightly. Combine peaches, lemon juice, corn syrup, ginger and flavoring in blender container. Purée. Add ⅓ of the whipped topping. Blend for 15 seconds. Pour into large bowl. Fold in remaining whipped topping and cubed cranberry sauce. Spoon into 9-inch square dish. Freeze, covered, for 2 hours or until soft-firm. Scoop into dessert glasses. Yield: 6 servings.

1   *16-ounce package frozen sweetened sliced peaches*
1   *tablespoon lemon juice*
¼   *cup light corn syrup*
½   *teaspoon ground ginger*
¼   *teaspoon almond extract*
12   *ounces whipped topping*
1   *8-ounce can Ocean Spray jellied cranberry sauce, cubed*

Mango and Lime Sorbet
Joan Dew, Tennessee

3   **cups chopped fresh mangos** *
1   **cup sugar**
3   **tablespoons lime juice** *
4   **sprigs of fresh mint** *
      * Seasonal

Reserve mango pits. Combine 1½ cups water and sugar in heavy saucepan. Heat until sugar is dissolved. Add mango pits. Simmer, covered, for 5 minutes. Remove and discard mango pits. Chill syrup in bowl set in cracked ice for 1 hour. Purée in syrup in blender container. Combine with lime juice in bowl. Chill for 2 hours or longer. ** Pour into ice cream freezer container. Freeze according to manufacturer's instructions. Scoop onto chilled dessert plates. Garnish with mint sprig. Yield: 4 servings.

** *Make ahead to this point.*

Frozen Colada Yogurt
Photograph for this recipe on page 2.

2   **cups vanilla yogurt**
¾ **cup coconut rum**
1   **8-ounce can crushed pineapple, drained**
3   **egg whites**
      Pinch of cream of tartar

Combine yogurt, rum and pineapple in bowl; mix well. Pour into freezer tray. Freeze until partially frozen. Beat egg whites with cream of tartar until stiff peaks form. Beat pineapple mixture in bowl until smooth. Fold in egg whites gently. Pour into freezer tray. Freeze until firm. Serve scoops of yogurt in pineapple shell.
Yield: 6 servings.

Key Lime Cake
Louise Scott, Florida

2   **tablespoons Key lime juice** *
1   **package lemon cake mix**
1   **package lemon instant pudding mix**
4   **eggs, beaten**
1   **cup oil**
2   **cups confectioners' sugar**
⅓ **cup Key lime juice** *
      * Seasonal

Combine 2 tablespoons lime juice, cake mix, pudding mix, eggs, oil and 1 cup water in mixer bowl; beat until smooth. Pour into greased 9x13-inch baking pan. Bake at 325 degrees for 45 minutes or until cake tests done. Cool for 10 minutes. Pierce with fork. Mix confectioners' sugar and ⅓ cup lime juice in small bowl. Pour over warm cake.
Yield: 16 servings.

Coconut-Chocolate Bars
Kitty Whitmire, Illinois

1   **package refrigerator crescent rolls**
2   **cups coconut**
1   **can sweetened condensed milk**
¼ **teaspoon almond extract**
6   **ounces chocolate chips**
2   **tablespoons peanut butter**

Press roll dough over bottom of 10x15-inch baking pan. Sprinkle with coconut. Mix condensed milk and almond extract in small bowl. Drizzle over coconut. Bake at 350 degrees for 25 minutes or until golden brown. Melt chocolate chips and peanut butter in saucepan or microwave; blend well. Spread over baked layer. Chill until set. Cut into bars.
Yield: 3 dozen.

Recipe on page 137.

Layered Fruit Compote
Marlene Blankely, Maryland

Combine milk, liqueur and pudding mix in mixer bowl. Beat at low speed for 1 minute. Add whipped topping. Beat for 1 minute longer. Place half the fruit in serving bowl. Spoon ⅔ of the pudding over fruit. Top with remaining fruit and pudding. Yield: 4 servings.

1¾ **cups milk**
1 **tablespoon orange liqueur**
1 **package vanilla instant pudding mix**
1 **cup whipped topping**
1 **cup blueberries ***
1 **cup melon balls ***
1 **cup raspberries ***
1 **cup sliced peaches ***
* Seasonal

Fresh Pear Tart
D'Lyn Loessin, Texas

Combine first 4 ingredients in bowl. Knead until blended. Pat over bottom and side of 9-inch springform tart pan. Prick with fork. Bake at 400 degrees for 10 minutes or until golden. Cool on wire rack. Soften gelatin in orange juice in saucepan for 1 minute. Cook over low heat until dissolved, stirring constantly. Remove from heat. Stir in brown sugar, marmalade and puréed pears. Chill for 40 minutes, stirring occasionally. Pour into prepared tart pan. Chill, covered, for 2 hours or until set. ** Place on serving plate; remove side of pan. Arrange sliced pears over top of tart. Brush with melted marmalade. Yield: 6 servings.

** *Make ahead to this point.*

¾ **cup flour**
6 **tablespoons butter**
3 **tablespoons sugar**
¼ **teaspoon allspice**
1 **envelope unflavored gelatin**
½ **cup orange juice**
3 **tablespoons brown sugar**
¼ **cup orange marmalade**
3 **ripe pears, puréed ***
3 **ripe pears, thinly sliced ***
¼ **cup orange marmalade, melted**
* Seasonal

Miniature Shoofly Pies
Kathy Snyder, Michigan

Cream 1 cup margarine and cream cheese in mixer bowl until light and fluffy. Add 2 cups flour; mix well. Shape into 16 balls. Press each over bottom and side of miniature muffin cup. Combine eggs, brown sugar, melted butter and vanilla in bowl; mix well. Spoon into prepared muffin cups. Combine sugar and 1½ cups flour in bowl. Cut in ½ cup margarine until crumbly. Sprinkle over tart filling. Bake at 400 degrees for 20 minutes.
Yield: 16 servings.

1 **cup margarine, softened**
6 **ounces cream cheese, softened**
2 **cups flour**
2 **eggs, beaten**
1½ **cups packed brown sugar**
2 **tablespoons melted butter**
¼ **teaspoon vanilla extract**
1 **cup sugar**
1½ **cups flour**
½ **cup margarine**

Recipe on page 137.

Fall

The first chill of Fall shakes us from our Summer laziness into a flurry of activity. Like the animals, scurrying about gathering hibernation treats, we are suddenly invigorated. Crisp scents fill the outdoors; foods are in their fullness; and already we are anticipating the exciting holidays ahead.

As the earth becomes a palette of golds, greens, yellows, and oranges, gardens and grapes are harvested; shiny new lunch boxes are packed for school; and hot soups begin to bubble in the pot again. Hearty stews, forgotten in the heat of Summer, are savored now as if they were entirely new. Pumpkins and gourds appear in rustic colors; the popcorn popper is hauled out; and spices for preserving late Summer's fruits and vegetables enter the air. Tart, juicy McIntoshes are sliced for apple pies and served up in flaky crusts under a slab of melted Cheddar. Fires and ovens are relit, and the sweet smell of yeast again perfumes the house.

Football season brings tailgate picnics which have progressed far beyond the fried chicken and potato salad fare of my youth. Nowadays, it's pâtés of veal and pork, vegetable terrines, marinated salads, flavorful casseroles, and imaginative quiches.

Hunting season brings game to the table—duck (never better than when roasted with a luscious cranberry glaze), rabbit, quail, and venison. Orchard fruits such as apples and pears are at their peak. Grapes are also plentiful. After months of Summer vegetables, these seasonal fruits offer a welcome change for salads. Among my favorite combinations: pears with bleu cheese; apple and fennel; grapefruit and avocado dressed with vinaigrette.

The kids are no sooner settled into the routine of a new school year than it's time to carve pumpkins into Jack-O-Lanterns, don outlandish costumes, and play trick-or-treat. Halloween treats have come full circle since my childhood. We were offered home-baked goodies and fresh fruits to fill our trick-or-treat bags, and someone in the neighborhood always gave a party where the adults dressed as witches and ghosts and had more fun than the kids! Years later, when my children went out on Halloween night, homemade Halloween cookies seemed to be a thing of the past. Happily, both the parties and the freshly made treats have returned. Chocolate cupcakes with orange icing, old-fashioned popcorn balls, candied apples, and rich chocolate fudge are once again finding their way into the sacks of little goblins and gremlins.

At the height of Fall, when the harvest has been gathered and before the cold of Winter sets in, man takes time to celebrate his triumph over nature. For many of us who love good food, Thanksgiving is the best of holidays. My Thanksgiving menu never varies. I serve the same dishes that my mother and grandmother prepared for their families, a tradition I cherish because it's a tangible connection with my heritage. We begin with cream of pumpkin soup, updated somewhat by serving it in a pumpkin shell and garnishing it with toasted pumpkin seeds, followed by Waldorf salad, whipped potatoes, giblet gravy, sweet potato soufflé topped with melted marshmallows, green bean casserole, yeast rolls, and roast turkey with the best-ever Southern corn bread dressing. (The secret is using homemade buttered croutons rather than day-old bread.) Desserts always include pecan pie, pumpkin pie, and fresh pear tart.

The only thing better than Thanksgiving is the leftovers. No one was more creative at using the last morsel of the holiday bird than my grandmother. We had creamed turkey on toast for breakfast; turkey hash sandwiches for lunch; Turkey Divan for dinner. There were also turkey potpie, Turkey à La King, and turkey croquettes. And when all that was gone, there was turkey-noodle soup!

Thanksgiving wasn't the only Fall food ritual that never varied at my grandmother's house. In October, she made spicy applesauce which we enjoyed throughout the Winter. Jars of spiced peaches she had put up in the Summer came out in early November, the perfect accompaniment for roast chicken, pork, or baked ham. After the first frost, there was always a big pot of collard greens, served with cracklin' bread to sop up the pot liquor. And by the middle of November, the Christmas fruitcakes were baked, drizzled with Brandy, Bourbon, or rum, wrapped in cheesecloth, and put away to "rest" until the holidays.

In contrast to the "down-home" cooking of Thanksgiving, Christmas meant the fanciest foods of the year—a time to bring out the family's finest crystal, china, and linen; to spruce up the house with cedar boughs, ribbons, candles, and pine cones. The festive and joyous spirit of the season demands the best one has to offer. Lobster bisque, scalloped oysters, roast pheasant with wild rice, and prime rib with Yorkshire pudding are among the foods I associate most with Christmas. And nothing brings my holiday spirit out more than a large bowl filled with ambrosia made of freshly grated coconut and juicy sweet oranges.

The celebration of Christmas centers on a child, so it is fitting that the season brings out the child in all of us. Is there anyone so "grown up" that he doesn't feel excited on Christmas morning when it's time to open gifts? My favorite presents are those I receive from the kitchens of thoughtful friends, and the ones I most enjoy giving are the ones I've made at home—meat and vegetable pâtés; peach and plum preserves; Brandied fruit; cookies and candies; barbecued pecans; herb vinegars; holiday breads—gifts to savor well into the New Year.

Fall spills over with foods that are not only deep and rich in tradition, but wonderful to taste—reason enough for a season of grand celebrations!

Fall Foods

*F*all is the season of celebrations which focus on the harvest of bountiful foods. The vegetables, fruits, and game abundant now reflect autumn's rich, warm colors and fill kitchens and holiday tables with the memorable aromas and tastes of which traditions are made.

Cranberries: Choose bright, plump cranberries with rich color. Store in refrigerator or freezer.

Persimmons: Choose plump, glossy, firm-tender persimmons and have attached caps which are free from spots and punctures. Store in refrigerator. Use as soon as possible.

Pomegranates: Choose medium to large pomegranates which are bright red or pink with unbroken skins. Store in refrigerator.

Tangelos and Tangerines: Choose plump, firm, heavy fruit which are free from punctures, mold, or blemishes. Store tangelos at room temperature and tangerines in refrigerator.

Pumpkins: Choose firm, bright, well-shaped, 6 to 7-inch pumpkins which are heavy for their size and free from scars and bruises. Store in cool place.

Rutabagas: Choose firm, heavy, smooth 2 to 3-pound rutabagas which are free from cuts or bruises. Store in cool place.

Winter squash: Choose hard-shelled, heavy Hubbard, Butternut and Acorn squash which have thick rinds and are free from sunken spots or mold.

Sweet Potatoes: Choose firm, bright, evenly-colored sweet potatoes which are free from soft spots, shriveling, and sunken spots. Store in cool, dry place, not in refrigerator.

Turnips: Choose firm, smooth, 2 to 3-inch turnips with fresh, crisp, green tops and no scars or roots. Store in refrigerator.

Beef and Game: Beef should be bright red with creamy-white fat. Tender cuts are from the rib, short loin, and sirloin. Less tender cuts may be leaner. Game birds should be firm and fresh smelling with little or no shot damage. Venison should be moist, velvety, and fresh smelling.

Menus

BREAKFASTS

Bountiful Breakfast

A Fall Breakfast for Four

Eggs Benedict	191
Breakfast Bread	178
Chilled Apple Juice	

Christmas Morning Brunch

A Make-Ahead Brunch for Eight

Christmas Morning Sausage Ring	204
Mixed Orange and Grapefruit Sections	
Easy Yogurt Coffee Cake	207

LUNCHES

Cozy Picnic Lunch

A Hearthside Lunch for Six

Hot Vegetable Sipper	167
Con Queso Rolls	170
Coleslaw with Apples and Carrots	
Honey Gingerbread	181

Impromptu Luncheon

A Pantry-Shelf Luncheon for Four

Fruited Ham Salad in Lettuce Cups	202
Buttered Green Peas	
Finger Rolls	
Pumpkin Mousse	196

Autumn Affair

A Tailgate Lunch for Six to Twelve

Olive-Nut Bread with Parmesan Spread	166
Fried Chicken	
Mexican Beans	192
Fresh Vegetable Tray	
Citrus Apple Cake	181

DINNERS

194	Corn Bread Dressing	*All-American*
	Roast Turkey	*Thanksgiving*
185	Cranberry-Pear Relish	*Dinner*
	Relish Tray	
192	Carrots in Orange Sauce	
199	Sweet Potato Pie	*A Traditional Dinner for Eight*
193	Cranberry Yams	
217	Fruit Juicy Eggnog	*Christmas Eve*
203	Spicy Rib Eye Roast	*Buffet*
	Brussels Sprouts and Carrots	
	Spiced Crab Apples	
199	Yogurt-Cranberry Pie	*A Holiday Dinner for Twelve*
211	Peppery Spice Cake	

SUPPERS

171	Double-Crusted Beef Pie	*Spooky*
	Buttered Green Beans	*Supper*
	Carrot-Raisin Salad	
180	Frozen Halloween Dessert	*A Halloween Supper for Five*
172	Smothered Quail	*Harvest*
177	Green Tomato Casserole	*Supper*
208	Sweet Potato Biscuits	
183	Hot Buttered Rum-Apple Pie	*A Fall Supper for Four*
212	Chocolate-Cherry Drops	*Nutcracker*
212	Chocolate Nutters	*Sweets*
198	Oatmeal Chippers	
213	Chocolate Spritz Cookies	
214	Holiday Fruit Bars	*A Holiday Cookie Exchange*
213	Macaroon Kisses	
215	Mini Chip Fruit and Nut Bars	
215	Mini Chip Peanut Butter Foldovers	
213	Chocolate Toffee Bars	

October

Olive-Nut Appetizer Bread with Parmesan Spread

Francine Caffey, New Mexico

1	**cup milk, scalded**
3	**tablespoons sugar**
2	**tablespoons butter**
2	**teaspoons salt**
2	**packages or 2 tablespoons dry yeast**
4½	**cups flour**
2	**cups shredded Cheddar cheese**
¾	**cup thinly sliced green olives**
¾	**cup chopped pecans ***
	* Seasonal

Combine milk, sugar, butter and salt in bowl. Cool to lukewarm. Dissolve yeast in 1 cup warm water in bowl. Add milk mixture and flour; mix well. Batter will be stiff. Add cheese, olives and pecans; mix well. Let rise, covered, until doubled in bulk. Knead on floured surface for 1 minute. Shape into 16-inch rope. Place in well-greased bundt pan; seal ends. Let rise until doubled in bulk. Bake at 350 degrees for 50 minutes. Remove to wire rack to cool. Place on serving plate; slice thinly. Serve with Parmesan Spread. Yield 30 servings.

Parmesan Spread

8	**ounces cream cheese, softened**
½	**cup Parmesan cheese**
1	**4-ounce can chopped green chilies, drained**
	* Seasonal

Combine all ingredients in bowl; mix well. Chill, covered, for several minutes. Spoon into serving dish. Serve at room temperature. Yield: 1½ cups.

Barbecued Pecans
Roy Musgrove, Texas

Combine first 4 ingredients in bowl; mix well. Stir in pecans. Spread in shallow baking pan. Bake at 300 degrees for 30 minutes, stirring frequently, or microwave on High for 6 minutes, stirring twice. Spread on paper towels. Let stand until completely cool. Sprinkle with salt. Store in airtight container. Yield: 4 cups.

¼ cup Worcestershire sauce
1 tablespoon catsup
⅛ teaspoon hot sauce
2 tablespoons melted butter
4 cups pecan halves *
Salt to taste
* Seasonal

Harvest Popcorn
Shirley Fryatt, Washington

Sprinkle popcorn with salt and butter in bowl. Stir in peanuts. Sprinkle with mixture of garlic powder, onion powder, lemon pepper and dillweed; mix gently. Spread in two 9x13-inch baking pans. Bake at 350 degrees for 6 minutes. Cool completely. Store in airtight container. Yield: 4½ quarts.

4 quarts popped popcorn
Salt to taste
3 tablespoons melted butter
2 cups salted peanuts *
½ teaspoon garlic powder
1 teaspoon each onion powder, lemon-pepper and dillweed
* Seasonal

Jalapeño Jelly
Stacy Goodman, Texas

Measure 1 cup green peppers and ¼ cup jalapeño peppers. Combine with vinegar and sugar in saucepan. Bring to a boil. Boil for 4 minutes; strain. Stir in pectin and green food coloring if desired. **Pour into hot sterilized jars, leaving ¼-inch headspace. Seal with 2-piece lids.** Process in boiling water bath for 5 minutes. Serve with cheese and crackers, Mexican food and other snacks. Yield: 4 cups.

4 green peppers, ground
8 to 10 jalapeño peppers, ground *
1 cup cider vinegar
2 pounds sugar
1 6-ounce bottle of pectin
* Seasonal

Hot Vegetable Sipper
Anita Raynes, Maryland

Sauté vegetables in oil in saucepan for 10 minutes. Add bouillon cube, seasonings and 3 cups water. Simmer, covered, for 15 to 20 minutes or until vegetables are tender. Pour into blender container. Process until smooth. Chill for several hours if desired. ** Pour into saucepan. Add 1 to 2 cups water to make of desired consistency. Heat to serving temperature. Pour into mugs. Yield: 6 servings.

** *Make ahead to this point.*

4 or 5 broccoli stems *
2 carrots, chopped
½ stalk celery, sliced
1 potato, peeled, chopped
1 onion, chopped
1 tablespoon oil
1 chicken bouillon cube
⅛ teaspoon each salt, pepper and garlic powder
* Seasonal

Vegetable-Fruit Soup

Joan Resor, California

2 **onions, chopped**
2 **potatoes, chopped**
2 **bananas, chopped**
2 **apples, chopped** *
2 **tomatoes, chopped** *
2 **carrots, chopped**
   Celery leaves, chopped
2 **packages dry chicken noodle**
   soup mix
2 **cups cream**
1 **teaspoon curry powder**
2 **tablespoons butter**
   Salt and pepper to taste
   * Seasonal

Combine onions, potatoes, bananas, apples, tomatoes, carrots and celery leaves. Combine with water to cover in large saucepan. Cook until tender. Drain, reserving liquid. Purée vegetable and fruit mixture in blender container, adding enough reserved liquid to process easily. Combine with remaining ingredients in saucepan; mix well. Bring to the boiling point over low heat, stirring frequently. Ladle into soup bowls. Serve immediately.
Yield: 6 servings.

Spanish Orange Salad

Elena O'Brien, Maryland

6 **oranges** *
1 **pomegranate** *
1 **tablespoon sugar**
½ **cup anisette**
   * Seasonal

Peel and thinly slice oranges. Peel pomegranate; separate seed carefully. Combine fruit in serving bowl. Sprinkle with sugar and anisette. Let stand for 1 to 2 hours.
Yield: 8 servings.

Spiral Vegetable Salad

Joyce Lusk, California

1 **16-ounce package frozen**
   broccoli and baby carrots
3 **cups cooked rotini**
1 **cup sliced mushrooms**
½ **cup slivered water chestnuts**
¾ **cup chopped sweet red pepper**
⅔ **cup Italian salad dressing**
   Pepper to taste
4 **slices crisp-fried bacon,**
   crumbled

Thaw frozen vegetables in colander under cold running water; drain on paper towels. Combine with macaroni, mushrooms, water chestnuts and red pepper in salad bowl. Add salad dressing and pepper; mix gently. Chill, covered, until serving time. Garnish with bacon just before serving.
Yield: 6 to 8 servings.

Taco Salad
Ella Kernodle, Missouri

Brown ground chuck in skillet, stirring until crumbly; drain. Stir in onion, seasonings and ⅓ cup salad dressing. Simmer for 5 minutes. Combine remaining ⅔ cup salad dressing, lettuce, radishes, tomatoes, corn and garbanzo beans in bowl; toss lightly. Layer corn chips, ground chuck mixture and vegetable mixture in serving bowl. Arrange avocado slices, olives, cheese and dollops of sour cream over top.
Yield: 6 servings. ✔ 🍎 🥄

1½	pounds ground chuck *
1	onion, chopped
½	teaspoon oregano
½	teaspoon salt
¼	teaspoon pepper
1	cup French salad dressing
½	head lettuce, torn
6	radishes, sliced
2	tomatoes, chopped
1	8-ounce can corn, drained
1	can garbanzo beans, drained
8	ounces corn chips
1	avocado *
12	ripe olives
1	cup shredded Cheddar cheese
1	cup sour cream

* Seasonal

Zesty Chicken Salad
Della Dewey, Ohio

Combine chicken, cheese, green pepper, onion and pickle in bowl; mix well. Add eggs; toss lightly. Blend mayonnaise, lemon juice, Tabasco sauce, horseradish and seasonings in small bowl. Add to salad; mix well. Chill until serving time.
Yield: 2 to 3 servings. ✔ 🥄 🍲

Serving suggestion: Serve in crisp lettuce cups, or use as sandwich filling or stuffing for tomatoes or cucumbers.

1	cup chopped cooked chicken *
¼	cup grated Cheddar cheese
2	tablespoons each chopped green pepper, onion and sweet pickle
3	hard-boiled eggs, chopped
½	cup mayonnaise
2	teaspoons lemon juice
½	teaspoon Tabasco sauce
½	teaspoon horseradish
¼	teaspoon each salt, pepper and paprika

* Seasonal

Crock•Pot Beef
Sandra Stokes, Kentucky

Combine beef, soup mix, soup and red wine in Crock•Pot; mix well. Drain water chestnuts and mushrooms. Add to beef mixture; mix well. Cook on Low for 8 to 12 hours or until beef is tender. Serve over rice or noodles.
Yield: 6 servings. 🥄 🍲

2	pounds stew beef*
1	envelope dry onion soup mix
1	can cream of mushroom soup
½	cup red wine
1	can sliced water chestnuts
1	4-ounce can mushrooms

* Seasonal

Oriental Steak Fingers

3	pounds strip steak *
⅓	cup soy sauce
⅓	cup Worcestershire sauce
2	tablespoons minced garlic
1½	tablespoons beer
	* Seasonal

Cut steak into 1-inch strips. Arrange in 8x12-inch glass baking dish. Pour soy sauce over steak. Marinate for 5 minutes. Pour mixture of Worcestershire sauce, garlic and beer over steak. Marinate, covered, for 5 minutes or in refrigerator for 1 hour. ** Microwave on Medium for 10 minutes. Turn steak strips over. Microwave on High for 4 to 5 minutes or until tender.
Yield: 4 to 6 servings.

** Make ahead to this point.

Skillet Lasagna
Angela Hersel, Idaho

1½	pounds ground beef *
½	cup chopped onion
2	cups cottage cheese
6	lasagna noodles
16	ounces tomato sauce
1	tablespoon parsley flakes
1	teaspoon each basil, oregano and garlic powder
½	teaspoon celery flakes
¼	teaspoon chili powder
2	cups shredded Cheddar cheese
	* Seasonal

Brown ground beef with onion in skillet, stirring frequently; drain. Spread evenly in skillet. Layer cottage cheese and uncooked noodles over top. Mix tomato sauce, seasonings and 1 cup water in bowl. Pour over noodles. Simmer, covered, for 35 minutes or until noodles are tender. Top with Cheddar cheese. Let stand for 5 minutes.
Yield: 6 servings.

Con Queso Rolls
Nancy Ingman, California

½	cup chopped green chilies *
3	green onions, chopped
½	cup chopped ripe olives
2	tablespoons olive oil
¼	cup tomato sauce
1½	teaspoons hot sauce
12	ounces Velveeta cheese, cubed
½	pound ground round
½	clove of garlic, chopped
18	small sourdough French rolls
	* Seasonal

Combine chilies, green onions, olives, olive oil, tomato sauce, hot sauce and cheese in bowl; mix well. Place crumbled ground round and garlic in 2-quart glass baking dish. Microwave on High for 4 to 6 minutes or until ground round is no longer pink; drain. Add cheese mixture; mix well. Slice tops from rolls; scoop out centers. Spoon ground beef mixture into rolls; replace tops. Wrap in waxed paper. Chill in refrigerator for several hours if desired. ** Microwave on Medium until heated through. Wrap in foil to keep warm.
Yield: 6 servings.

** Make ahead to this point.

Double-Crusted Beef Pie

Mary Hamilton, Ohio

Combine flour, ¼ cup potato flakes, sugar, soda and cream of tartar in bowl. Cut in butter until crumbly. Stir in milk and mayonnaise. Roll half the dough on floured surface; fit into pie plate. Sprinkle with ½ cup cheese. Brown ground beef and onion in skillet, stirring frequently; drain. Stir in next 5 ingredients; season to taste. Spoon into prepared pie shell. Sprinkle with ½ cup cheese. Top with remaining dough; trim edge and cut vents. Spread mixture of ½ cup potato flakes and melted butter over top. Bake at 350 degrees for 30 minutes. Cut into wedges.
Yield: 6 servings.

2	*cups flour*
¼	*cup instant potato flakes*
1	*tablespoon sugar*
1	*teaspoon soda*
1	*teaspoon cream of tartar*
6	*tablespoons butter*
½	*cup milk*
½	*cup mayonnaise*
½	*cup shredded Cheddar cheese*
1	*pound lean ground beef **
½	*cup chopped onion*
½	*cup instant potato flakes*
1	*egg, beaten*
½	*cup catsup*
1	*tablespoon sweet pickle relish*
1	*tablespoon prepared mustard*
	Salt and pepper to taste
½	*cup shredded Cheddar cheese*
½	*cup instant potato flakes*
2	*tablespoons melted butter*
	* Seasonal

Sweet and Sour Rabbit

Kevin Gursky, Texas

Combine eggs, ¼ cup flour, salt and 2 tablespoons water in bowl; mix well. Chill for 1 hour. ** Bone rabbit; cut into 1-inch pieces. Coat pieces with 1 cup flour. Dip 1 piece at a time into chilled batter. Deep-fry in 375-degree oil until golden brown; drain. Heat 1 cup pineapple juice and sugar in saucepan, stirring until sugar dissolves. Stir in mixture of cornstarch and ¼ cup pineapple juice. Cook until mixture thickens, stirring constantly. Add drained pineapple, vinegar and mustard; mix well. Serve warm with rabbit.
Yield: 6 servings.

** *Make ahead to this point.*

2	*eggs, beaten*
¼	*cup flour*
1	*teaspoon salt*
1	*2 to 3-pound rabbit*
1	*cup flour*
	Oil for deep frying
1	*cup pineapple juice **
2	*tablespoons sugar*
1	*tablespoon cornstarch*
¼	*cup pineapple juice **
1	*8-ounce can crushed pineapple, drained **
2	*tablespoons vinegar*
2	*teaspoons mustard*
	* Seasonal

Chorizo Breakfast
Pat Mendenhall, California

1½	**pounds chorizo**
6	**eggs**
1	**10-ounce can corn, drained**
1	**cup cooked rice**
12	**flour tortillas**
	Salsa

Crumble or slice chorizo into skillet. Cook until brown, stirring frequently. Add eggs 1 at a time, stirring constantly. Stir in drained corn and rice. Cook until eggs are of desired consistency. Spoon onto tortillas; fold or roll to enclose filling. Place on serving plate. Serve with salsa.
Yield: 12 servings.

Chicken in Blankets
Dorothy Graham, California

1	**package frozen patty shells, thawed**
4	**chicken breast filets ***
4	**thin slices ham**
4	**thin slices Swiss cheese**
1	**teaspoon dillseed**
1	**recipe white sauce**
	* Seasonal

Roll each patty shell into rectangle on floured surface. Pound chicken breasts thin. Place 1 filet on each rectangle. Top each with ham and cheese. Roll to enclose filling; fold ends over. Place seam side down in buttered baking dish. Bake at 375 degrees for 40 minutes or until brown. Stir dillseed into warm white sauce. Serve over chicken rolls.
Yield: 4 servings.

Foil-Wrapped Chicken
Noreen K. Frost, New Mexico

3	**cups 1-inch pieces boned chicken ***
2	**tablespoons each oil, soy sauce and Sherry**
2	**tablespoons sugar**
2	**tablespoons cornstarch**
2	**tablespoons sliced green onion**
1	**tablespoon chopped parsley**
1	**clove of garlic, minced**
	* Seasonal

Combine chicken with remaining ingredients in bowl; mix well. Marinate, covered, at room temperature for 2 hours or in refrigerator overnight. ** Divide into 4 portions on squares of heavy-duty aluminum foil. Fold foil to enclose chicken. Place on baking sheet or grill. Bake at 500 degrees for 10 minutes or over hot coals for 10 to 15 minutes until chicken is tender.
Yield: 3 servings.

** *Make ahead to this point.*

Smothered Quail
Patsy McLemore, Texas

4	**quail ***
	Salt and pepper to taste
4	**red potatoes, thickly sliced**
1	**cup sliced mushrooms**
1	**cup chopped celery stalks with leaves**
8	**green onions and tops, sliced**
2	**tablespoons red wine**
	* Seasonal

Sprinkle quail with salt and pepper. Brown in oil-coated cast-iron skillet. Remove quail. Fry potatoes in pan drippings until almost tender. Arrange quail on top. Add mushrooms, celery, sliced green onions and wine. Simmer, covered, for 30 minutes. Remove to serving platter.
Yield: 4 servings.

Company Turkey Divan

Denise Adams, North Carolina

Cut broccoli into serving pieces. Cook broccoli in a small amount of water in saucepan or microwave on High until tender-crisp; drain. Place in 6 greased individual casseroles. Blend flour, salt and shortening in saucepan. Cook until bubbly, stirring constantly. Stir in broth gradually. Cook until thickened, stirring constantly; remove from heat. Add blue cheese; stir until melted. Whisk in cream. Spoon ¼ cup sauce into each dish. Top with turkey slices. Stir half the Parmesan cheese into remaining sauce. Spoon over turkey. Sprinkle with remaining Parmesan cheese. Chill in refrigerator if desired. ** Bake at 375 degrees for 15 minutes or until bubbly. Broil for 1 minute or until brown.
Yield: 6 servings. ≋ ⊟

** *Make ahead to this point.*

2	**bunches broccoli, trimmed ***
¼	**cup flour**
½	**teaspoon salt**
¼	**cup melted butter**
1	**cup chicken broth**
¼	**cup crumbled blue cheese**
1	**cup whipping cream**
6	**to 12 slices cooked turkey breast**
¾	**cup Parmesan cheese**
	* Seasonal

Fish Amandine

Deedra Massey, New Mexico

Sauté almonds in butter in skillet until light brown; remove with slotted spoon. Place fish in skillet. Cook until golden brown and easily flaked, turning once. Sprinkle with salt and pepper. Remove to warm serving dish. Add lemon juice and almonds to skillet; stir to deglaze. Cook until heated through. Pour over fish.
Yield: 4 servings. ↙

¼	**cup slivered almonds ***
¼	**cup butter**
1	**pound fish fillets ***
½	**teaspoon salt**
	Pepper to taste
2	**teaspoons lemon juice**
	* Seasonal

Baked Parmesan Fish

Thelma Jackson, California

Roll up fish fillets. Place seam side down in ungreased baking dish. Sprinkle with salt and pepper. Blend sour cream, Parmesan cheese, paprika and tarragon in bowl. Spread over fish. Bake at 350 degrees for 20 minutes or microwave on High until fish flakes easily. Top with green onions and tomato slices.
Yield: 4 servings. ↙ ⊙ ≋

1	**pound small fish fillets ***
½	**teaspoon salt**
⅛	**teaspoon pepper**
½	**cup sour cream**
1	**tablespoon Parmesan cheese**
¼	**teaspoon paprika**
⅛	**teaspoon tarragon**
3	**green onions, sliced**
1	**tomato, thinly sliced**
	* Seasonal

Vegetarian Pasta
Mary Foreman, Colorado

4 ounces mushrooms, sliced
1 stalk celery, chopped
1 onion, chopped
1 clove of garlic, minced
4 ounces tofu, crumbled
2 tablespoons butter
2 tablespoons chopped parsley
¼ cup Parmesan cheese
8 ounces tomato sauce
1 16-ounce can tomatoes
½ cup wine
8 ounces pasta
2 tablespoons half and half
1 teaspoon basil
1 tablespoon butter

Sauté mushrooms, celery, onion, garlic and tofu in 2 tablespoons butter in skillet. Add parsley, cheese, tomato sauce, tomatoes and wine; mix well. Simmer for 30 minutes. Cook pasta just until tender using package directions; drain. Combine with half and half, 1 teaspoon basil and 1 tablespoon butter in bowl; toss to coat well. Spoon onto serving platter. Pour sauce over top. Sprinkle with additional Parmesan cheese.
Yield: 6 servings.

Jerusalem Artichoke Patties
Viola Holmes, California

2 cups sliced mushrooms
1 onion, sliced
1 clove of garlic, minced
¼ cup oil
1 carrot, grated
2 cups grated Jerusalem artichokes *
1 cup whole wheat flour
2 eggs, beaten
Tabasco sauce to taste
Oil for frying
* Seasonal

Sauté mushrooms, onion and garlic in ¼ cup oil in skillet. Combine with carrot, artichokes, flour, eggs and Tabasco sauce in bowl; mix well. Drop by rounded tablespoonfuls into ⅛-inch hot oil in skillet. Flatten into patties with back of spoon. Cook until light brown on both sides; drain on paper towel. Arrange on serving plate.
Yield: 20 to 24 patties.

Broccoli-Rice Casserole
Caroll Mealy, Maryland

1 bunch broccoli, chopped *
1 green pepper, chopped
2 hot banana peppers, chopped
1 onion, chopped
2 stalks celery, chopped
1 stick margarine
2 cups rice, cooked
2 cans Cheddar cheese soup
1 can cream of mushroom soup
1 cup grated Cheddar cheese
* Seasonal

Reserve several broccoli flowerets for garnish. Sauté remaining broccoli, peppers, onion and celery in margarine in skillet until tender-crisp. Add rice; mix well. Combine soups in large bowl. Stir in broccoli and rice mixture. Spoon into greased 9x13-inch baking dish. Sprinkle with cheese. Bake at 350 degrees for 30 minutes or until brown and bubbly. Garnish with reserved broccoli flowerets.
Yield: 8 to 10 servings.

Recipe on page 185.

Mashed Rutabagas and Potatoes Supreme

Pearl McCauley, Michigan

Peel and chop rutabaga and potatoes. Dissolve bouillon cube in 2 cups boiling water in saucepan. Add rutabaga, potatoes, salt and sugar. Simmer until vegetables are tender. Drain and mash vegetables. Add pepper, cheese and onion; beat until fluffy. Spoon into serving dish.
Yield: 6 servings.

1	*large rutabaga* *
3	*potatoes* *
1	*chicken bouillon cube*
2	*teaspoons salt*
1	*tablespoon sugar*
¼	*teaspoon pepper*
1	*cup grated Cheddar cheese*
2	*tablespoons chopped onion*
	* Seasonal

Sweet Potato-Apple Scallop

Dorothy Merritt, Maryland

Cook sweet potatoes in boiling water in saucepan or microwave on High until tender. Cool. Peel and slice sweet potatoes and apples. Layer sweet potatoes, apples and mixture of brown sugar, butter, salt and pineapple ½ at a time in buttered 1-quart baking dish. Pour pineapple juice over layers. Chill in refrigerator if desired. ** Bake, covered, at 350 degrees for 30 minutes. Bake, uncovered, until apples are tender and top is brown.
Yield: 6 servings.

** *Make ahead to this point.*

2	*sweet potatoes* *
2	*tart apples* *
½	*cup packed brown sugar*
¾	*cup butter*
1	*teaspoon salt*
1	*cup crushed pineapple*
¾	*cup pineapple juice*
	* Seasonal

Green Tomato Casserole

Sarah McCreight, North Carolina

Slice tomatoes. Layer tomatoes, seasonings, butter and cheese ⅓ at a time in greased casserole. Bake at 350 degrees for 30 minutes or until tomatoes are tender. Sprinkle with cracker crumbs. Drizzle with melted butter. Bake for 5 minutes longer. Yield: 4 servings.

4	*green tomatoes, sliced*
1	*teaspoon salt*
½	*teaspoon pepper*
1	*tablespoon butter*
1	*cup grated cheese*
1	*cup cracker crumbs*
1	*tablespoon butter, melted*

Mock Noodles Romanoff

Myrtle Stevens, Oklahoma

Cook noodles according to package directions; drain. Combine with cottage cheese, sour cream, onion, garlic, salt and Worcestershire sauce in bowl; mix well. Spoon into greased casserole. Sprinkle with cheese. Chill in refrigerator for several hours if desired. ** Bake at 350 degrees for 40 minutes. Yield: 12 servings.

** *Make ahead to this point.*

10	*ounces noodles*
2	*cups cottage cheese*
2	*cups sour cream*
1	*tablespoon minced onion*
1	*large clove of garlic, minced*
1	*teaspoon salt*
1	*teaspoon Worcestershire sauce*
½	*cup grated cheese*

Recipes on pages 176, 183 and 216.

Vegetable Puff Verde
Joan Maynard, Maryland

10	ounces frozen French-style green beans
10	ounces frozen lima beans
10	ounces frozen tiny green peas
3	green peppers
3	green onions, chopped
1½	cups whipping cream
1½	cups mayonnaise
¾	cup grated Cheddar cheese
	Salt and pepper to taste

Thaw frozen vegetables; drain well. Cut green peppers into strips. Combine all vegetables in greased shallow 3-quart casserole. Chill for several hours if desired. ** Whip cream in bowl until stiff peaks form. Add mayonnaise, cheese and seasonings; mix well. Spoon over vegetables. Bake at 325 degrees for 40 minutes or until puffed and brown.
Yield: 12 servings.

** Make ahead to this point.

Easy Fruit Bread
Helen Dewey, Ohio

4	cups flour
3	cups sugar
1	teaspoon salt
2	teaspoons each soda, cinnamon and nutmeg
1	small jar each prune, plum and applesauce baby food
6	eggs
2	teaspoons vanilla extract
2	cups oil
1½	cups chopped nuts *
	* Seasonal

Combine dry ingredients in bowl. Add baby food, eggs, vanilla and oil; mix well. Stir in nuts. Fill greased and floured 4x8-inch loaf pans ½ full. Bake at 350 degrees for 35 minutes or until loaves test done. Cool in pans for several minutes. Remove to wire rack to cool completely.
Yield: 4 or 5 loaves.

Breakfast Bread
Vera Hansen, Ohio

⅓	cup margarine, softened
⅓	cup sugar
2	eggs
1	cup orange juice *
2	teaspoons grated orange rind
2	cups flour
1½	cups cornflakes, crushed
1	tablespoon baking powder
½	teaspoon salt
½	cup chopped nuts *
½	cup raisins *
	* Seasonal

Cream margarine and sugar in mixer bowl until light and fluffy. Mix in eggs, orange juice and rind. Add mixture of flour, cornflake crumbs, baking powder and salt; mix well. Stir in nuts and raisins. Pour into greased and floured loaf pan. Bake at 350 degrees for 50 minutes or until bread tests done. Yield: 12 servings.

Easy Coffee Cake
Deanna Rowe, Indiana

Combine 1½ cups cake mix, yeast, flour, eggs and ⅔ cup water in mixer bowl. Beat for 2 minutes. Spread in greased 9x13-inch cake pan. Spoon pie filling over dough. Mix remaining cake mix and butter in bowl until crumbly. Sprinkle over pie filling. Bake at 375 degrees for 30 minutes. Combine confectioners' sugar, corn syrup and 1 tablespoon water in small bowl; mix well. Drizzle over coffee cake. Serve warm or cold.
Yield: 12 servings.

1	*package yellow cake mix*
1	*package or 1 tablespoon dry yeast*
1	*cup flour*
2	*eggs*
1	*can cherry pie filling*
5	*tablespoons butter, melted*
1	*cup confectioners' sugar*
1	*tablespoon corn syrup*

Special Apricot Muffins
Rebecca Jackson, Texas

Combine flour, baking powder, sugar, salt, and soda in bowl; make well in center. Mix egg, oil, milk, yogurt and dried apricots in bowl. Pour into well in dry ingredients; mix just until moistened. Fill greased muffin cups ⅔ full. Mix 2 tablespoons flour, brown sugar, pecans and ½ teaspoon cinnamon in bowl. Cut in butter until crumbly. Sprinkle over muffins. Bake at 400 degrees for 20 minutes or until golden brown. Serve warm.
Yield: 1 dozen.

2	*cups flour*
2	*teaspoons baking powder*
½	*cup sugar*
½	*teaspoon each salt, soda*
½	*teaspoon each nutmeg, cinnamon*
1	*egg, beaten*
⅓	*cup oil*
⅓	*cup milk*
8	*ounces peach yogurt*
½	*cup chopped dried apricots*
2	*tablespoons flour*
2	*tablespoons brown sugar*
2	*tablespoons chopped pecans*
½	*teaspoon cinnamon*
2	*tablespoons butter*

Midnight Muffins
Dorine Jones, California

Beat eggs, milk, vanilla and butter in bowl until smooth. Add mixture of dry ingredients and pecans; stir just until moistened. Fill lightly greased muffin cups ⅔ full. Bake at 400 degrees for 15 minutes or until muffins test done. Cool on wire rack. Drizzle mixture of confectioners' sugar and orange juice over top. Serve warm.
Yield: 1 dozen.

2	*eggs*
¾	*cup milk*
1	*teaspoon vanilla extract*
¼	*cup melted butter*
1½	*cups flour*
½	*cup cocoa*
1	*tablespoon baking powder*
⅓	*cup sugar*
¼	*teaspoon salt*
½	*cup chopped pecans*
1	*cup confectioners' sugar*
2	*to 3 tablespoons orange juice*

Cheese Torte
Joey Speir, New Mexico

6	ounces Zwieback, crushed
1	cup sugar
1	teaspoon cinnamon
¼	cup melted butter
24	ounces dry curd cottage cheese
1	cup sugar
4	eggs
1	cup whipping cream
¼	cup flour
¼	teaspoon salt
	Juice and grated rind of ½ lemon

Mix Zwieback crumbs with 1 cup sugar, cinnamon and butter in bowl. Reserve ¼ cup for topping. Press remaining crumbs over bottom and side of 9-inch springform pan. Combine cottage cheese, 1 cup sugar, eggs, cream, flour, salt, lemon juice and rind in blender container. Process until smooth. Pour into prepared pan. Sprinkle with reserved crumbs. Bake at 325 degrees for 1 hour. Turn off oven. Let torte stand in closed oven for 1 hour. Place on serving plate; remove side of pan. Chill in refrigerator.
Yield: 12 servings.

Fruit Topping
Bonnie Roelofs, Tennessee

1	11-ounce can mandarin oranges
1	29-ounce can sliced peaches
3	tablespoons tapioca
½	cup sugar
	Dash of salt
1	6-ounce can frozen orange juice concentrate, thawed
1	10-ounce package frozen strawberries, thawed
2	bananas, sliced
1	pound cake, sliced

Drain oranges and peaches, reserving juice. Add enough water to reserved juice to measure 2½ cups. Combine 1 cup juice, tapioca, sugar and salt in saucepan. Let stand for 5 minutes. Cook over medium heat until thickened and clear, stirring constantly. Add remaining 1½ cups reserved liquid juice. Combine orange juice concentrate, strawberries, oranges and peaches in bowl. Stir in tapioca. Chill until serving time. Add bananas just before serving. Serve over pound cake slices.
Yield: 15 servings.

Frozen Halloween Dessert
Jennifer Buzard, New Mexico

20	Oreo cookies, crushed
⅓	cup melted margarine
½	gallon orange sherbet
2	squares baking chocolate
½	cup sugar
1	small can evaporated milk
1	cup chopped pecans *
	* Seasonal

Mix cookie crumbs and margarine in bowl. Press into 9x13-inch dish. Freeze until firm. Spread sherbet over crumb layer. Freeze until firm. Add chocolate, sugar and evaporated milk. Melt in double boiler. Cook until thickened, stirring constantly. Cool. Drizzle over sherbet. Sprinkle with pecans. Freeze until serving time.
Yield: 12 servings.

Frozen Papaya Soufflé

Photograph for this recipe on page 2.

Combine sugar and ½ cup water in double boiler. Cook over direct heat for 5 minutes or until syrupy. Cool for 5 minutes. Beat egg yolks until thick. Add syrup gradually, beating constantly. Cook over hot water until thickened, stirring constantly. Place pan in bowl of ice water. Beat with electric mixer until chilled and thickened. Fold in whipped cream, papaya purée and rum. Pour into 1-quart soufflé dish with collar. Freeze until firm. Remove collar. Press walnuts around side of soufflé. Garnish with papaya slices.
Yield: 8 servings.

½ **cup sugar**
7 **egg yolks**
1 **cup whipping cream, whipped**
1¼ **cups papaya purée ***
¾ **cup Coco Ribe coconut rum**
¾ **cup finely chopped walnuts**
 Papaya slices *
 * Seasonal

Citrus Apple Cake

Elizabeth Tregeser, Maryland

Sprinkle apples with mixture of cinnamon and 3 tablespoons sugar in bowl. Combine remaining ingredients in mixer bowl; mix well. Layer batter and apples ⅓ at a time in greased and floured tube pan. Bake at 350 degrees for 1¾ to 2 hours or until cake tests done. Cool on wire rack. Invert onto serving plate. Yield: 12 servings.

6 **large apples, thinly sliced ***
2 **teaspoons cinnamon**
3 **tablespoons sugar**
3 **cups flour**
1 **tablespoon baking powder**
2½ **cups sugar**
½ **teaspoon salt**
1 **cup oil**
⅓ **cup orange juice ***
4 **eggs, beaten**
2½ **teaspoons vanilla extract**
 * Seasonal

Honey Gingerbread

Lois E. Park, California

Cream shortening and sugar in mixer bowl until light and fluffy. Add eggs 1 at a time, beating well after each addition. Add honey in fine stream, beating constantly. Add sifted dry ingredients alternately with sour milk, mixing well after each addition. Pour into greased and floured 8x8-inch baking pan. Bake at 350 degrees for 40 minutes or until toothpick inserted in center comes out clean. Serve warm or cold with whipped cream or lemon sauce.
Yield: 12 servings.

¼ **cup shortening**
½ **cup sugar**
2 **eggs**
½ **cup honey ***
1½ **cups flour**
½ **teaspoon soda**
¼ **teaspoon salt**
¼ **teaspoon ginger**
½ **teaspoon cinnamon**
⅛ **teaspoon cloves**
½ **cup sour milk**
 * Seasonal

Almond Gingersnaps
Bertha DeVeaux, Maryland

1	**cup butter, softened**
1	**cup sugar**
3½	**cups flour**
1	**teaspoon soda**
½	**teaspoon salt**
1	**tablespoon ginger**
2	**teaspoon each cinnamon, cloves**
½	**cup molasses**
1	**cup sliced almonds**

Cream butter and sugar in mixer bowl until light and fluffy. Add mixture of dry ingredients alternately with molasses, mixing well after each addition. Mix in almonds. Knead on floured surface until well mixed. Shape into 2-inch diameter rolls. Wrap in waxed paper. Chill in refrigerator. ** Cut into thin slices. Place on greased cookie sheet. Bake at 325 degrees for 8 minutes or until light brown. Cool on wire rack. Yield: 8 dozen.

** *Make ahead to this point.*

Lemon-Glazed Persimmon Bars
Clara Sampson Berryessa, California

1	**egg, beaten**
1	**cup sugar**
1½	**cups finely chopped dates ***
1½	**teaspoons lemon juice**
1	**teaspoon soda**
1¾	**cups flour**
½	**teaspoon salt**
1	**teaspoon each cinnamon, nutmeg**
¼	**teaspoon cloves**
1	**cup persimmon pulp ***
1	**cup chopped walnuts**
1	**cup confectioners' sugar**
2	**tablespoons lemon juice**
	* Seasonal

Combine egg, sugar and dates in bowl; mix well. Stir in 1½ teaspoons lemon juice and soda. Add mixture of flour, salt and spices alternately with persimmon pulp, mixing well after each addition. Stir in walnuts. Spread in greased and floured 10x15-inch baking pan. Bake at 350 degrees for 25 minutes or until light brown. Cool for 5 minutes. Glaze with mixture of confectioners' sugar and 2 tablespoons lemon juice. Cool completely. Cut into bars. Yield: 4 dozen.

Gobblin' Fudge
Erma Lee Sellers, Mississippi

1	**cup margarine**
8	**ounces Velveeta cheese**
1½	**teaspoons vanilla extract**
2	**pounds confectioners' sugar**
½	**cup cocoa**
1	**cup chopped pecans**

Melt margarine and cheese together in double boiler, stirring frequently. Add vanilla. Mix confectioners' sugar and cocoa in bowl. Add cheese mixture; mix well. Spread in buttered 9x13-inch dish. Sprinkle with pecans; press in pecans lightly. Let stand until firm. Cut into squares. Yield: 3 pounds.

Hot Buttered Rum-Apple Pie

Kathy Lindsey, California

Melt ¼ cup margarine and brown sugar in large skillet. Stir in rum, lemon rind and juice and nutmeg. Add apples; mix well. Simmer, covered, for 10 minutes or until apples are tender. Cool slightly. Spoon into pie shell. Mix flour and sugar in bowl; cut in ¼ cup margarine until crumbly. Mix in almonds. Sprinkle over apples. Bake at 375 degrees for 35 minutes. Serve hot.
Yield: 12 servings.

¼	*cup margarine*
½	*cup packed brown sugar*
¼	*cup light rum*
1	*teaspoon grated lemon rind* *
1	*tablespoon lemon juice* *
1	*teaspoon nutmeg*
8	*cups sliced peeled apples* *
1	*unbaked 9-inch pie shell*
½	*cup flour*
½	*cup sugar*
¼	*cup margarine*
¼	*cup sliced almonds* *

* Seasonal

Fluffy Banana Tarts

Photograph for this recipe on page 176.

Prepare pudding mix according to package directions using 1 cup milk. Fold in whipped topping. Chill until serving time. Melt chocolate with butter in saucepan over very low heat, stirring constantly. Cool. Dip 1 end of 8 banana slices into chocolate. Chill until chocolate is firm. Place remaining banana slices in Cookie Tart Shells. Drizzle with remaining chocolate. Fill with pudding mixture. Decorate with chocolate-covered banana slices. Serve immediately.
Yield: 8 servings.

1	*small package pistachio instant pudding and pie filling mix*
1	*cup cold milk*
4	*ounces whipped topping*
9	*squares sweet cooking chocolate*
2	*tablespoons margarine*
2	*medium bananas, sliced*

Cookie Tart Shells

Cream butter and sugar in mixer bowl until light and fluffy. Add egg whites, 1 at a time, beating well after each addition. Stir in flour, almonds and flavoring. Spread 2 tablespoons at a time into 6-inch rounds on greased baking sheet. Bake at 350 degrees for 7 to 8 minutes or until edges are light brown. Grease bottoms of several 2-inch diameter glasses. Place hot cookies over glasses. Shape into cups making fluted edge. Cool. Remove glass carefully.
Yield: 8 tart shells.

¼	*cup butter or margarine, softened*
⅓	*cup sugar*
2	*egg whites*
⅓	*cup flour*
¼	*cup ground almonds*
⅛	*teaspoon almond extract*

Oktoberfest Steamer

Andrea Ball, Minnesota

Combine juice and spice in saucepan. Cook over low heat or in microwave on Medium until steaming. Pour into mugs. Add cinnamon stick to each mug. Serve hot.
Yield: 3 servings.

1	*cup each apple juice, cranberry juice and orange juice*
1	*tablespoon each cinnamon, cloves*
3	*4-inch cinnamon sticks*

November

Beef Wellington Appetizers

½ **pound beef tenderloin**
½ **cup teriyaki marinade**
1 **2-crust package pie crust mix**
2 **2-ounce jars chicken liver pâté**
1 **egg, beaten**

Cut tenderloin into ½x1-inch pieces. Marinate in teriyaki marinade for 1 hour. Prepare pie crust mix using package directions. Roll into two 9x12-inch rectangles; cut into 2x3-inch strips. Drain tenderloin. Spread a small amount of pâté on each piece. Place beef piece on each pastry strip; fold pastry to enclose filling, sealing edge. Brush with beaten egg. Place on greased baking sheet. Chill for several hours if desired. ** Bake at 425 degrees for 20 minutes. Arrange on serving plate.
Yield: 3 dozen.

** *Make ahead to this point.*

Cheese Tarts
Bev Delucry, Ontario, Canada

1 **onion, chopped**
8 **slices crisp-fried bacon, crumbled**
2 **cups grated mozzarella cheese**
24 **baked tartlet shells**
24 **mushroom slices**

Sauté onion in skillet until tender. Layer bacon, onion and cheese in tartlet shells. Top with mushroom slice. Place on baking sheet. Bake at 400 degrees until heated through and cheese melts. Arrange on serving plate.
Yield: 2 dozen.

Cranberry-Pear Relish

Photograph for this recipe on page 175.

Combine pears in syrup, wine, cinnamon stick and cloves in saucepan. Bring to a boil. Simmer, covered, for 10 minutes. Remove pears; strain syrup. Combine cranberries, brown sugar and syrup in saucepan. Simmer, covered, for 15 minutes or until cranberries pop. Stir in mixture of cornstarch and 2 tablespoons water. Cook for 1 minute, stirring constantly. Reserve 6 pear halves; chop remaining pears. Add chopped pears, oranges and walnuts to syrup. Cool. Pour into serving bowl. Arrange reserved pear halves on top. Chill in refrigerator.
Yield: 6 servings.

- 2 *16-ounce cans pear halves*
- 1/3 *cup dry white wine*
- 1 *2-inch cinnamon stick*
- 1/4 *teaspoon whole cloves*
- 2 *cups whole cranberries **
- 1/3 *cup packed brown sugar*
- 2 *tablespoons Argo cornstarch*
- 2 *oranges, chopped, peeled **
- 1/3 *cup coarsely chopped walnuts*
  * Seasonal

Mulligatawny

Combine lentils with cold water to cover in saucepan. Bring to a boil over low heat. Add beef bouillon and pepper pods. Cook, covered, for 1 hour or until tender, adding additional water if necessary. Sauté onions and garlic in oil in skillet. Add seasonings; mix well. Stir into lentil mixture. Add sour cream and lemon juice just before serving. **Remove pepper pods.** Ladle into soup bowls.
Yield: 10 servings.

- 1 *pound dry lentils*
- 3 *to 5 tablespoons instant beef bouillon*
- 1 *to 3 pods of red pepper*
- 2 *onions, chopped*
- 4 *cloves of garlic, minced*
- 1/4 *cup oil*
- 2 *tablespoons dry mustard*
- 3 *tablespoons cumin*
- 1 *teaspoon turmeric*
- 1½ *cups sour cream*
  Juice of 5 lemons *
  * Seasonal

Turkey Soup

Beulah Jelley, Ohio

Brown turkey with onion flakes in 4-quart saucepan. Add celery, green beans, carrots, mushrooms, cabbage, tomatoes and tomato juice; mix well. Stir in seasonings. Add enough water to make of desired consistency. Simmer for 2 hours, adding water if necessary. **Remove bay leaf.** Ladle into serving bowls.
Yield: 8 servings.

Note: May substitute ground beef for turkey.

- 2 *pounds ground fresh turkey **
- 2 *teaspoons onion flakes*
- 2 *cups chopped celery*
- 2 *cups green beans*
- 1 *cup sliced carrots*
- 1 *cup sliced mushrooms*
- 2 *cups shredded cabbage*
- 4 *cups canned tomatoes*
- 4 *cups tomato juice*
- 1 *tablespoon Worcestershire sauce*
- 2 *teaspoons basil*
- 1 *teaspoon oregano*
- 1 *teaspoon garlic powder*
- 1 *bay leaf*
  * Seasonal

Crunchy Cranberries

Jerri Dickson, Oklahoma

2	*cups sugar*
2½	*tablespoons unflavored gelatin*
4	*cups cranberries* *
1	*medium orange* *
1	*cup chopped celery*
1	*cup chopped nuts* *
	Crisp lettuce leaves
1	*cup yogurt*
	* Seasonal

Combine sugar with 1 cup water in saucepan. Cook to consistency of thin syrup, stirring frequently. Soften gelatin in ½ cup cold water. Add to syrup; stir until dissolved. Grind cranberries and unpeeled orange. Add to gelatin mixture with celery and nuts; mix well. Pour into mold. Chill until firm. ** Unmold onto lettuce-lined serving plate. Serve with yogurt. Yield: 16 servings.

** *Make ahead to this point.*

Marinated Avocado and Mushroom Salad

Bonnie Fairbanks, California

1	*medium avocado, sliced* *
1	*cup sliced mushrooms*
2	*thin slices onion, separated*
¼	*cup dry white wine*
2	*tablespoons vinegar*
¼	*cup oil*
½	*teaspoon sugar*
¼	*teaspoon basil*
¼	*teaspoon salt*
	Bibb lettuce leaves
	* Seasonal

Combine avocado, mushrooms and onion rings in salad bowl. Combine wine, vinegar, oil, sugar, basil and salt in covered jar; shake to blend well. Pour over salad. Chill, covered, for 2 hours or longer. ** Drain. Serve on Bibb lettuce-lined plates. Yield: 4 servings.

** *Make ahead to this point.*

California Crab Louis

Mrs. Lyle Abel, California

1	*cup mayonnaise*
¼	*cup whipping cream*
¼	*cup chili sauce*
¼	*cup chopped green pepper*
¼	*cup chopped green onions*
1	*teaspoon lemon juice*
	Dash of salt
2	*7-ounce cans crab meat*
3	*avocados* *
	Crisp lettuce leaves
	Paprika to taste
1	*tomato*
2	*hard-boiled eggs*
1	*lemon*
1	*cup ripe olives*
	* Seasonal

Combine mayonnaise, whipping cream, chili sauce, green pepper, green onions, lemon juice and salt in bowl; mix well. Add crab meat; mix well. Cut avocados into halves; place on lettuce-lined plates. Fill with crab mixture; sprinkle with paprika. Cut tomato, hard-boiled eggs and lemon into wedges. Arrange tomato, egg, lemon wedges and olives around avocados.
Yield: 6 servings.

Serving suggestion: May serve crab mixture in tomato cups formed by cutting each tomato into wedges to but not through bottom and opening slightly.

Homemade Salad Seasoning
Pam Stibitz, Michigan

Combine all ingredients in bowl; mix well. Spoon into airtight 1-quart container. Store for up to 4 months. Use to season salads, baked potatoes, eggs or other dishes as desired. Yield: 48 tablespoons. ↙ ⟁ ⊟ ✳

Gift suggestion: This seasoning makes a welcome gift when packaged in small decorative jars. Be sure to include a copy of the recipe and your own special suggestions for use.

2 **cups Parmesan cheese**
½ **cup sesame seed**
3 **tablespoons celery seed**
2 **tablespoons poppy seed**
2 **tablespoons parsley flakes**
1 **tablespoon onion flakes**
2 **teaspoons paprika**
2 **teaspoons salt**
½ **teaspoon each garlic salt, dillseed and pepper**

Honey-Mustard Dressing
Donna Wilterink, California

Blend vinegar, mayonnaise and mustard in bowl. Add sugar, onion, honey and parsley. Season to taste; mix well. Whisk in oil gradually. Store in covered container in refrigerator. Yield: 2¼ cups. ↙ ⟁ ⊟

Serving suggestion: Use on spinach, mixed green, citrus, or pasta salads.

¼ **cup vinegar**
1 **cup mayonnaise**
1 **teaspoon mustard**
1 **teaspoon sugar**
1 **teaspoon chopped onion**
½ **cup honey ***
1 **tablespoon chopped parsley**
   Salt and pepper to taste
½ **cup oil**
   * Seasonal

Italian Roast Beef Sandwiches
Laura J. Salers, Maryland

Cut 6 to 8 deep slashes in roast. Mix celery, parsley, cheese and garlic powder in small bowl. Insert 2 to 3 teaspoons celery mixture and 2 or 3 butter slices into each slash. Place roast in baking pan. Sprinkle with salt and pepper. Bake at 400 degrees for 30 to 40 minutes. Reduce temperature to 325 degrees. Add 3 to 4 cups water to pan. Bake for 3 hours or until tender, basting occasionally. Remove roast to plate; reserve pan juices. Cool. Chill roast and juices for several hours to overnight. ** Slice roast thinly. Skim juices. Place sliced roast in juices in saucepan. Simmer until heated through. Serve roast on heated hard rolls. Yield: 8 to 12 sandwiches. ⊟

*** Make ahead to this point.*

1 **4-pound sirloin tip roast**
3 **tablespoons minced celery**
2 **tablespoons minced parsley**
1 **to 2 tablespoons Parmesan cheese**
¼ **teaspoon garlic powder**
1 **stick butter, sliced**
   Salt and pepper to taste
8 **to 12 hard rolls, split**

Veal and Pork Country Pâté
Joan Dew, Tennessee

4 ounces mushrooms, chopped
1 medium onion, minced
1 clove of garlic, minced
¼ cup dry Sherry
1 teaspoon salt
¼ teaspoon pepper
½ teaspoon thyme leaves
⅛ teaspoon nutmeg
8 ounces lean ground pork *
8 ounces ground veal
2 ounces ground pork fat
¼ cup pistachios *
1 egg
2 tablespoons finely chopped parsley
8 ounces sliced bacon
¼ cup finely chopped parsley
   * Seasonal

Sauté mushrooms, onion and garlic in oil in skillet over medium heat until tender; do not brown. Add Sherry, salt, pepper, thyme and nutmeg. Simmer for 5 minutes. Combine with meats, pistachios, egg and 2 tablespoons parsley in bowl; beat with wooden spoon until well mixed. Line bottom and sides of 4x8-inch loaf pan with bacon slices, overlapping slightly and leaving overhang. Pack meat into prepared pan; fold overhanging bacon over top to completely enclose mixture. Rap pan sharply on counter top to remove any air bubbles. Bake at 350 degrees for 1¼ hours. Cover pâté with foil-covered cardboard cut to fit snuggly inside pan. Weight top with canned goods. Refrigerate for overnight to 1 week. Remove weights and cardboard. Dip pan in hot water for 15 seconds; loosen pâté from side of pan with spatula. Invert onto serving plate; scrape off excess fat. Garnish with remaining parsley. Serve with crackers and grapes. Yield: one 2-pound pâté.

Apple-Glazed Pork Chops
Rosalind Lehman, Michigan

4 to 8 pork chops *
¼ cup flour
½ teaspoon salt
⅛ teaspoon pepper
½ teaspoon dry mustard
2 tablespoons margarine
2 apples, peeled, sliced *
⅓ cup raisins *
2 tablespoons flour
2 tablespoons brown sugar
1½ cups apple juice *
½ teaspoon cinnamon
   * Seasonal

Coat pork chops with mixture of ¼ cup flour, salt, pepper and dry mustard. Brown on both sides in margarine in skillet. Arrange in single layer in baking dish. Layer apples and raisins over pork chops. Stir 2 tablespoons flour and brown sugar into drippings in skillet. Stir in apple juice gradually. Cook until thickened, stirring constantly. Pour over pork chops. Sprinkle with cinnamon. Bake, covered, at 350 degrees for 1 hour. Yield: 4 servings.

Curried Chicken
Mary Holcomb, Texas

6 frozen breaded chicken breast filets, thawed
¼ cup butter
1 tablespoon curry powder
1½ cups white wine
1 cup cream
3 cups chopped celery
2 large apples, chopped *
1 cup rice, cooked
   * Seasonal

Cut chicken into bite-sized pieces. Brown in butter in skillet. Stir in curry powder and wine. Bring to a boil. Stir in cream. Sprinkle celery over top; reduce heat. Simmer, covered, for several minutes. Add apples. Simmer, covered, just until apples are tender. Serve over hot cooked rice. Yield: 6 servings.

Oven-Baked Pancake with Sausage

Terrie Null, California

Combine first 3 ingredients in bowl; mix well. Sift flour, baking powder, 1½ tablespoons sugar and salt together. Add to egg mixture; beat until smooth. Pour into greased 10x15-inch baking pan. Arrange sausages over top. Bake at 450 degrees for 15 minutes. Combine remaining ingredients in saucepan; mix well. Cook over low heat for 5 minutes or until thickened, stirring constantly. Cut pancake into serving portions. Serve with hot fruit sauce.
Yield: 15 servings.

- 3 eggs, beaten
- 3 tablespoons melted butter
- 1½ cups milk
- 1¾ cups sifted flour
- 4 teaspoons baking powder
- 1½ tablespoons sugar
- 1 teaspoon salt
- 2 pounds brown and serve sausage links
- 3 tablespoons sugar
- 2 teaspoons cornstarch
- 3 cups apricot nectar
- 2 tablespoons lemon juice

Venison Supreme

Shirley Charlier, Michigan

Cut venison into ½-inch cubes. Coat with mixture of flour, salt and pepper. Brown in shortening in skillet. Add mushrooms and onion. Sauté until onion is tender. Stir in tomato juice, oregano, bay leaf and ½ cup water. Simmer for 25 minutes or until venison is tender. Add sour cream and celery. Simmer, covered, for 15 minutes. **Remove bay leaf.** Spoon hot noodles into ring on serving platter. Spoon venison into center. Yield: 6 servings.

- 1 pound venison *
- ¼ cup flour
- 1 teaspoon salt
- ½ teaspoon pepper
- ¼ cup shortening
- ½ cup sliced mushrooms
- ¼ cup chopped onion
- 1 cup tomato juice
  Oregano to taste
- ½ bay leaf
- ¾ cup sour cream
- 1 cup chopped celery
- 8 ounces noodles, cooked
  * Seasonal

Honey-Glazed Chicken

Grace Hanley, Maryland

Cut unpeeled orange into quarters. Place in small baking dish. Place 1 chicken breast filet over each orange quarter. Mix orange juice, salt, pepper and ginger in small bowl. Pour over chicken. Bake at 375 degrees for 20 minutes. Brush with honey. Bake for 10 minutes or until tender, basting frequently with mixture of wine and orange rind.
Yield: 4 servings.

- 1 orange *
- 4 chicken breast filets *
- ½ cup orange juice *
- 1 teaspoon salt
- ¼ teaspoon pepper
- ¼ teaspoon ginger
- ½ cup honey *
- ½ cup red wine
  Grated rind of 1 orange
  * Seasonal

Turkey and Stuffing Pie
Thelma Gentry, Ohio

1	*package herb stuffing mix*
¾	*cup chicken broth*
1	*egg, beaten*
½	*cup melted butter*
1	*4-ounce can mushrooms*
½	*cup chopped onion*
1	*tablespoon butter*
3	*cups chopped cooked turkey* *
1	*cup peas*
1	*can chicken gravy*
2	*tablespoons chopped pimento*
1	*teaspoon Worcestershire sauce*
1	*teaspoon parsley flakes*
¼	*teaspoon thyme*
2	*teaspoons flour*
4	*slices American cheese*
	* Seasonal

Combine stuffing mix, chicken broth, egg and ½ cup butter in bowl; mix well. Press over bottom and side of 10-inch pie plate. Drain mushrooms, reserving liquid. Sauté mushrooms and onion in 1 tablespoon butter in skillet. Add turkey, peas, gravy, pimento, Worcestershire sauce, parsley and thyme. Blend flour with reserved mushroom liquid. Stir into turkey mixture. Cook until thickened and bubbly, stirring constantly. Spoon into prepared pie plate. Bake at 325 degrees for 20 minutes. Cut cheese slices into strips. Arrange in lattice-pattern over top. Bake for 5 minutes longer. Cut into wedges. Yield: 6 servings.

Stuffed Bluefish
Michael Ford, Maryland

12	*ounces stuffing mix*
1	*cup Shoe Peg corn*
½	*cup golden raisins* *
½	*cup chopped English walnuts* *
2	*tablespoons rum*
¼	*to ½ cup Chablis*
½	*teaspoon cayenne pepper*
1	*medium bluefish*
1	*Bermuda onion, sliced*
1	*orange, sliced* *
1	*lemon, sliced* *
1	*lime, sliced* *
	* Seasonal

Combine stuffing mix, corn, raisins, walnuts, rum, Chablis and pepper in bowl; mix well. Let stand for 1 hour. Rinse fish inside and out; pat dry and place on large foil sheet. Spoon stuffing into cavity. Layer half the onion and citrus slices over stuffing; secure with skewers. Arrange remaining slices over fish. Seal foil. Vent foil with fork. Cook over hot coals for 45 minutes or until fish flakes easily. Yield: 4 servings.

Super Supper Casserole
Clara Landrus, California

1	*large bunch broccoli* *
2	*cups corn bread crumbs*
1	*can mushroom soup*
1	*13-ounce can salmon, drained*
1	*tablespoon lemon juice*
2	*large tomatoes, sliced*
1	*cup shredded Cheddar cheese*
	* Seasonal

Separate broccoli into flowerets. Cook in a small amount of lightly salted water in saucepan, or microwave until tender-crisp; drain. Layer crumbs, soup, salmon, lemon juice and broccoli in 2-quart baking dish. Arrange tomato slices over top. Bake at 350 degrees for 30 minutes or until heated through. Sprinkle cheese over top. Bake until cheese melts. Yield: 4 servings.

Crab Quiche
Deloris Barton, California

Layer cheese, crab meat and chopped green onions in pie shell. Combine eggs, cream, salt, pepper, lemon rind, dry mustard and mace in bowl; beat well. Pour into pie shell. Sprinkle with almonds. Bake at 325 degrees for 45 minutes or until set. Let stand for 10 minutes before serving.
Yield: 6 servings.

4	ounces Swiss cheese, shredded
1	7-ounce can crab meat
2	green onions, chopped
1	unbaked 9-inch pie shell
3	eggs
1	cup light cream
½	teaspoon salt
	Pepper to taste
½	teaspoon grated lemon rind
¼	teaspoon dry mustard
	Dash of mace
¼	cup sliced almonds

Eggs Benedict

Sauté onion in 2 tablespoons butter. Stir in mushroom soup. Heat until bubbly; reduce heat. Break eggs into soup mixture. Cook, covered, until eggs are set. Toast English muffins; top with additional butter. Place ham on muffins; top each with egg and mushroom sauce.
Yield: 4 servings.

¼	cup chopped onion
2	tablespoons butter
1	can cream of mushroom soup
4	eggs
2	English muffins, split
4	slices baked ham, grilled

Walnutburgers
Sandy Gill, Michigan

Combine walnuts, cheese, bread crumbs, wheat germ, onion, sesame seed, parsley, soy sauce, garlic, thyme and milk powder in bowl; mix well. Beat eggs in bowl. Add to nut mixture; mix well. Shape into patties. Chill in refrigerator if desired. ** Heat oil in skillet over medium heat. Brown patties on both sides in oil. Drain on paper towel. Arrange on serving plate.
Yield: 5 servings.

** *Make ahead to this point.*

1	cup ground walnuts *
1	cup shredded Cheddar cheese
½	cup bread crumbs
¼	cup wheat germ
½	cup chopped onion
2	tablespoons sesame seed
1	tablespoon chopped parsley
1	teaspoon soy sauce
2	cloves of garlic, chopped
¼	teaspoon thyme
2	tablespoons nonfat dry milk powder
4	eggs
¼	cup (about) oil
	* Seasonal

Crock•Pot Mexican Beans

Sally Richardson, Michigan

1	**16-ounce can kidney beans**
1	**16-ounce can butter beans**
1	**16-ounce can pork and beans**
1	**onion, chopped**
6	**slices crisp-fried bacon, crumbled**
½	**cup sugar**
⅓	**cup packed brown sugar**
1	**tablespoon chili powder**
2	**teaspoons Worcestershire sauce**

Drain kidney beans and butter beans. Combine with pork and beans and onion in Crock•Pot. Stir in bacon, sugars and seasonings; mix well. Cook on Low for 5 to 8 hours. Yield: 6 servings.

Note: May bake in covered casserole at 300 degrees for 2 hours or longer.

Carrots in Orange Sauce

Edythe Koerzendorfer, California

3	**tablespoons margarine**
½	**cup sugar**
1½	**tablespoons cornstarch**
3	**tablespoons frozen orange juice concentrate**
	Salt to taste
2	**cups hot cooked carrots**

Combine melted margarine, sugar and cornstarch in saucepan; mix well. Stir in orange juice concentrate, salt and 1 cup water gradually. Cook until thickened, stirring constantly, or microwave on High, stirring twice. Serve over hot cooked carrots. Yield: 4 servings.

Deep-Fried Cauliflower

Loleta Kalsbeek, California

1	**head cauliflower ***
1	**cup milk**
1	**cup (or more) flour**
1	**egg, beaten**
2	**tablespoons milk**
½	**teaspoon salt**
1	**package cornflake crumbs**
	Oil for deep frying
	* Seasonal

Separate cauliflower into flowerets. Dip flowerets into milk; coat well with flour. Dip in mixture of egg, 2 tablespoons milk and salt. Roll in cornflake crumbs; press crumbs firmly over surface to coat well. Deep-fry in 375-degree oil for 1½ to 2 minutes or until golden brown; drain. Arrange on serving plate. Yield: 6 to 8 servings.

Serving suggestion: Deep-fried cauliflower can also be served with horseradish dipping sauce as an appetizer.

Stove-Top Potato Scallop

Louise Feldpausch, Michigan

Combine potatoes, celery, onion, bouillon cube, parsley, salt and 1¼ cups water in saucepan. Cook until vegetables are tender. Stir in mixture of flour and milk. Cook until thickened, stirring constantly. Add cheese. Cook until cheese melts, stirring constantly. Spoon into serving dish. Yield: 6 servings. ✔ 🫕

3	*cups chopped potatoes*
½	*cup chopped celery*
¼	*cup chopped onion*
1	*chicken bouillon cube*
1	*teaspoon parsley flakes*
¼	*teaspoon salt*
2	*tablespoons flour*
1½	*cups milk*
2	*cups shredded cheese*

Cranberry Yams

Robin Williams, Texas

Combine flour, brown sugar, oats and cinnamon in bowl. Cut in margarine until crumbly. Mix 1 cup oats mixture with drained yams and cranberries in bowl; toss to mix well. Pour into baking dish. Chill in refrigerator if desired. ** Top with remaining oats mixture. Bake at 350 degrees for 35 minutes or until light brown. Yield: 8 servings. ✔ 🫕 🍲

** *Make ahead to this point.*

½	*cup flour*
½	*cup packed brown sugar*
½	*cup oats*
1	*teaspoon cinnamon*
⅓	*cup margarine*
4	*cups chopped cooked yams* *
2	*cups fresh cranberries* *
	* Seasonal

Vegetable Casserole

Dorothy Hedrick, Ohio

Separate cauliflower and broccoli into small flowerets. Cook in a small amount of water in saucepan or microwave until tender-crisp; drain. Add drained whole kernel corn and mushrooms. Combine cream-style corn, cheese and soup in bowl; mix well. Fold into cauliflower mixture. Pour into greased 9x13-inch baking dish. Chill in refrigerator if desired. ** Sprinkle mixture of butter and crumbs over top. Bake at 375 degrees for 30 minutes or until bubbly. Yield: 12 to 15 servings. ✔ 🫕 🍲

** *Make ahead to this point.*

1	*head cauliflower* *
1	*bunch broccoli* *
1	*17-ounce can whole kernel corn*
1	*4-ounce can mushrooms*
1	*17-ounce can cream-style corn*
2	*cups shredded Swiss cheese*
1	*can cream of celery soup*
2	*tablespoons melted butter*
1½	*cups soft rye bread crumbs*
	* Seasonal

Microwave Stir-Fry Vegetables
Leonore Fergus, Ohio

3	medium onions
1	tablespoon oil
1	tablespoon butter
3	stalks celery
1	carrot
1	green pepper
1	cup broccoli flowerets *
1	cup cauliflowerets *
3	cups sliced cabbage
½	cup sliced green onions
½	to 1 cup chopped cooked chicken *
½	cup sliced mushrooms

* Seasonal

Cut onions into quarters lengthwise. Combine with oil and butter in 3-quart glass baking dish. Microwave on High for 3 minutes. Slice celery and carrot diagonally. Cut green pepper into ½-inch strips. Add celery, carrot, green pepper, broccoli, cauliflower, cabbage and green onions to baking dish. Microwave, covered, for 4 minutes, stirring once. Stir in chicken and mushrooms. Microwave for 4 to 6 minutes longer, stirring once. Let stand for several minutes. Serve with rice. Yield: 6 to 8 servings.

Rice Timbales
Wendy Moritz, Texas

1	cup rice
½	cup heavy cream
¾	cup shredded Monterey Jack cheese
¼	cup chopped pecans
¼	cup chopped green onions
	Dash of red pepper
2	eggs, beaten
8	ounces thinly sliced ham
1	tablespoon melted butter
1	tablespoon flour
1	cup milk
¾	cup shredded Cheddar cheese
1½	teaspoons mustard

Cook rice according to package directions. Scald cream in saucepan. Add to rice with Monterey Jack cheese, pecans, green onions, red pepper and eggs; mix well. Line 4 buttered 10-ounce custard cups with ham slices, fitting to edge of cups. Fill with rice mixture. Place in baking pan. Add boiling water to half the depth of cups. Bake at 350 degrees for 30 minutes or until set. Blend butter and flour in saucepan. Cook for 1 minute, stirring constantly. Stir in milk gradually. Cook until thickened, stirring constantly. Add Cheddar cheese and mustard; blend well. Unmold timbales onto serving plate. Serve with cheese sauce.
Yield: 4 servings.

Corn Bread Dressing
Louise Barker, Tennessee

¼	cup finely chopped onion
1	cup finely chopped celery
½	cup butter
3	cups toasted bread cubes
3	cups crumbled corn bread
2	eggs, slightly beaten
1	teaspoon salt
½	teaspoon pepper
1	teaspoon poultry seasoning
½	teaspoon sage
2	to 3 cups broth

Sauté onion and celery in butter in saucepan. Remove from heat. Add bread cubes and corn bread; mix well. Add mixture of eggs, seasonings and broth; mix well. Spoon dressing into 9x13-inch baking dish. Chill in refrigerator if desired. ** Bake at 350 degrees until light brown and crisp around edges. Yield: 8 to 12 servings.

** Make ahead to this point.
Note: Dressing may be used for stuffing turkey.

Corn Stuffing Balls
LaVonne Benton, California

Combine butter and 1½ cups water in large saucepan. Heat until butter melts. Remove from heat. Add stuffing mix; mix well. Add corn, eggs and parsley; mix well. Add a small amount of water if necessary to make of desired consistency. Shape into balls; arrange in buttered shallow baking dish. Refrigerate, covered, for 1 hour. ** Bake, uncovered, at 400 degrees for 15 minutes. Place on serving plate. Yield: 8 servings.

** *Make ahead to this point.*

- ¾ cup butter
- 12 ounces stuffing mix
- 2 cups whole kernel corn, drained
- 2 eggs, beaten
- ½ cup chopped parsley

Pineapple-Spice Scones
Garett Massey, New Mexico

Combine flour, baking powder, salt and ⅓ cup sugar in bowl. Cut in butter until crumbly. Make well in center. Add pineapple; stir just until mixed. Dough will be sticky. Knead 10 to 12 times on lightly floured surface. Roll ¼ inch thick; cut with floured 2½-inch biscuit cutter. Place on ungreased baking sheet. Brush with milk. Mix almonds, 1 tablespoon sugar and cinnamon in bowl. Sprinkle over scones. Bake at 425 degrees for 15 minutes or until golden brown. Serve warm. Yield: 2 dozen.

- 3 cups flour
- 2½ teaspoons baking powder
- ½ teaspoon salt
- ⅓ cup sugar
- ¾ cup butter
- 1 8-ounce can juice-pack crushed pineapple
- 2 tablespoons milk
- 3 tablespoons chopped almonds
- 1 tablespoon sugar
- ½ teaspoon cinnamon

Sweet Potato Muffins
Audrey Fisher, Virginia

Combine flour, ½ cup sugar, brown sugar, baking powder, salt and pecans in bowl; mix well. Make well in center. Mix sweet potatoes, milk, butter and eggs in bowl. Pour into well in dry ingredients; stir just until moistened. Fill greased muffin cups ⅔ full. Sprinkle with mixture of cinnamon and ¼ cup sugar. Bake at 425 degrees for 25 minutes or until brown. Yield: 1⅓ dozen.

- 1¾ cups flour
- ½ cup sugar
- 1 tablespoon brown sugar
- 1 tablespoon baking powder
- 1 teaspoon salt
- ½ cup chopped pecans *
- 1¼ cups mashed cooked sweet potatoes *
- ¾ cup milk
- ¼ cup melted butter
- 2 eggs, beaten
- ½ teaspoon cinnamon
- ¼ cup sugar
- * Seasonal

Microwave Boston Brown Bread

Jane Cooley, Washington

1	*cup buttermilk*
½	*cup molasses*
½	*cup raisins* *
½	*teaspoon each baking powder, soda and salt*
½	*cup whole wheat flour*
¼	*cup all-purpose flour*
½	*cup yellow cornmeal*
	* Seasonal

Combine buttermilk and molasses in bowl; mix well. Add raisins, baking powder, soda and salt; mix well. Add flours and cornmeal. Stir just until moistened. Pour into well-greased 4-cup glass measure. Cover loosely with plastic wrap; secure with rubber band. Microwave on Medium for 8½ to 9½ minutes or just until set. Let stand, uncovered, for 10 minutes. Remove to wire rack. Let stand for 5 minutes before slicing. Yield: 8 servings.

Whole-Grain Bread

Jeannette Katt, Michigan

¼	*cup honey* *
¼	*cup molasses*
2	*packages or 2 tablespoons dry yeast*
⅔	*cup nonfat dry milk powder*
2	*eggs*
2	*teaspoons oil*
2	*tablespoons salt*
½	*cup quick-cooking oats*
½	*cup wheat germ*
½	*cup bran cereal*
2	*cups whole wheat flour*
2½	*to 3¼ cups all-purpose flour*
	* Seasonal

Combine honey, molasses, yeast and 1¾ cups warm water in large bowl. Let stand, covered, for 10 minutes or until frothy. Add dry milk powder, eggs, oil and salt; mix well. Add oats, wheat germ, cereal and whole wheat flour; mix well. Add enough all-purpose flour to make moderately stiff dough. Knead on floured surface for 5 to 8 minutes. Place in greased bowl, turning to grease surface. Let rise, covered, until doubled in bulk. Divide into 2 portions. Let rest for 10 minutes. Shape into loaves; place in greased loaf pans. Let rise until doubled in bulk. Bake at 350 degrees for 40 minutes. Remove to wire rack to cool.
Yield: 2 loaves.

Pumpkin Mousse

Karlon Blythe, New Mexico

1	*envelope whipped topping mix*
½	*cup milk*
½	*teaspoon vanilla extract*
1	*small package vanilla instant pudding mix*
⅔	*cup milk*
1	*cup pumpkin purée* *
¾	*teaspoon pumpkin pie spice*
	* Seasonal

Prepare whipped topping according to package directions, using ½ cup milk and ½ teaspoon vanilla. Prepare pudding mix according to package directions, using ⅔ cup milk. Add pumpkin and spice. Fold in ⅔ of the whipped topping gently. Spoon into dessert glasses. Swirl remaining whipped topping on top. Chill until serving time.
Yield: 4 servings.

Tangerine Sunshine Cake

Combine cake mix, pudding mix, 4 teaspoons tangerine rind, tangerine juice, eggs, oil and 1 cup water in mixer bowl. Beat at medium speed for 4 minutes. Pour into well-greased 10-inch bundt pan. Bake at 350 degrees for 50 minutes or until cake tests done. Cool in pan for 5 minutes. Invert onto serving plate to cool completely. Sprinkle with confectioners' sugar. Prepare topping mix with milk according to package directions, omitting vanilla. Peel tangerines and separate into segments. Add to whipped topping with 2 teaspoons grated rind. Serve with cake.
Yield: 12 servings.

1 *package yellow cake mix*
1 *small package vanilla instant pudding mix*
4 *teaspoons grated tangerine rind*
3 *tablespoons fresh tangerine juice **
4 *eggs*
1/3 *cup oil*
1/4 *cup confectioners' sugar*
1 *envelope whipped topping mix*
1/2 *cup milk*
2 *tangerines **
2 *teaspoons grated tangerine rind*
* Seasonal

Spiced Apple Cookies

Edna Ehle, Ohio

Combine raisins with water to cover in saucepan. Bring to a boil; remove from heat. Let stand, covered, for 5 minutes; drain. Cream shortening and brown sugar in mixer bowl until light and fluffy. Beat in egg and milk. Add sifted dry ingredients; mix well. Stir in walnuts, apple and raisins. Drop by rounded teaspoonfuls onto ungreased cookie sheet. Bake at 375 degrees for 8 to 10 minutes or until brown. Remove to wire rack to cool.
Yield: 3 1/2 dozen.

1 *cup raisins **
1/2 *cup shortening*
1 1/3 *cups packed brown sugar*
1 *egg*
1/4 *cup milk*
2 1/4 *cups flour*
1/2 *teaspoon salt*
1 *teaspoon each soda, cinnamon*
1/2 *teaspoon each cloves, nutmeg*
1 *cup chopped walnuts **
1 *cup chopped unpeeled apple **
* Seasonal

Honey-Carob Brownies

Karen Schaefer, New Mexico

Blend butter, carob powder and honey in bowl. Add eggs and vanilla; mix well. Add mixture of flour, baking powder and salt; mix well. Stir in walnuts. Pour into greased 8-inch baking dish. Bake at 350 degrees for 40 minutes. Cool on wire rack. Cut into squares.
Yield: 16 brownies.

1/2 *cup butter, melted*
1/2 *cup carob powder*
1 *cup honey **
2 *eggs, well beaten*
1 *teaspoon vanilla extract*
1 *cup sifted whole wheat pastry flour*
1 *teaspoon baking powder*
1/4 *teaspoon salt*
1/2 *cup chopped walnuts **
* Seasonal

Oatmeal Chippers

Photograph for this recipe on Cover.

½   **cup butter, softened**
½   **cup packed brown sugar**
⅓   **cup sugar**
1   **egg**
½   **teaspoon vanilla extract**
1   **cup flour**
½   **teaspoon soda**
½   **teaspoon salt**
¼   **cup milk**
1   **cup semisweet miniature chocolate chips**
1¼   **cups oats**
½   **cup chopped nuts ***
    * Seasonal

Cream butter, brown sugar and sugar in bowl. Add egg and vanilla; mix well. Add mixture of flour, soda and salt alternately with milk, mixing well after each addition. Stir in chocolate chips, oats and nuts. Drop by teaspoonfuls onto lightly greased cookie sheet. Bake at 375 degrees for 10 to 12 minutes. Cool on wire rack.

Yield: 4 dozen.

Mincemeat Chiffon Pie

1⅓   **cups graham cracker crumbs**
2   **tablespoons sugar**
¼   **cup melted butter**
¼   **cup sugar**
1   **envelope unflavored gelatin**
⅛   **teaspoon salt**
2   **eggs, separated**
1   **cup milk**
¼   **cup sugar**
1   **cup whipping cream**
1   **cup mincemeat**
2   **tablespoons grated orange rind**

Combine graham cracker crumbs and 2 tablespoons sugar in bowl; mix well. Stir in butter. Press over bottom and side of buttered 9-inch pie plate. Bake at 350 degrees for 5 minutes. Cool on wire rack. Combine ¼ cup sugar, gelatin and salt in saucepan. Beat egg yolks with milk in bowl. Stir into gelatin mixture. Let stand to soften gelatin. Cook over low heat until gelatin is dissolved, stirring constantly. Chill until thick. Beat egg whites in bowl until soft peaks form. Add ¼ cup sugar gradually, beating until stiff. Fold into gelatin mixture. Fold in stiffly whipped cream, mincemeat and grated orange rind. Spoon into cooled crust. Chill until set.

Yield: 6 to 8 servings.

Mystery Pecan Pie

Patricia Doyle, Maryland

1   **cup flour**
½   **teaspoon salt**
⅓   **cup shortening**
8   **ounces cream cheese, softened**
⅓   **cup sugar**
1   **egg**
1   **teaspoon vanilla extract**
¼   **teaspoon salt**
1¼   **cups chopped pecans ***
3   **eggs**
¼   **cup sugar**
1   **cup light corn syrup**
1   **teaspoon vanilla extract**
    * Seasonal

Combine flour and ½ teaspoon salt in bowl. Cut in shortening until crumbly. Add 3 to 4 tablespoons cold water gradually, mixing just until moistened. Roll dough on floured surface. Fit into 9-inch pie plate. Beat cream cheese, ⅓ cup sugar, 1 egg, 1 teaspoon vanilla and ¼ teaspoon salt in bowl until creamy. Spread in prepared pie plate. Sprinkle pecans over top. Combine 3 eggs, ¼ cup sugar, corn syrup and 1 teaspoon vanilla in bowl; beat until well blended. Pour over pecans. Bake at 375 degrees for 35 minutes or until center is firm. Cool on wire rack.

Yield: 6 to 8 servings.

Sweet Potato Pie

Ruth G. White, Maryland

Combine eggs, allspice, butter, cream cheese, sugar and vanilla in bowl; mix well. Mix cornstarch and ¼ cup cold water. Stir cornstarch mixture into egg mixture. Add sweet potato and nuts; mix well. Pour into pie shell. Bake at 425 degrees for 10 minutes. Reduce temperature to 325 degrees. Bake for 35 to 45 minutes longer.
Yield: 6 to 8 servings.

Note: May substitute 1 cup flaked coconut for nuts.

2	eggs, beaten
2	teaspoons allspice
1½	sticks butter, melted
6	ounces cream cheese, softened
2	cups sugar
1	teaspoon vanilla extract
1	tablespoon cornstarch
1½	cups mashed cooked sweet potato *
1	cup chopped nuts *
1	unbaked 9-inch pie shell
	* Seasonal

Yogurt-Cranberry Pie

Anita M. Wilson, Ohio

Dissolve gelatin in ¾ cup boiling water in medium bowl. Stir in yogurt and cranberry sauce. Chill for 45 to 60 minutes or until mixture mounds when dropped from spoon, stirring occasionally. Fold in whipped topping. Pour into pie shells. Chill for 4 hours or longer.
Yield: 2 pies.

1	6-ounce package orange gelatin
2	cups vanilla yogurt
2	cups whole cranberry sauce *
2	cups whipped topping
2	butter-flavored crumb pie shells
	* Seasonal

Mulled Cranberry Cup

Lucia Scoville, North Dakota

Combine juices, spices, salt and sugar in saucepan. Bring to the boiling point. Pour into mugs.
Yield: 4 servings.

4	cups cranberry juice *
⅔	cup unsweetened grapefruit juice
½	teaspoon each cloves, cinnamon
¼	teaspoon each allspice, salt
	Sugar to taste
	* Seasonal

Hot Buttered Rum Mix

Joyce New, Washington

Blend ice cream and butter in bowl. Add sugars; blend well. Stir in spices. Store in freezer in airtight container. ** Place 2 tablespoons mixture in mug. Add boiling water; mix well. Add rum if desired.
Yield: 30 servings.

** *Make ahead to this point.*

1	quart vanilla ice cream, softened
3	sticks butter, softened
1	pound brown sugar
1	pound confectioners' sugar
1½	teaspoons cinnamon
½	teaspoon each nutmeg, cloves
	Rum to taste

December

Blender Pâté

Doris Wolverton, Maryland

12	**ounces boned chicken**
1	**medium onion, chopped**
2	**tablespoons bread crumbs**
1	**tablespoon flour**
1	**egg**
¼	**cup melted margarine**
½	**cup evaporated skim milk**
	Parsley sprigs

Combine all ingredients in blender container. Process for 1 minute or until smooth. Pour into buttered ring mold; cover with foil. Place in baking pan with ½-inch hot water. Bake at 375 degrees for 45 minutes or until pâté pulls from side of mold. Unmold onto serving plate. Garnish with parsley sprigs. Serve warm pâté with crackers.

Yield: 10 to 20 servings.

Fruited Cranberry Relish

Faye Rice, California

4	**large oranges ***
1	**lemon ***
6	**large apples ***
8	**cups fresh cranberries ***
2	**cups sugar**
	* Seasonal

Cut unpeeled oranges, lemons and apples into wedges; discard seed and core. Put all fruit through food grinder. Add sugar; mix well. Chill, covered, for 2 days to several weeks. Serve as holiday relish.

Yield: 10 cups.

Quick Lobster Bisque

Faye Jones, Connecticut

Blend soups in saucepan. Stir in cream and milk gradually. Add seasonings. Cook over low heat for 10 minutes, stirring frequently. Add lobster. Heat to serving temperature. Stir in Sherry. Ladle into soup bowls. Sprinkle with chives. Yield: 6 servings.

1	*can cream of mushroom soup*
1	*can cream of asparagus soup*
1	*cup cream*
1½	*cups milk*
¼	*teaspoon seafood seasoning*
	Salt and pepper to taste
2	*cups chopped cooked lobster* *
½	*cup Sherry*
¼	*cup chopped chives*
	* Seasonal

Shrimp and Corn Chowder

Don Buckalew, Texas

Sauté green onions, garlic and cayenne pepper in butter in skillet until onion is tender. Add soup, cream cheese and milk. Cook until blended, stirring frequently. Stir in shrimp and corn. Bring to a boil; reduce heat. Simmer, covered, for 10 minutes or until shrimp turn pink, stirring occasionally. Ladle into soup bowls. Yield: 6 servings.

½	*cup chopped green onions*
1	*clove of garlic, minced*
⅛	*teaspoon cayenne pepper*
1	*tablespoon butter*
2	*cans cream of potato soup*
3	*ounces cream cheese, softened*
1½	*soup cans milk*
2	*cups peeled shrimp* *
1	*cup whole kernel corn*
	* Seasonal

Spiced Cranberry Ring

Linda Alpern, Maryland

Dissolve gelatin, salt and spices in 2 cups boiling water in bowl. Add cranberry sauce and orange rind; mix well. Chill until partially set. Fold in chopped orange and apple. Pour into 6-cup mold. Chill until firm. ** Unmold onto serving plate. Garnish as desired. Yield: 12 servings.

** *Make ahead to this point.*

6	*ounces raspberry gelatin*
¼	*teaspoon each salt, cinnamon*
	Pinch of cloves
2	*cups whole cranberry sauce*
2	*tablespoons grated orange rind*
1	*cup chopped orange sections* *
1	*cup chopped apples* *
	* Seasonal

Pear and Grape Salad

Cut pears vertically into halves; remove cores. Place cut side down on lettuce-lined salad plates. Blend cream cheese and French dressing in bowl. Spread over pears. Press grapes cut side down into cream cheese to resemble grape clusters. Chill until serving time. Yield: 8 servings.

4	*ripe pears, peeled* *
	Crisp lettuce leaves
8	*ounces cream cheese, softened*
2	*tablespoons French dressing*
4	*cups black seedless grape halves*
	* Seasonal

Microwave Hot Bean Salad

Joyce Horvath, Ohio

6	*slices bacon*
	Vinegar
1	*tablespoon cornstarch*
¼	*cup sugar*
1	*16-ounce can wax beans*
1	*16-ounce can green beans*
1	*16-ounce can kidney beans*
1	*medium onion, sliced into rings*

Microwave bacon in glass baking dish on High for 5 minutes or until crisp. Drain and crumble bacon, reserving drippings. Add enough vinegar to drippings to measure ½ cup. Blend with cornstarch and sugar in 2-quart glass baking dish. Microwave on High for 3 minutes or until thickened, stirring twice. Drain beans well. Stir in drained beans and onion. Sprinkle bacon over top. Microwave on High for 4 to 5 minutes or until heated through.

Yield: 8 to 10 servings.

Cauliflower Delight

Sharon Johnson, Texas

1	*head cauliflower* *
2	*stalks celery, chopped*
1	*green pepper, chopped*
1	*2-ounce jar pimento*
¾	*cup sliced stuffed olives*
8	*ounces Cheddar cheese, cubed*
8	*ounces Caesar salad dressing*
1	*cup sour cream*
3	*tablespoons olive juice*
	* Seasonal

Cut cauliflower into flowerets. Combine cauliflower, celery, green pepper, drained pimento, olives and cheese in serving bowl. Blend salad dressing, sour cream and olive juice in bowl. Pour over cauliflower mixture; mix well. Chill for several hours to overnight.

Yield: 8 to 10 servings.

Fruited Ham Salad

Katherine Wilson, Tennessee

⅔	*cup sugar*
1	*teaspoon paprika*
1	*teaspoon mustard*
1	*teaspoon celery seed*
½	*cup vinegar*
1	*tablespoon lemon juice*
⅓	*cup honey* *
1	*cup oil*
3	*mandarin oranges* *
2	*grapefruit* *
2	*cups fresh pineapple chunks* *
2	*cans chunk-style ham*
1	*cup chopped celery*
	Crisp lettuce cups
	* Seasonal

Combine sugar, paprika, mustard, celery seed, vinegar, lemon juice, honey and oil in blender container. Process until smooth. Separate oranges and grapefruit into sections. Combine oranges, grapefruit, pineapple chunks, ham and celery in bowl. Add enough dressing to moisten. Chill for several hours if desired. ** Spoon into lettuce cups. Serve with remaining dressing.

Yield: 4 servings.

** *Make ahead to this point.*

Apricot Waldorf Salad in Croissants
Catherine Bates, California

Drain and chop apricots, reserving 2 tablespoons syrup. Sprinkle apple with lemon juice. Combine apple, apricots, chicken, celery and pecans in bowl. Sprinkle with salt. Blend cream cheese with reserved apricot syrup. Add to apricot mixture; mix well. Chill, covered, until serving time. ** Place spinach leaves on bottom halves of croissants; spread with apricot mixture. Cover with croissant tops.
Yield: 4 servings.

** *Make ahead to this point.*

1 **8-ounce can apricot halves**
1 **small apple, chopped ***
1 **tablespoon lemon juice ***
1 **cup chopped cooked chicken ***
¼ **cup chopped celery**
¼ **cup chopped pecans ***
⅛ **teaspoon salt**
3 **ounces cream cheese, softened**
4 **croissants, split**
  Spinach leaves
  * Seasonal

Spicy Rib Eye Roast

Trim excess fat from roast; pat with mixture of pepper and cardamom. Marinate in mixture of next 5 ingredients in refrigerator overnight; turn occasionally. ** Drain roast; discard marinade. Place on foil in shallow baking pan; insert meat thermometer. Seal foil tightly. **Be sure foil does not touch thermometer.** Bake at 325 degrees for 2 hours or to 140 degrees on meat thermometer for rare or 160 degrees for medium. Remove to serving platter. Garnish with spiced crab apples and parsley.
Yield: 12 servings.

** *Make ahead to this point.*

1 **6-pound boneless rib eye roast**
⅓ **cup cracked pepper**
½ **teaspoon cardamom**
1 **cup reduced-sodium soy sauce**
¾ **cup red wine vinegar**
1 **tablespoon tomato paste**
1 **teaspoon paprika**
½ **teaspoon garlic powder**
  Spiced crab apples
  Parsley

Crêpes Ensenada
Ginny Wilfahrt, California

Cut Monterey Jack cheese into ½-inch strips. Cut chilies into ¼-inch strips. Place 1 slice ham, 1 strip cheese and 1 strip chili on each tortilla; roll to enclose filling. Place in greased 9x13-inch baking dish. Blend butter and flour in saucepan. Stir in milk gradually. Cook until thickened, stirring constantly. Add Cheddar cheese and mustard. Cook until cheese melts. Pour over tortillas. Sprinkle with paprika. Chill for several hours if desired. ** Bake at 350 degrees for 45 minutes or until bubbly.
Yield: 6 to 12 servings.

** *Make ahead to this point.*

1 **pound Monterey Jack cheese**
1 **4-ounce can whole green chilies**
12 **thin slices ham**
12 **flour tortillas**
2 **sticks butter, melted**
½ **cup flour**
4 **cups milk**
3 **cups grated Cheddar cheese**
1 **teaspoon dry mustard**
  Paprika to taste

Christmas Morning Sausage Ring

Mrs. Arnold Johnson, Kansas

2	*pounds sausage*
1½	*cups cracker crumbs*
2	*eggs, slightly beaten*
½	*cup milk*
¼	*cup minced onion*
1	*cup finely chopped apple* *
	* Seasonal

Combine all ingredients in bowl; mix well. Pack lightly into greased 6-cup ring mold. Chill for several hours. ** Unmold onto baking sheet. Bake at 325 degrees for 1 hour. Remove to serving plate. Spoon scrambled eggs into center of sausage ring. Yield: 8 servings.

** Make ahead to this point.

Orange-Herbed Chicken Breasts

M.A. Sparks, Maryland

4	*chicken breasts, skinned*
½	*cup yogurt*
1	*tablespoon mayonnaise*
¼	*cup flour*
2	*to 4 tablespoons oil*
1	*onion, sliced*
	Juice of 1 orange *
	Grated rind of ½ orange
½	*teaspoon tarragon*
¼	*teaspoon garlic powder*
2	*oranges, peeled, sliced* *
	* Seasonal

Dip chicken breasts in mixture of yogurt and mayonnaise; coat with flour. Brown lightly in a small amount of oil in skillet. Add onion, orange juice, orange rind, tarragon and garlic powder. Simmer, covered, for 30 minutes or until tender. Cut orange slices into halves. Add to skillet. Heat to serving temperature. Arrange chicken breasts on serving platter. Spoon orange sauce over top.
Yield: 4 servings.

Turkey Hash

Jean Vitelli, Maryland

1	*onion, chopped*
2	*tablespoons butter*
1	*cup sliced mushrooms*
1	*clove of garlic, minced*
4	*cups chopped cooked turkey* *
2	*to 3 cups leftover stuffing*
1	*cup heavy cream*
¼	*cup chopped parsley*
	Nutmeg to taste
3	*tablespoons shredded Swiss cheese*
	Cranberry sauce
	* Seasonal

Sauté onion in butter in skillet until tender. Add mushrooms and garlic. Sauté over medium heat for 3 minutes. Add turkey and stuffing. Cook for 5 minutes or until heated through, stirring frequently. Stir in cream, parsley and nutmeg. Cook for 4 minutes or until browned on bottom. Sprinkle with cheese. Broil until cheese browns. Serve with cranberry sauce.
Yield: 6 servings.

Smoked Duck
Clayton Hester, Texas

Wash duck; wipe dry inside and out. Place duck in foil baking pan. Pour Sherry over top. Marinate in refrigerator overnight. ** Chop apple, celery, onion and jalapeño pepper. Combine with sausage, seasonings and croutons in bowl. Rub duck with drippings. Stuff with sausage mixture. Place in smoker. Cook for 4 hours or longer, using manufacturer's instructions. Yield: 4 servings.

** *Make ahead to this point.*

Note: May bake at 350 degrees for 3 hours.

1	*mallard duck* *
	Sherry
½	*apple* *
1	*stalk celery*
1	*small onion*
1	*jalapeño pepper*
½	*cup sausage*
	Salt, pepper and garlic to taste
1	*cup croutons*
	Bacon drippings
	* Seasonal

Shellfish Paella
Kathleen Boulos, Maryland

Sauté onion and garlic in oil in saucepan until tender. Add rice and saffron. Sauté for 5 minutes. Stir in bay leaf and 2 cups broth. Simmer, covered, for 10 minutes. Stir in 1 cup broth and shrimp. Simmer, covered, for 5 minutes. Add clams, mussels and additional broth if necessary. Cook for 10 minutes or until shells open. **Discard unopened shells and bay leaf.** Add peas, pimento and seasonings. Heat to serving temperature. Ladle into bowls.
Yield: 6 servings.

1	*large onion, chopped*
2	*cloves of garlic, chopped*
¼	*cup oil*
1½	*cups rice*
⅛	*teaspoon saffron*
1	*bay leaf*
3	*cups (or more) chicken broth*
1	*pound shelled shrimp* *
18	*clams, scrubbed* *
18	*mussels, scrubbed* *
1	*cup peas*
2	*tablespoons chopped pimento*
	Salt and pepper to taste
	* Seasonal

Food Processor Cheese Soufflé
Ellen Jansson, Iowa

Combine eggs, cream, Parmesan cheese, mustard, salt and pepper in food processor container fitted with steel blade. Process until smooth. Add Cheddar cheese and cream cheese, processing constantly until smooth. Process for 5 seconds longer. Pour into buttered soufflé dish. Bake at 375 degrees until light brown and set.
Yield: 6 servings.

6	*eggs*
½	*cup heavy cream*
¼	*cup Parmesan cheese*
½	*teaspoon mustard*
½	*teaspoon salt*
¼	*teaspoon pepper*
2	*cups grated Cheddar cheese*
11	*ounces cream cheese, cubed*

Spinach-Artichoke Casserole

Marian Swain, Florida

1 **16-ounce can artichoke hearts**
8 **ounces cream cheese**
1 **stick butter**
2 **10-ounce packages frozen chopped spinach, thawed**
1 **cup bread crumbs**

Drain artichoke hearts; cut into quarters. Arrange in greased 9x9-inch baking dish. Melt cream cheese and butter in saucepan or microwave. Stir in well-drained spinach. Spread over artichokes. Chill in refrigerator for several hours if desired. ** Top with bread crumbs. Bake at 350 degrees for 20 minutes or until bubbly.
Yield: 4 to 6 servings.

** *Make ahead to this point.*

Tri-Color Vegetable Terrine

Joan Dew, Tennessee

½ **tablespoon unsalted butter**
1¼ **pounds carrots, peeled**
2 **medium onions, chopped**
1 **2-pound cauliflower ***
1 **egg**
2 **egg whites**
¼ **teaspoon salt**
⅛ **teaspoon nutmeg**
   Freshly ground pepper to taste
1 **egg**
1 **egg white**
3 **to 4 tablespoons freshly grated Romano cheese**
3 **tablespoons finely chopped shallots**
¼ **teaspoon salt**
2 **pounds fresh spinach, stemmed**
2 **cloves of garlic, chopped**
2 **tablespoons unsalted butter**
¼ **teaspoon salt**
1 **egg**
1 **egg white**
   * Seasonal

Butter 2-quart rectangular terrine mold with ½ tablespoon butter; place buttered waxed paper in bottom. Place in refrigerator. Slice carrots ¼ inch thick. Steam carrots and ⅓ of the onions for 16 minutes or until very tender. Cut cauliflower into large flowerets. Steam cauliflower covered with half the remaining onions for 20 minutes or until stems are tender; drain on paper towels. Process 1 egg and 2 egg whites in food processor for 30 seconds. Add steamed carrot mixture, ¼ teaspoon salt, nutmeg and pepper to taste. Process for 1 minute. Pour carefully into prepared mold, smoothing top. **Do not leave any carrot mixture on side of mold.** Process 1 egg and 1 egg white in food processor for 30 seconds. Add steamed cauliflower mixture, cheese, shallots, ¼ teaspoon salt and pepper. Process for 1 minute, scraping container side once. Spread evenly over carrot layer. **Do not leave any cauliflower mixture on side of mold.** Add enough hot water to large baking dish to come ⅔ up side of mold. Place in preheated 350-degree oven. Cook spinach in a very small amount of water in saucepan over high heat for 3 minutes or until just wilted. Drain and press out excess moisture. Sauté remaining onions and garlic in 2 tablespoons butter in heavy skillet for 3 minutes. Stir in spinach, ¼ teaspoon salt and pepper; remove from heat. Process 1 egg and 1 egg white in food processor for 30 seconds. Add spinach mixture. Process for 1 minute, scraping container side once. Press out excess moisture if necessary. Spread spinach mixture carefully over cauliflower layer. Cover with buttered waxed paper. Place in prepared waterbath. Bake for 1 hour and 10 minutes. Let stand at room temperature for 20 minutes. Loosen from side of mold with knife; unmold onto serving platter. Cool for 5 minutes. Slice carefully. Terrine is fragile.
Yield: 12 servings.

Pine Nut Rice

Mary R. Lawrence, Maryland

Cook rice according to package directions. Combine hot rice with onion, pine nuts, pimentos, olive oil and seasonings in serving bowl; mix well. Serve immediately.
Yield: 12 to 15 servings.

3	*cups rice*
2	*cups chopped onion*
2	*cups pine nuts **
6	*pimentos, chopped*
½	*teaspoon olive oil*
½	*teaspoon Tabasco sauce*
1½	*teaspoons paprika*
½	*teaspoon salt*
½	*teaspoon pepper*
	* Seasonal

Oyster Stuffing

Tony Matesic, Maryland

Combine bouillon cubes, poultry seasoning and 2 cups water in saucepan. Bring to a boil, stirring until bouillon dissolves; remove from heat. Sauté celery, onion and mushrooms in butter in saucepan. Add bouillon and remaining ingredients; mix well. Spoon into greased casserole. Chill in refrigerator for several hours if desired. ** Bake, covered, at 450 degrees for 1 hour. Bake, uncovered, for 15 minutes longer or until brown and crisp around edge.
Yield: 12 servings.

** *Make ahead to this point.*

3	*chicken bouillon cubes*
1	*teaspoon poultry seasoning*
2	*cups chopped celery*
1	*cup chopped onion*
1	*cup sliced mushrooms*
¼	*cup butter*
11	*ounces croutons*
9	*slices rye bread, diced, dried*
1	*pound celery sausage*
2	*eggs*
1	*teaspoon caraway seed*
¼	*teaspoon each salt and pepper*
2	*pints small oysters **
	* Seasonal

Easy Yogurt Coffee Cake

Colleen Slaughter, Nevada

Combine cake mix, egg, pecans and yogurt in bowl; mix well with wooden spoon. Pour into greased and floured 8-inch square cake pan. Sprinkle mixture of sugar and cinnamon over batter. Bake at 350 degrees for 25 minutes. Cool. Cut into squares. Yield: 8 servings.

1	*1-layer package yellow cake mix*
1	*egg*
½	*cup chopped pecans **
1	*carton fruit-flavored yogurt*
3	*tablespoons sugar*
½	*teaspoon cinnamon*
	* Seasonal

Tangelo Muffins
Janet Chamberlain, California

1	*large tangelo* *
1	*cup raisins* *
2	*small carrots, chopped*
2	*eggs*
1	*cup milk*
¼	*cup oil*
4	*cups buttermilk baking mix*
1½	*cups sugar*
¼	*cup wheat germ*
⅓	*cup flour*
½	*cup sugar*
1½	*teaspoons cinnamon*
¼	*cup butter*
½	*cup chopped nuts* *
	* Seasonal

Chop unpeeled tangelo; discard core. Place in blender container. Process for several seconds. Add raisins, carrots, eggs, milk and oil. Process until well mixed but not smooth. Combine baking mix, 1½ cups sugar, wheat germ and tangelo mixture in bowl; stir just until moistened. Fill greased muffin cups ⅔ full. Combine flour, ½ cup sugar and cinnamon in small bowl. Cut in butter until crumbly. Add nuts; mix well. Sprinkle over muffins. Bake at 400 degrees for 15 minutes or until light brown.
Yield: 2 to 2½ dozen.

Sweet Potato Biscuits
Reta Hamilton, Texas

2½	*cups flour*
½	*teaspoon soda*
1	*tablespoon baking powder*
1	*cup sugar*
6	*tablespoons shortening*
1	*cup buttermilk*
2	*cups mashed cooked sweet potatoes* *
	* Seasonal

Mix flour, soda, baking powder and sugar in bowl. Cut in shortening until crumbly. Add buttermilk and sweet potatoes; mix well. Knead on lightly floured surface. Roll ½ inch thick; cut with biscuit cutter. Place on greased baking sheet. Bake at 425 degrees for 20 minutes or until brown.
Yield: 2 dozen.

Whole Wheat-Yogurt Dinner Rolls
Sherri Mitchell, Indiana

4	*cups sifted all-purpose flour*
2	*cups whole wheat flour*
2	*packages or 2 tablespoons dry yeast*
½	*cup sugar*
¾	*cup milk, scalded*
2	*eggs, beaten*
2	*teaspoons salt*
½	*cup yogurt*
¾	*cup melted butter*

Mix all-purpose flour and whole wheat flour in bowl. Dissolve yeast and sugar in ½ cup 110 to 115-degree water in large bowl. Add half the flour mixture, milk, eggs, salt and yogurt; mix well. Add butter and remaining flour. **Do not knead.** Chill, covered, for 4 hours to overnight. ** Roll into 3 circles on floured surface. Cut each into 16 wedges. Roll from wide end; shape into crescents. Place on greased baking sheet. Let rise for 3 hours or until doubled in bulk. Bake at 400 degrees for 15 minutes.
Yield: 4 dozen.

*** Make ahead to this point.*

Holiday Bread
Mary Smith, Ohio

Cream sugar and shortening in bowl until light and fluffy. Add eggs and bananas; mix well. Add mixture of flour, salt and soda; mix well. Stir in pecans, chocolate chips and cherries. Pour into greased and floured loaf pan. Bake at 350 degrees for 1 hour or until loaf tests done. Cool in pan for 10 minutes. Remove to wire rack to cool completely.
Yield: 12 servings.

1	cup sugar
½	cup shortening
2	eggs, beaten
3	bananas, mashed
2	cups flour
⅛	teaspoon salt
1	teaspoon soda
¼	cup chopped pecans
¼	cup chocolate chips
½	cup chopped maraschino cherries

Carolers' Stollen
Jackie Carlisle, Texas

Dissolve yeast in ½ cup lukewarm water in large bowl. Stir in lukewarm milk. Sift in 6 cups flour and salt; mix well. Let rise, covered, in warm place until doubled in bulk. Add 1½ cups butter, sugar, lemon rind, egg yolks and Brandy; mix well. Add 4 cups flour gradually, mixing until mixture forms ball. Add fruits and pecans gradually. Knead on floured surface for 3 to 5 minutes or until smooth and elastic. Divide into 5 portions. Shape each into loaf; place in greased loaf pan. Make 2 or 3 lengthwise slashes in each loaf. Let rise until doubled in bulk. Bake at 350 degrees for 1 hour or until golden brown. Remove from pans. Cool on wire rack for 10 minutes. Drizzle ¼ cup butter over each loaf. Sprinkle with confectioners' sugar. Cool completely. Store, wrapped in plastic wrap, in cool place.
Yield: 5 loaves.

2	packages or 2 tablespoons dry yeast
3½	cups milk, scalded
6	cups flour
1	teaspoon salt
1½	cups butter, melted
1½	cups sugar
2	teaspoons grated lemon rind
5	egg yolks
¼	cup Brandy
4	cups flour
1	pound raisins *
1	pound mixed candied fruit
8	ounces candied cherries
1	pound pecans, chopped *
1¼	cups melted butter
½	cup confectioners' sugar
	* Seasonal

Microwave Sweet Potato Pudding
Jane Gabel, Texas

Peel and grate sweet potatoes. Combine with eggs, sugar, corn syrup and butter in bowl. Stir in orange rind and salt. Spoon into glass baking dish. Microwave on High for 30 minutes, stirring every 10 minutes. Let stand until set.
Yield: 6 servings.

Serving suggestion: Serve as vegetable or with whipped cream as dessert if desired.

2	pounds sweet potatoes *
3	eggs, beaten
½	cup sugar
1	cup dark corn syrup
½	cup butter, softened
2	tablespoons grated orange rind
1	teaspoon salt
	* Seasonal

Pumpkin Crumble

Sharon Rocha, California

3½ cups pumpkin purée *
1 large can evaporated milk
1 cup sugar
3 eggs
4 teaspoons pumpkin pie spice
1 2-layer package yellow cake mix
¾ cup melted butter
½ cup chopped pecans *
    * Seasonal

Combine pumpkin, evaporated milk, sugar, eggs and spice in bowl; mix well. Pour into buttered 9x13-inch baking dish. Layer cake mix, butter and pecans on top. Bake at 350 degrees for 1 hour or until set. Spoon into dessert dishes. Serve warm or cool with whipped cream.
Yield: 12 servings.

Friendship Fruit

Ruth Heinaman, Florida

1½ cups canned sliced peaches
1½ cups canned pineapple
1½ cups fruit cocktail
1 package or 1 tablespoon dry yeast
3 cups sugar

Combine all ingredients in glass container; mix well. Let stand, loosely covered, for 3 weeks, stirring daily. Serve over pound cake or ice cream or use in one of the following cakes. Replenish by adding additional 1 cup sugar and 1½ cups fruit every 2 weeks. Let stand for 3 days before using.
Yield: 16 servings.

Friendship Butter Cake

1 2-layer package golden butter cake mix
1½ cups Friendship Fruit
⅔ cup oil
4 eggs, beaten
1 cup chopped nuts

Combine all ingredients in bowl; mix well. Pour into greased and floured bundt pan. Bake at 350 degrees for 1 hour or until cake tests done. Cool in pan on wire rack for 10 minutes. Invert onto serving plate to cool completely.
Yield: 16 servings.

Friendship Orange Cake

1 2-layer package orange cake mix
1½ cups Friendship Fruit
¼ cup oil
4 eggs
1¾ cups confectioners' sugar
¼ cup lemon juice

Combine cake mix, Friendship Fruit, oil and eggs in bowl; mix well. Pour into greased and floured bundt pan. Bake at 325 degrees for 45 minutes. Blend confectioners' sugar and lemon juice in small bowl. Drizzle half the mixture over hot cake in pan. Cool for 10 minutes. Invert onto serving plate. Drizzle remaining glaze over cake.
Yield: 16 servings.

Friendship Bundt Cake

1 2-layer package white cake mix
1 small package vanilla instant pudding mix
4 eggs
⅔ cup oil
1 cup drained Friendship Fruit
1 cup chopped nuts

Combine cake mix and pudding mix in bowl; mix well. Add eggs, oil and 1 cup water; mix well. Stir in Friendship Fruit and nuts. Pour into greased and floured bundt pan. Bake at 350 degrees for 50 minutes or until cake tests done. Cool in pan for 10 minutes. Invert onto serving plate. Frost or glaze if desired. Yield: 16 servings.

Chocolate Fruitcakes

Linda Sue James, Missouri

Cream butter and sugar in mixer bowl until light and fluffy. Add potatoes and eggs; mix well. Add mixture of dry ingredients alternately with sour milk, mixing well after each addition. Stir in fruit and nuts. Pour into 2 greased and floured 5x9-inch loaf pans. Bake at 325 degrees for 1 hour or until cakes test done. Cool in pans for 10 minutes. Remove to wire rack to cool completely. Store, wrapped in foil, for several days before serving.

Yield: 2 fruitcakes.

1	cup butter, softened
2	cups sugar
2	cups mashed potatoes
4	eggs
2	cups flour
½	cup cocoa
1½	teaspoons cinnamon
1	teaspoon each nutmeg, salt
¼	teaspoon cloves
2	teaspoons soda
¾	cup sour milk
1	cup mixed candied fruit
2	cups raisins *
1	cup chopped nuts *
	* Seasonal

Peppery Spice Cake

Kristy Cartwright, Indiana

Cream shortening, cloves, cinnamon, pepper, vanilla and soda in large bowl. Add sugar and brown sugar gradually; mix well. Beat in eggs 1 at a time. Sift flour, baking powder and salt together. Add flour mixture to creamed mixture alternately with buttermilk, mixing well after each addition. Pour into 3 greased and floured 9-inch round cake pans. Bake at 375 degrees for 25 minutes or until cake tests done. Cool in pans for 10 minutes. Remove to wire rack to cool completely. Frost as desired.

Yield: 12 to 16 servings.

¾	cup shortening
½	teaspoon cloves
1½	teaspoons cinnamon
½	teaspoon pepper
1½	teaspoons vanilla extract
¾	teaspoon soda
1	cup sugar
¾	cup packed light brown sugar
3	eggs
2½	cups sifted cake flour
1	teaspoon baking powder
1	teaspoon salt
1	cup buttermilk

Yogurt Fudge Cake

Kelly Bouldin, New Mexico

Mix flour, sugar, soda and baking powder in bowl. Melt chocolate in double boiler over hot water. Add mixture of butter, yogurt, vanilla and eggs; blend well. Add to dry ingredients; stir until well mixed. Stir in chocolate chips. Pour into greased and floured tube pan. Bake at 350 degrees for 45 to 50 minutes or until cake tests done. Cool in pan for 30 minutes. Invert onto cake plate. Cool completely. Frost with favorite fudge frosting or garnish with light sifting of confectioners' sugar.

Yield: 16 servings.

2	cups flour
1	cup sugar
1	teaspoon soda
1	teaspoon baking powder
3	squares semisweet chocolate
¼	cup butter, softened
1½	cups yogurt
1	teaspoon vanilla extract
2	eggs, beaten
1	cup chocolate chips

Christmas Candy
Mrs. John C. Martin, Alabama

3	cups sugar
1	cup light corn syrup
1½	cups light cream
1	teaspoon vanilla extract
8	ounces black walnuts *
8	ounces almonds *
8	ounces pecans *
8	ounces candied pineapple
8	ounces candied cherries
	* Seasonal

Combine sugar, corn syrup and cream in saucepan. Bring to a boil, stirring constantly. Boil for 8 minutes or to 235 degrees on candy thermometer, soft-ball stage, stirring constantly. Remove from heat; stir in vanilla. Beat until mixture thickens and becomes lighter in color. Stir in nuts and fruits. Spread in buttered 10x15-inch pan. Let stand until completely cool. Cut into squares. Let ripen in airtight container for 2 weeks before serving. Yield: 3 pounds.

Chocolate-Cherry Drops
Photograph for this recipe on Cover.

1¼	cups butter, softened
2	cups sugar
2	eggs
2	teaspoons vanilla extract
2½	cups flour
¾	cup cocoa
1	teaspoon each soda, salt
2	cups chopped drained maraschino cherries
1	cup chopped nuts *
72	maraschino cherry halves
	* Seasonal

Cream butter and sugar in mixer bowl until light and fluffy. Add eggs and vanilla; beat until smooth. Add mixture of flour, cocoa, soda and salt; mix well. Stir in chopped cherries and nuts. Chill in refrigerator for 30 minutes. Drop by teaspoonfuls onto ungreased cookie sheet. Top with cherry halves. Bake at 350 degrees for 10 minutes or until crisp around edge. Cool on wire rack.
Yield: 6 dozen.

Chocolate Nutters
Photograph for this recipe on Cover.

1	cup butter, softened
1	cup confectioners' sugar
¼	cup cocoa
1¾	cups flour
6	ounces cream cheese, softened
1	cup confectioners' sugar
2	tablespoons cocoa
1	egg, separated
1	teaspoon vanilla extract
1	cup chopped pecans *
36	candied cherry halves
	* Seasonal

Cream butter and 1 cup confectioners' sugar in large mixer bowl until light and fluffy. Mix in ¼ cup cocoa. Beat in flour gradually. Chill for 30 minutes. Beat cream cheese in small mixer bowl. Add 1 cup confectioners' sugar, 2 tablespoons cocoa, egg yolk and vanilla; beat until smooth. Shape dough into 1-inch balls. Dip into lightly beaten egg white; roll in chopped pecans. Place 1 inch apart on ungreased cookie sheet. Make indentation in center of each with thumb. Fill each with 1 teaspoonful cream cheese mixture. Bake at 350 degrees for 12 minutes or until filling is set. Cool on cookie sheet for 2 minutes. Top each with cherry half. Remove to wire rack to cool completely. Store in refrigerator.
Yield: 3 dozen.

Chocolate Spritz Cookies

Photograph for this recipe on Cover.

Cream butter, sugar, egg and vanilla in large mixer bowl until light and fluffy. Add mixture of flour, cocoa and salt gradually; mix well. Press through cookie press onto **cool** ungreased cookie sheet. Bake at 350 degrees for 5 minutes or until set. Remove to wire rack. Cool completely.
Yield: 4½ dozen. ⛴ ✳

Note: When using the same cookie sheet for successive batches, be sure sheet is completely cool before pressing on additional dough.

1	*cup butter, softened*
⅔	*cup sugar*
1	*egg*
1	*teaspoon vanilla extract*
2¼	*cups flour*
⅓	*cup unsweetened cocoa*
½	*teaspoon salt*

Chocolate Toffee Bars

Photograph for this recipe on Cover.

Cream butter with sugar and brown sugar in mixer bowl until fluffy. Beat in egg yolk and vanilla. Add flour; mix well. Pat into 9x13-inch baking pan. Brush with lightly beaten egg white. Bake at 350 degrees for 25 minutes or until light brown. Cool for 5 minutes. Sprinkle with chocolate chips. Let stand until melted; spread to cover top. Sprinkle with nuts; press lightly into chocolate. Chill until set. Cut into bars.
Yield: 3 dozen. ✓4 ⛴

1	*cup butter, softened*
½	*cup sugar*
½	*cup packed brown sugar*
1	*egg, separated*
1	*teaspoon vanilla extract*
2	*cups flour*
1½	*cups semisweet miniature chocolate chips*
¾	*cup nuts **
	* Seasonal

Macaroon Kisses

Photograph for this recipe on Cover.

Cream butter, cream cheese and sugar in bowl until light and fluffy. Add egg yolk, almond extract and orange juice; mix well. Add mixture of flour, baking powder and salt gradually; mix well. Stir in 3 cups coconut. Chill, covered, for 1 hour. Shape into balls; roll in remaining coconut. Place on ungreased cookie sheet. Bake at 350 degrees for 10 minutes or until light brown on bottom. Press chocolate kiss into center of each cookie. Cool for 1 minute. Remove cookies to wire rack to cool completely.
Yield: 4½ dozen. ⛴

⅓	*cup butter, softened*
3	*ounces cream cheese, softened*
¾	*cup sugar*
1	*egg yolk*
2	*teaspoons almond extract*
2	*teaspoons orange juice **
1¼	*cups flour*
2	*teaspoons baking powder*
¼	*teaspoon salt*
1	*14-ounce package flaked coconut*
1	*9-ounce package chocolate kisses*
	* Seasonal

Holiday Fruit Bars

Photograph for this recipe on Cover.

½	cup butter, softened
¾	cup packed brown sugar
1	egg
½	teaspoon vanilla extract
1¼	cups flour
½	teaspoon each soda, salt
2	tablespoons light brown sugar
2	tablespoons milk
1	tablespoon melted butter
1	egg
⅓	cup flour
½	teaspoon each soda, cinnamon
¼	teaspoon salt
¾	cup semisweet miniature chocolate chips
1	cup chopped mixed raisins and dried apricots *
½	cup chopped mixed candied red and green cherries
½	cup coarsely chopped nuts *
	* Seasonal

Cream ½ cup butter, ¾ cup brown sugar, 1 egg and vanilla in bowl. Add mixture of flour, ½ teaspoon soda and ½ teaspoon salt; mix well. Spread in lightly greased 9x13-inch baking pan. Bake at 350 degrees for 12 to 15 minutes or until light brown. Blend 2 tablespoons brown sugar, milk, melted butter and 1 egg in bowl. Add mixture of ⅓ cup flour, ½ teaspoon soda, ½ teaspoon cinnamon and ¼ teaspoon salt; mix well. Spread over baked layer. Top with mixture of chocolate chips, fruit and nuts. Bake for 15 minutes longer. Cool. Cut into bars.

Yield: 3 dozen.

Italian Fig Bars

Connie Zoria, California

3	pounds white Calimyrna figs *
3	pounds raisins *
1	pound each toasted almonds, walnuts *
1	small jar orange marmalade
2	cups honey *
1	cup sweet wine
1	tablespoon each allspice, cinnamon
1½	teaspoons nutmeg
9	cups flour
¼	cup baking powder
4	cups sugar
1	teaspoon salt
2	cups shortening
6	eggs, beaten
1	tablespoon vanilla extract
1	large can evaporated milk
1	pound confectioners' sugar
¼	cup butter, melted
3	tablespoons milk
2	teaspoons vanilla extract
	* Seasonal

Put figs, raisins and nuts through food grinder. Combine with marmalade, honey, wine and spices in bowl; mix well. Sift flour, baking powder, sugar and salt into bowl. Cut in shortening until crumbly. Add eggs, 1 tablespoon vanilla and evaporated milk; mix well. Divide into several portions. Roll each into strip on floured surface. Spread fig mixture down 1 side of strip. Fold dough over to enclose filling; seal edges. Place on ungreased baking sheet. Repeat with remaining dough and filling. Bake at 350 degrees for 10 minutes or until brown. Cool. Combine confectioners' sugar, butter, milk and 2 teaspoons vanilla in bowl; beat until smooth. Spread over cooled strips. Cut into bars.

Yield: 12 dozen.

Mini Chip Fruit and Nut Bars

Photograph for this recipe on Cover.

Cream butter and brown sugar in large mixer bowl until light and fluffy. Add egg and vanilla; blend well. Add mixture of flour, baking powder, salt and cinnamon; mix well. Stir in fruits, nuts and ½ cup chocolate chips. Spread in greased 9x13-inch baking pan. Bake at 375 degrees for 25 minutes or until light brown. Cool in pan. Dissolve sugar in 3 tablespoons water in small saucepan. Bring to a boil; remove from heat. Add 1 cup chocolate chips; stir until melted. Blend in marshmallow creme. Stir in 1 to 2 tablespoons hot water, 1 teaspoonful at a time, until glaze is of desired consistency. Spread over baked layer. Let stand until set. Cut into bars. Yield: 3 dozen.

½ cup butter, softened
1 cup packed light brown sugar
1 egg
1 teaspoon vanilla extract
1½ cups flour
½ teaspoon baking powder
½ teaspoon salt
¼ teaspoon cinnamon
½ cup golden raisins *
½ cup chopped dried apricots *
½ cup chopped prunes *
½ cup coarsely chopped pecans *
½ cup semisweet miniature chocolate chips
⅓ cup sugar
1 cup semisweet miniature chocolate chips
3 tablespoons marshmallow creme
* Seasonal

Mini Chip-Peanut Butter Foldovers

Photograph for this recipe on Cover.

Cream butter and cream cheese in mixer bowl until fluffy. Mix in flour. Divide into 2 portions. Chill, wrapped in plastic wrap, for several minutes. **Melt chocolate chips in double boiler over hot, not boiling water.** Blend inn peanut butter; remove from heat. Add confectioners' sugar and peanuts; mix well. Roll chilled dough into two 12½-inch squares on lightly floured surface. Cut each into twenty-five 2½-inch squares. Place 2 teaspoons filling in center of each square. Fold 2 corners to center to partially enclose filling; press corners to seal. Place ½ inch apart on ungreased cookie sheet. Bake at 350 degrees for 15 minutes or until light brown. Cool on wire rack. Yield: 4 dozen.

Note: May cut dough into 2½-inch circles, fill with 1 teaspoon chocolate mixture and fold over to form crescent, sealing edge with fork.

1 cup butter, softened
6 ounces cream cheese, softened
2½ cups flour
1 to 1½ cups miniature chocolate chips
¾ cup creamy peanut butter
½ cup confectioners' sugar
½ cup chopped unsalted peanuts

Apple-Cranberry Pie

Photograph for this recipe on page 176.

3	cups sliced peeled apples *
1½	cups cranberries *
¼	cup sugar
1	small package raspberry gelatin
1	small package vanilla pudding and pie filling mix
1	baked 9-inch pie shell
1	recipe pie pastry
	Whipped topping
	* Seasonal

Combine apples, cranberries, 1½ cups water and sugar in saucepan. Bring to a boil. Simmer for 5 minutes, stirring frequently. Add gelatin and pie filling; mix well. Bring to a boil, stirring constantly; remove from heat. Let stand for 5 minutes. Pour into pie shell. Chill for 4 hours or until set. Roll pastry thin on floured surface. Cut with cookie cutter. Place on baking sheet. Bake at 425 degrees for 8 minutes. Cool. Arrange on pie. Garnish with whipped topping. Yield: 6 to 8 servings.

Pumpkin-Ice Cream Pie

Blanche Keller, Ohio

¾	cup pumpkin *
¼	cup honey *
½	teaspoon cinnamon
¼	teaspoon each cloves, ginger
¼	teaspoon salt
1	quart vanilla ice cream
½	cup chopped pecans *
1	baked pie shell
1	cup whipped cream
12	pecan halves *
	* Seasonal

Combine pumpkin, honey, spices and salt in saucepan. Bring to a boil, stirring constantly. Cool. Beat softened ice cream in bowl until smooth. Add pecans and pumpkin mixture. Pour into pie shell. Freeze until firm. Garnish with whipped cream and pecan halves. Yield: 6 to 8 servings.

Raspberry-Orange Cream Cheese Pie

Photograph for this recipe on page 176.

8	ounces cream cheese, softened
⅓	cup sugar
1	cup sour cream
1	tablespoon grated orange rind
1	teaspoon vanilla extract
8	ounces whipped topping
1	baked 9-inch graham cracker pie shell
¼	cup raspberry jam, strained

Beat cream cheese until fluffy. Add sugar gradually, beating until light and fluffy. Fold in sour cream, orange rind and vanilla. Fold in whipped topping until blended. Spoon into pie shell. Chill for 4 hours. ** Arrange orange sections in circle on chilled filling. Spoon jam over oranges and center of pie. Yield: 6 to 8 servings.

** *Make ahead to this point.*

Swiss Bavarian Pie

Soften gelatin in 1 cup milk in medium saucepan. Add mixture of ⅔ cup sugar and cocoa. Bring to a boil over medium heat, stirring constantly; remove from heat. Add butter; stir until melted. Blend in ⅔ cup milk and ¾ teaspoon vanilla. Chill until thick, stirring occasionally. Whip ½ cup whipping cream in bowl until stiff peaks form. Fold gently into chilled mixture. Pour into pie shell. Chill until firm. ** Combine next 5 ingredients in bowl; beat until stiff. Decorate pie with spiced whipped cream. Garnish with chocolate curls. Yield: 6 to 8 servings.

*** Make ahead to this point.*

1	envelope unflavored gelatin
1	cup milk
⅔	cup sugar
⅓	cup cocoa
2	tablespoons butter
⅔	cup milk
¾	teaspoon vanilla extract
½	cup whipping cream
1	baked 9-inch pie shell
½	cup whipping cream
1	tablespoon sugar
¼	teaspoon vanilla extract
¼	teaspoon cinnamon
	Dash of nutmeg
	Bittersweet chocolate curls

Fruit Juicy Eggnog

Brian Jones, New Mexico

Beat eggs in mixer bowl until thick and lemon-colored. Add honey gradually, beating constantly; set aside. Combine apricot nectar, orange juice, lemon juice and dry milk powder in blender container. Process until smooth. Add strawberries. Process until smooth. Add egg mixture gradually, processing constantly. Pour into covered container. Chill until serving time. ** Mix well; pour into glasses. Garnish with mint leaf and lemon twist. Yield: 4 servings.

*** Make ahead to this point.*

2	eggs
2	tablespoons honey *
1	cup apricot nectar
⅔	cup orange juice *
1	tablespoon lemon juice
½	cup nonfat dry milk powder
1	cup frozen sweetened strawberries, partially thawed
	Mint leaves and lemon twists for garnish
	* Seasonal

Syllabub

Justine Jones, Maryland

Combine first 5 ingredients in bowl; stir until sugar is dissolved. Chill in refrigerator. ** Beat egg whites until foamy. Add ¼ cup sugar 1 tablespoon at a time, beating until stiff peaks form. Combine chilled cider mixture, milk and cream in bowl; beat until frothy. Pour into punch bowl. Drop meringue by spoonfuls on top. Sprinkle with nutmeg. Ladle into punch cups with meringue puff on each. Yield: 6 cups.

*** Make ahead to this point.*

3	cups apple cider *
¼	cup lemon juice *
3	tablespoons grated lemon rind
1	cup sugar
1	teaspoon light corn syrup
2	egg whites
¼	cup sugar
2	cups milk
1	cup light cream
	Nutmeg to taste
	* Seasonal

Calorie Chart

Almonds, shelled, ¼ cup . . . 213
Apples: 1 med 70
   chopped, ½ cup 30
Apple juice, 1 cup 117
Applesauce: sweet, ½ cup . . 115
   unsweetened, ½ cup 50
Apricots: fresh, 3 55
   canned, ½ cup 110
   dried, 10 halves 100
Apricot nectar, 1 cup 140
Asparagus: fresh, 6 spears . . . 19
   canned, ½ cup 18
Avocado, 1 med 265
Bacon, 2 sl. crisp-cooked . . 90
Banana, 1 med. 100
Beans: baked, ½ cup 160
   dry, ½ cup 350
   green, ½ cup 20
   lima, ½ cup 95
   soy, ½ cup 95
Bean sprouts, ½ cup 18
Beef, cooked, 3 oz:
   roast, rib 375
   roast, heel of round 165
   steak, sirloin 330
Beer, 12 oz. 150
Beets, cooked, ½ cup 40
Biscuit, from mix, 1 90
Bologna, all meat, 3 oz. . . . 235
Bread: roll, 1 85
   white, 1 slice 65
   whole wheat, 1 slice 55
Bread crumbs, dry, 1 cup . . . 390
Broccoli, cooked, ½ cup 20
Butter, 1 tbsp. 100
Buttermilk, 1 cup 90
Cabbage: cooked, ½ cup 15
   fresh, shredded, ½ cup . . . 10
Cake: angel food, 1/12 140
   devil's food, 1/12 195
   yellow, 1/12 200
Candy: caramel, 1 oz. 115
   chocolate, sweet, 1 oz. . . . 145
   hard candy, 1 oz. 110
   marshmallows, 1 oz. 90
Cantaloupe, ½ med 60
Carrots, cooked, ½ cup 23
   fresh, 1 med. 20
Catsup, 1 tbsp. 18
Cauliflower: cooked, ½ cup . . 13
   fresh, ½ lb. 60
Celery, chopped, ½ cup 8
Cereals: bran flakes, ½ cup . . 53
   cornflakes, ½ cup 50
   oatmeal, cooked, ½ cup . . . 65

Cheese: American, 1 oz. . . 105
   Cheddar, 1 oz. 113
   cottage: creamed, ½ cup . 130
     uncreamed, ½ cup 85
   cream, 1 oz. 107
   mozzarella, 1 oz. 80
   Parmesan, 1 oz. 110
   Velveeta, 1 oz. 84
Cherries:
   canned, sour, ½ cup 53
   fresh, sweet, ½ cup 40
Chicken, meat only, 4 oz. serving:
   broiled 155
   canned, boned 230
   roast, dark meat 210
   roast, light meat 207
Chilies: green, fresh, ½ lb. . . 62
   red, fresh, ½ lb. 108
Chili powder, 1 tbsp. 51
Chocolate, baking, 1 oz. . . . 143
Cocoa mix, 1-oz. package . . . 115
Cocoa powder, 1/3 cup 120
Coconut, shredded, ¼ cup . . 166
Coffee 0
Corn: cream-style, ½ cup . . . 100
   whole kernel, ½ cup 85
Corn bread, 1x4-inch piece . 125
Corn chips, 1 oz. 130
Cornmeal, ½ cup 264
Cornstarch, 1 tbsp. 29
Crab meat: fresh, 3 oz. 80
   canned, 3 oz. 85
Crackers: graham, 1 square . . 28
   Ritz, each 17
   saltine, 2-in. square 13
Cracker crumbs, ½ cup 281
Cranberries: fresh, ½ lb. . . . 100
   juice, cocktail, 1 cup 163
   sauce, ½ cup 190
Cream: half-and-half, 1 tbsp. . 20
   heavy, 1 tbsp. 55
   light, 1 tbsp. 30
Creamer, imitation dry, 1 tsp. . 10
Cucumber, 1 med. 30
Dates, chopped, ½ cup 244
Eggs: 1 whole, large 80
   1 white 17
   1 yolk 59
Eggplant, cooked, ½ cup 19
Fish sticks, 5 200
Flour:
   all-purpose: 1 cup 420
     1 tbsp. 28
   rye: 1 cup 286
   whole wheat, 1 cup 400

Fruit cocktail, canned, ½ cup . 98
Garlic, 1 clove 2
Gelatin, unflavored, 1 env. . . . 25
Grapes: fresh, ½ cup 35-50
   juice, 1 cup 170
Grapefruit: fresh, ½ med. . . . 60
   juice, unsweetened, 1 cup . 100
Ground beef, lean, 3 oz. . . . 185
   regular, 3 oz. 245
Haddock, fried, 3 oz. 140
Ham, 3 oz. servings:
   boiled 200
   country-style 335
   cured, lean 160
   fresh, roast 320
Honey, 1 tbsp. 65
Ice cream, ½ cup 135
Ice milk, ½ cup 96
Jams and preserves, 1 tbsp. . . 54
Jellies, 1 tbsp. 55
Jell-O, ½ cup 80
Lamb, leg roast, 3 oz. 185
   rib chop, 3 oz. 175
Lemonade, sweetened, 1 cup . 110
Lemon juice, 1 tbsp. 4
Lentils, cooked, ½ cup 168
Lettuce, 1 head 40
Liver, beef, fried, 2 oz. 130
   chicken, simmered, 2 oz. . . 88
Lobster, 2 oz. 55
Macaroni, cooked, ½ cup . . . 90
Mango, 1 fresh 134
Margarine, 1 tbsp. 100
Mayonnaise, 1 tbsp. 100
Milk: whole, 1 cup 160
   skim, 1 cup 89
   2-percent, 1 cup 145
   condensed, 1 cup 982
   evaporated, 1 cup 345
Muffin, plain 120
Mushrooms: canned, ½ cup . . 20
   fresh, 1 lb. 123
Mustard, brown, 1 tbsp. 13
   prepared, yellow, 1 tbsp. . . 10
Nectarine, 1 fresh 30
Noodles: egg, cooked, ½ cup . 100
   fried, chow mein, 2 oz. . . 275
Oil, cooking, salad, 1 tbsp. . . 120
Okra, cooked, 8 pods 25
Olives: green, 3 lg. 15
   ripe, 2 lg. 15
Onion: chopped, ½ cup 32
   dehydrated flakes, 1 tbsp. . 17
   green, 6 20
Orange: 1 whole 65

Peaches: fresh, 1 med. 35
   canned, ½ cup 100
   dried, ½ cup 210
Peanuts, roasted, 1 cup 420
Peanut butter, 1 tbsp. 100
Pears: fresh, 1 med. 100
   canned, ½ cup 97
   dried, ½ cup 214
Peas: black-eyed, ½ cup 70
   green, canned, ½ cup 83
   green, frozen, ½ cup 69
Pecans, chopped, ½ cup 400
Peppers: sweet green, 1 med. . 14
   sweet red, 1 med. 19
Perch, white, 4 oz. 50
Pickles: dill, 1 lg. 15
   sweet, 1 average 30
Pie, ⅙ serving:
   apple 420
   cherry 402
   custard 330
   pumpkin 321
Pimento, canned, 1 avg. 10
Pineapple: fresh, ½ cup 36
   canned, ½ cup 90
   juice, 1 cup 135
Plums: fresh, 1 med. 30
   canned, 3 101
Popcorn: plain, popped, 1 cup . 23
   with oil and salt 40
Pork, cooked, lean:
   Boston butt, roasted, 4 oz. . 280
   chop, broiled, 3.5 oz. 260
   loin, roasted, 4 oz. 290
Potato chips, 10 med. 114
Potatoes, white:
   baked, 1 sm. with skin 93
   boiled, 1 sm. 70
   French-fried, 10 pieces . . . 175
   hashed brown, ½ cup 177
   mashed, ½ cup 90
Potatoes, sweet:
   baked, 1 avg. 155
   candied, 1 avg. 295
   canned, ½ cup 110

Prune: 1 lg. 19
   dried, cooked, ½ cup 137
   juice, 1 cup 197
Puddings, pie fillings, prepared:
   banana, ½ cup 165
   butterscotch, ½ cup 190
   chocolate, ½ cup 190
   lemon, ½ cup 125
Puddings, instant, prepared:
   banana, ½ cup 175
   butterscotch, ½ cup 175
   chocolate, ½ cup 200
   lemon, ½ cup 180
Pumpkin, canned, ½ cup 38
Raisins, dried, ½ cup 231
Rice: cooked, white, ½ cup . . . 90
   cooked, brown, ½ cup . . . 100
   precooked, ½ cup 105
Salad dressings, commercial:
   blue cheese, 1 tbsp. 75
   French, 1 tbsp. 70
   Italian, 1 tbsp. 83
   mayonnaise, 1 tbsp. 100
   mayonnaise-type, 1 tbsp. . . 65
   Russian, 1 tbsp. 75
   Thousand Island, 1 tbsp. . . 80
Salami, cooked, 2 oz. 180
Salmon: canned, 4 oz. 180
   steak, 4 oz. 220
Sardines, canned, 3 oz. 75
Sauces: barbecue, 1 tbsp. . . . 17
   hot pepper, 1 tbsp. 3
   soy, 1 tbsp. 9
   Tartar 74
   white, med., ½ cup 215
   Worcestershire, 1 tbsp. 15
Sauerkraut, ½ cup 21
Sausage, cooked, 2 oz. 260
Sherbet, ½ cup 130
Shrimp: cooked, 3 oz. 50
   canned, 4 oz. 130
Soft drinks, 1 cup 100
Soup, 1 can, condensed:
   chicken with rice 116
   cream of celery 215

cream of chicken 235
cream of mushroom 331
tomato 220
vegetable-beef 198
Sour cream, ½ cup 240
Spaghetti, cooked, ½ cup 80
Spinach: fresh, ½ lb. 60
   cooked, ½ cup 20
Squash: summer, ½ cup 15
   winter, ½ cup 65
Strawberries, fresh, ½ cup . . . 23
Sugar: brown, ½ cup 410
   confectioners', ½ cup 240
   granulated: ½ cup 385
      1 tbsp. 48
Syrups: chocolate, 1 tbsp. . . . 50
   corn, 1 tbsp. 58
   maple, 1 tbsp. 50
Tomatoes: fresh, 1 med. 40
   canned, ½ cup 25
   juice, 1 cup 45
   paste, 6 oz. can 150
   sauce, 8 oz. can 34
Toppings: caramel, 1 tbsp. . . . 70
   chocolate fudge, 1 tbsp. . . . 65
   Cool Whip, 1 tbsp. 14
   Dream Whip, 1 tbsp. 8
   strawberry, 1 tbsp. 60
Tortilla, corn, 1 65
Tuna: canned in oil, 4 oz. . . . 230
   canned in water, 4 oz. . . . 144
Turkey: dark, roasted, 4 oz. . 230
   light, roasted, 4 oz. 200
Veal: cutlet, broiled, 3 oz. . . . 185
   roast, 3 oz. 230
Vegetable juice cocktail, 1 cup . 43
Vinegar, 1 tbsp. 2
Waffles, 1 130
Walnuts, chopped, ½ cup . . . 410
Water chestnuts, ½ cup 25
Watermelon, fresh, ½ cup . . . 26
Wheat germ, 1 tbsp. 29
Yogurt: plain, 1 cup 153
   plain, skim milk, 1 cup . . . 123
   with fruit, 1 cup 260

Index

ACCOMPANIMENTS
Apple Butter, Crock•Pot, 15
Chutney, Tomato-Apple, 119
Jam
    Blueberry Freezer, 81
    Pineapple-Zucchini, 146
    Strawberry-Honey Freezer, 65
Jelly
    Jalapeño, 167
    Mint, 66
    Paradise, 118
Marmalade, Mystery, 81
Pickles
    Okra, 134
    Peach, 119
Relish, Cranberry
    Fruited, 200
    Pear, 185
Sauces, see Sauces
APPETIZERS
Artichoke Puffs, 80
Beef Wellington, 184
Berry-Yogurt Grapefruit, 80
Blender Pâté, 200
Caviar Pie, 14
Cheese
    Curried Bites, 30
    Tarts, 184
Cornmeal-Cheddar Snaps, 64
Crab Mousse, 94
Curried Tidbits, 42
Dips
    Broccoli, Golden, 42
    Garlic-Cheese Vegetable, 118
    Ginger Fluffy, 94
    Tapenade, 65
    Tomato, Tangy, 65
May Poles, 81
Mexican Won Tons, 43
Mushroom Party Snacks, 14
Olive-Nut Bread with Parmesan
      Spread, 166
Oyster Roll, Smoked, 43
Pâté, Blender, 200
Spreads
    Cheese, Bengali, 64
    Parmesan, 166
    Salmon, 134
Vegetable Canapés, 146
BEEF
Burgundy for Two, 99
Chili, Baked, 33
Chowder, Smoky Beef, 15
Reuben Casserole, 46
Roasts
    Brisket, Marinated, 99
    Pot
        Irish, 46
        Taco, 32
    Rib Eye, Spicy, 203
    Tenderloin, Stuffed, 17
Salad, Broccoli and, 17

Steak
    Fingers, Oriental, 170
    Flank, Marinated, 122
    T-Bones, Marinated, 149
Stew
    Brunswick, Mama Cook's, 44
    Crock•Pot, 169
Stir-Fry
    Sukiyaki, 69
    and Vegetables, 137
BEVERAGES
Champagne, Mock, 29
Cold Quack, 41
Cranberry Cup, Mulled, 199
Eggnog, Fruit Juicy, 217
Mix
    Buttered Rum, Hot, 199
    Cocoa Mocha, 29
Piña Colada Flip, 57
Punch, Fruit Medley, 111
Steamer, Oktoberfest, 183
Strawberry-Lemon Spritzer, 79
Syllabub, 217
Brunswick Stew, Mama Cook's, 44
BREADS
Biscuits, Sweet Potato, 208
Coffee Cake
    Butterscotch Breakfast, 107
    Easy, 179
        Yogurt, 207
Corn Bread Olé, 130
French Toast, Peaches
      and Cream, 143
Herb-Buttered, 107
Loaves
    Quick
        Boston Brown, 196
        Breakfast, 178
        Fruit, Easy, 178
        Ham and Cheese, 76
        Holiday, 209
        Lemon Spice, 91
        Loquat, 52
        Mini Chip Cranberry-Nut, 38
        Onion, Baked Loaf, 26
        Squash, 131
    Yeast
        Cheddar, 154
        Cheesy Potato-Rye Ring, 55
        Mushroom, 39
        Sprouted Herb, 107
        Stollen, Carolers', 209
        Whole-Grain, 196
Muffins
    Applesauce, 39
    Apricot, Special, 179
    Blueberry Ice Cream, 130
    Midnight, 179
    Orange, Fresh, 91
    Peach Upside-Down, 144
    Peanut Butter-Bran, 26
    Pear-Bran, 108

    Pineapple Upside-Down, 52
    Sweet Potato, 195
    Tangelo, 208
Pancakes, Blueberry-Cheese, 143
Popovers, Cheese, 38
Rolls
    Butterscotch, Breakfast, 107
    Cinnamon, Easy Mix, 154
    Crescents, Cheesy Tomato, 131
    Mini Chip Swirl Buns, 39
    Multi-Grain, 55
    Onion-Poppy Seed, 55
    Quick Batter Mix, 27
    Whole Wheat-Yogurt, 208
Scones, Pineapple-Spice, 195
Sourdough with Garlic Spread, 143
Waffles
    Chocolate, 154
    Night-Before Yeast, 27
    Pecan, 77
CAKES
Apple, Citrus, 181
Butterscotch Carrot, 78
Cherry-Chocolate Chip, 110
Friendship, 210
Fruitcakes, Chocolate, 211
Fudge, Yogurt, 211
Gingerbread, Honey, 181
Grapefruit, Ruby Red, 28
Key Lime, 156
Maple Syrup, 28
Pear-Cheese, 56
Raspberry, Fresh, 133
Spice, Peppery, 211
Tangerine Sunshine, 197
CANDIES
Chocolate Crunchies, 77
Christmas, 212
Fudge, Gobblin', 182
CHICKEN
Barbecued, Mexicana, 149
in Blankets, 172
Breasts
    Italiano, 48
    Orange-Herbed, 204
    Stuffed with Crab Meat, 21
    in Yogurt-Mustard Sauce, 150
Broiled
    and Fruit, 48
    Lemon, 70
Buttermilk, 47
Curried, 188
Foil-Wrapped, 172
Fruited, 125
Honey-Glazed, 189
Kabobs, Marinated, 126
Lemon
    Broiled, 70
    Cold, 139
    Stir-Fried Sesame, 85
Lienz in Cornmeal Shell, 138
Nuggets, 73

Orange-Herbed Breasts, 204
Pâté, Blender, 200
Piccata, 100
Pizza, Upside-Down, 21
Rolls, Special, 85
Salad
    Garden-Style, 83
    and Rice, 16
    Zesty, 169
Stew, Calabasa, 126
Stir-Fried
    and Broccoli, 100
    Sesame-Lemon, 85
COOKIES
Almond Gingersnaps, 182
Apple
    Orange Squares, 41
    Spiced, 197
Bars
    Apple-Orange, 41
    Brownies
        Honey-Carob, 197
        Irish Cream, 57
        Saucepan, Quick, 29
    Chocolate
        Coconut, 156
        Toffee, 213
    Fig, Italian, 214
    Fruit
        Holiday, 214
        Mini Chip and Nut, 215
    Lemon-Glazed Persimmon, 182
Chocolate
    Cherry Drops, 212
    Nutters, 212
    Spritz, 213
Garden, 110
Macaroon Kisses, 213
Mini Chip Foldovers, 215
Oatmeal Chippers, 198
Shortbread, Pecan, 56
Tart Shells, 183
Cornish Game Hens with Wild Rice, 34
CROCK·POT
Apple Butter, 15
Beans, Mexican, 192
Beef, 169
Pizza Casserole, 18
Potatoes, au Gratin, 89
Turkey Gumbo, 35
DESSERTS
Cake, see Cakes
Candy, see Candies
Cheesecake, Fruited, 77
Cookies, see Cookies
Cranberry-Pear Crisp, 27
Crêpes, Cottage Cheese, 110
Fruit
    Compote, Layered, 159
    Cups
        Fiesta, 91
        Frozen, 108

with Dessert Cheese, 155
    Friendship, 210
    Southwestern Delight, 28
    Sparkling, 144
    Topping, 180
Halloween, Frozen, 180
Ice Cream
    Apricot-Grapefruit, 144
    Coconut-Strawberry Mold, 109
    Colada, Frozen Yogurt, 156
    Mango-Lime Sorbet, 156
    Peach
        Ginger, Cranberry, 155
        Praline, 133
    Rocky Road, 111
    Straw-Ba-Nut, 93
Lemon Cream and Berries, 92
Mousse
    Chocolate, Quick, 131
    Mocha, 93
    Pumpkin, 196
Peaches, Poached, 132
Pies, see Pies
Pizza, Old Glory, 132
Pumpkin, 163
    Crumble, 210
    Mousse, 196
Raspberry Pudding, 108
Rhubarb, Easy, 109
    Soufflé, Strawberry, 78
Shortcake, Angel, 132
Soufflé
    Papaya, Frozen, 181
    Raspberry, Hot, 56
    Strawberry-Rhubarb, 78
Strawberry
    Angel, Raspberry Sauce, 40
    Parfaits, Yogurt and Rice, 40
    San Remo, and Yogurt, 109
    Soufflé, Rhubarb, 78
    Tango, 92
Sweet Potato Pudding, 209
Tortes
    Blueberry-Sour Cream, 155
    Cheese, 180
    Cherry Angel, 92
Zucchini Crisp, 145
GAME
Duck, 163
    Dandelion Salad, 96
    Orange Spice, 86
    Smoked, 205
Quail, Smothered, 163, 172
Rabbit, Sweet and Sour, 171
Venison Supreme, 163, 189
GROUND BEEF
Argentinean, 47
Burgers, Independence, 122
Casseroles
    Cavatini, Baked, 122
    Coronado, 138
Crock·Pot Pizza Casserole, 18

Lasagna, Skillet, 170
Meatballs con Queso, 84
Meat Loaves
    French, 34
    Oriental, 83
    Working Girl's, 149
Pie, Double-Crusted, 171
Sandwiches
    Rolls, Con Queso, 170
    Stroganoff, 33
Soups, 43, 66
HAM
and Broccoli Pie, 70
    Soufflé, 47
Crêpes Ensenada, 203
Eggs Benedict, 191
Rolls
    Omelet, 102
    with Spinach, 85
Salad, Fruited, 202
Sandwiches, Burrito, 17
Slice, Fruited, 149
LAMB
Pie, Shepherd's, 99
Roast
    Leg of, 84
    Triple-Crown, 84
MEATLESS MAIN DISHES
Casserole, Garden Medley, 151
Egg
    Cheese Casserole, Easy, 87
    Omelets with Spanish Sauce, 127
    Quiche, Zucchini Tomato, 140
    Soufflé
        Cheese, Food Processor, 205
        Spinach, 88
Pasta
    Fettucini, Spinach, 102
    Garden, 128
    Lasagna
        Easter Brunch, 74
        Tofu, 88
    Tetrazzini, Mushroom, 36
Tofu
    Lasagna, 88
    Salad, 97
Walnutburgers, 191
PIES
Apple, 41
    Buttered Rum, Hot, 183
    Cranberry, 216
    Sugarless, 29
Banana Black Bottom, 79
Blueberry, Special, 111
Chocolate
    Cream Cheese, 93
    Swiss Bavarian, 217
Cranberry
    Apple, 216
    Yogurt, 199
Lemon Ribbon Alaska, 145
Mincemeat Chiffon, 198

Peach, Hurry-Up, 57
Pecan, Mystery, 198
Pumpkin-Ice Cream, 216
Raspberry-Orange, 216
Shoofly, Miniature, 159
Strawberry Cream, 79
Sweet Potato, 199
PORK
Beans, Baked, Grandma
　　　　　Schmitt's, 151
Chops
　Apple-Glazed, 188
　with Orange Rice, 69
Ham, see Ham
Pâté, and Veal, 188
Ribs, Baked, and Sauerkraut, 18
Roast, Spit-Barbecued, 138
Sausage, see Sausage
Sweet and Sour, 100
SALADS
Dressings
　Gazpacho, 98
　Herb, 68
　Homemade Seasoning, 187
　Honey-Mustard, 187
　Roquefort, 98
　Yogurt, 97
Fruit
　Apricot, Frozen, 44
　Citrus, 16
　Cranberry
　　Crunchy, 186
　　Spiced Ring, 201
　Della Robbia, 148
　Melon, Minted Ring, 95
　Mixed, 135
　Orange, Spanish, 168
　Peaches and Cream, 120
　Pear and Grape, 201
　Pineapple-Berry Boats, 82
　Winter Cups, 31
Lucky Fruited Green, 45
Main Dish
　Beef and Broccoli, 17
　Chicken
　　Garden-Style, 83
　　and Rice, 16
　　Zesty, 169
　Crab
　　Louis, California, 186
　　Oriental, 97
　Duck, Dandelion, 96
　Ham, Fruited, 202
　Lobster, 148
　Scallop, Ship Ahoy, 32
　Shrimp, Aegean, 121
　Taco, 169
　Tofu, 97
　Tuna
　　Niçoise, 68
　　Shoestring, 97
Pasta

with Herb Dressing, 68
Molded, 46
Rotini, Spinach, 45
Spiral Vegetable, 168
Spring Barley, 83
Vegetable
　Avocado and Mushroom,
　　Marinated, 186
　Barley, Spring, 83
　Cauliflower Delight, 202
　Bean, Microwave, Hot, 202
　Confetti, 136
　Greek, 45
　　Tomato, 121
　Hominy, 121
　Mixed, 32, 67, 96,
　Mushroom
　　and Avocado, Marinated, 186
　　Fresh, 96
　Potato, Secret, 136
　Slaw, Super, 16
　Tomatoes
　　Greek, 121
　　à la Russe, 148
　　Sicilian, 136
　Vinaigrette, Spring, 96
SANDWICHES
Beef
　Italian, 187
　Tortilla Roll-Ups, 98
Burrito, 17
Chicken
　Picnic Pita, 137
Fruit
　Apricot Waldorf Salad, 203
　Salad Pitas, 98
Rolls, con Queso, 170
Stroganoff, 33
SAUCES
Barbecue, Vinegar-Based, 135
Cucumber, 95
Fruity, 95
No-Cook Pizza, 81
SAUSAGE
Cassoulet, Easy, 18
Chorizo Breakfast, 172
Chowder, and Vegetable, 31
Pancake, Oven-Baked, 189
Ring, Christmas Morning, 204
Squash, Acorn Stuffed, 34
Tahoe Brunch, 70
Topping, O'Topper, 49
SEAFOOD
Bluefish, Stuffed, 190
Cioppino, 87
Clams, 11
Crab Meat, 11
　Bisque, Ten-Minute, 31
　Louis, California, 186
　Mousse, 94
　Quiche, 191
　Salad, Oriental, 97

Strata, 22
Fish, 115
　Amandine, 173
　Parmesan, Baked, 173
Flounder in Sour Cream Sauce, 101
Haddock-Shrimp Bake, 21
Lasagna, 139
Lobster
　Bisque, Quick, 201
　Salad, 148
Oyster, 11, 43
Paella, Shellfish, 205
Perch Turbans à la Newburg, 73
Salmon
　Baked, 86
　Casserole, Super Supper, 190
　Linguine, 101
　Steaks, Grilled Marinated, 127
Scallops, 11
　Coquilles St. Jacques, 35
　Salad, Ship Ahoy, 32
Shrimp, 11
　Casserole, 50
　Chowder, and Corn, 201
　Glazed Trout, 87
　Green Peppers Stuffed with, 127
　Haddock, Bake, 21
　Ratatouille Stir-Fry, 150
　Salad, 121, 73
Sole
　Fillet with Dill Sauce, 126
　Stuffed, 139
Trout, Shrimp-Glazed, 87
Tuna
　Casserole
　　Basque, 101
　　Mandarin, 74
　　Moussaka, Cheesy, 151
　　and Rice, Cheesy, 22
　Salad
　　Niçoise, 68
　　Shoestring, 97
　Topping, O'Topper, 49
SIDE DISHES
Barley-Mushroom Casserole, 37
Fettucini, Tomato and Basil, 130
Grits, Two-Alarm, 25
Hominy, 121
Noodles
　Romanoff, Mock, 177
　Sour Cream, 25
Rice
　Curried, 129
　Pepper, Casserole, 38
　Pilaf, Spring, 104
　Pilau Brown, 26
　Pine Nut, 207
　Ring, Spring, 90
　Risotto, 142
　Timbales, 194
　Twice as Nice, 52
Stuffing

Corn, Balls, 195
Corn Bread, 194
Oyster, 207

SNACKS
Cornmeal-Cheddar Snaps, 64
Nutrition, 147
Pecans, Barbecued, 167
Popcorn, 30, 167

SOUPS
Asparagus Marseilles, 82
Avocado, 135
Barley-Cheese, 15
Beef
    and Meatball, 66
    Smoky Chowder, 15
    Taco, 43
Bisque, 31, 201
Carrot, Chilled, 66
Chowder
    Beef, Smoky, 15
    Shrimp and Corn, 201
    Vegetable, 31, 44
Crab Bisque, Ten-Minute, 31
Cucumber, Danish-Style, 119
Curried, Cool, 95
Fruit, Vegetable, 168
Gazpacho, Make-Ahead, 120
Lemon, Cold, 147
Lobster Bisque, Quick, 201
Mulligatawny, 185
Nectarine, 135
Sausage and Vegetable Chowder, 31
Shrimp and Corn Chowder, 201
Spinach-Rice, 82
Sunset, 67
Turkey, 185
Vegetable
    Fruit, 168
    Sipper, Hot, 167
Zucchini, Chilled, 147

STIR-FRY
Beef
    Sukiyaki, 69
    and Vegetables, 137
Chicken
    and Broccoli, 100
    Sesame-Lemon, 85
Turkey Teriyaki, 86
Vegetables, Microwave, 194

TARTS
Banana, Fluffy, 183
Cookie Shells, 183
Peach, French, 145
Pear, 40, 159

TURKEY
Burrito Sandwiches, 17
Divan, Company, 173
Gumbo, Crock•Pot, 35
Hash, 204
Lasagna, and Spinach, 150
Pie, and Stuffing, 190
Soup, 185
Teriyaki, 86

VEAL
Audrey, 69
Pâté, Pork and, 188
Scallopini, 125

VEGETABLES
Artichoke
    Jerusalem, Patties, 174
    Spinach-Casserole, 206
Asparagus, 61
    Custard, 88
    Sesame, 89
    with Three-Cheese Sauce, 74
Beans
    Baked, 36, 151
    Dilly, and Carrots, 102
    Green
        Casserole, 152
        Cheesy, 89
        Italian, 128
        Tartare, 75
        with Tomatoes, 140
    Mexican, 192
Beets, Nippy, 128
Broccoli, 61
    Casserole
        Nutty, 89
        Rice, 174
    Puff, 48
Brussels Sprouts, 11, 36
Cabbage
    Mallum, 75
    Skillet, 50
Calabasitas, Microwave, 140
Carrots in Orange Sauce, 192
Casserole, 193
Cauliflower
    Deep-Fried, 192
    Parmesan, 103
Chard, Baked Swiss, 103
Corn, 115
    Fresh, Pudding, 128
    Monterey Bake, 152
    Peppers, 141
Cucumbers, Fried, 141
Eggplant, 115, 152

Endive, Belgian, 11, 37
Fresh
    in Cheese Sauce, 104
    Ghivetch, 76
Medley, Creamed, 51
Mushrooms, 11
    Fritters, 24
    Oriental, 75
    and Potato Skillet, 50
Mustard Green Patties, 24
Okra, Italiano, 129
Onion, Fried Vidalia, Rings, 103
Parsnip, 11, 24
Peas, 61, 90
    Black-eyed, 22, 23
Peppers, 115, 141
Potatoes, 61
    Baked Sliced, 129
    Crispy Cheese, 76
    Crock•Pot au Gratin, 89
    Glorious, 25
    Gourmet, 90
    Hasselback, 141
    Italian, 103
    Mushroom and, Skillet, 50
    O'Topper, 49
    Party, 153
    Puffs, Speedy, 37
    Scalloped, 51, 193
Puff Verde, 178
Ratatouille
    Savannah, 142
    Topping, O'Topper, 49
Rutabagas, 163, 177
Soups, see Soups
Spinach, 11
    Creamed, 51
    Artichoke Casserole, 206
Squash, 163
    Spaghetti, Italiano, 153
    Summer, Orange-Dilled, 104
    Stir-Fry, Microwave, 194
Sweet Potatoes, 163
    Apple Scallop, 177
    Cranberry Yams, 193
Terrine, Tri-Color, 206
Tomatoes
    Green, Casserole, 177
    Baked Stuffed, 142
        Zucchini, 129
Turnips, 163
Zucchini
    Dilled, Rice Bake, 153
    Stuffed Tomatoes, 129

ACRYLIC COOKBOOK HOLDER
A WELCOME AID FOR EVERY HOME

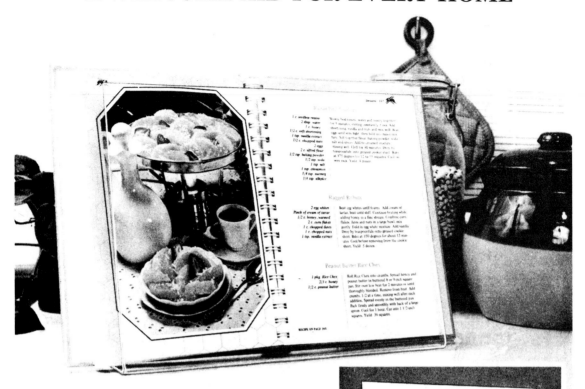

Protect your favorite cookbook from mixing splashes.

Your cookbook sits firmly at an easy-to-read angle, opened to your working recipe, protected from sticky fingers, mixing splatters and accidental spills. Hands-free convenience not only for cooking but also for sewing...working on crafts...even plumbing chores or hobbies. The holder can be wiped clean with a damp sponge. Sturdy acrylic holder is 9¾" by 12½" to support even large books.

Buy several at the low price of $7.95 plus .95 postage and handling for each cookbook holder ordered. Place your order by calling **toll free 1-800-251-1520,** or by sending your check, money order or charge card (VISA or MasterCard) information to:

The Southwestern Company
P.O. Box 1408
Nashville, Tennessee 37202

No COD orders, please.

Please allow 30 days for delivery.

If not completely delighted, you may return cookbook holder within 30 days for a full refund. Call our toll-free number for return information.